RaumFragen: Stadt – Region – Landschaft

Series Editor

Olaf Kühne, Forschungsbereich Geographie, Eberhard Karls Universität Tübingen, Tübingen, Germany

Sebastian Kinder, Forschungsbereich Geographie, Eberhard Karls Universität Tübingen, Tübingen, Germany

Olaf Schnur, Bereich Forschung, vhw – Bundesverband für Wohnen und Stadtentwicklung e.V., Berlin, Germany

RaumFragen: Stadt – Region – Landschaft | SpaceAffairs: City – Region – Landscape

Im Zuge des „spatial turns" der Sozial- und Geisteswissenschaften hat sich die Zahl der wissenschaftlichen Forschungen in diesem Bereich deutlich erhöht. Mit der Reihe „RaumFragen: Stadt – Region – Landschaft" wird Wissenschaftlerinnen und Wissenschaftlern ein Forum angeboten, innovative Ansätze der Anthropogeographie und sozialwissenschaftlichen Raumforschung zu präsentieren. Die Reihe orientiert sich an grundsätzlichen Fragen des gesellschaftlichen Raumverständnisses. Dabei ist es das Ziel, unterschiedliche Theorieansätze der anthropogeographischen und sozialwissenschaftlichen Stadt- und Regionalforschung zu integrieren. Räumliche Bezüge sollen dabei insbesondere auf mikro- und mesoskaliger Ebene liegen. Die Reihe umfasst theoretische sowie theoriegeleitete empirische Arbeiten. Dazu gehören Monographien und Sammelbände, aber auch Einführungen in Teilaspekte der stadt- und regionalbezogenen geographischen und sozialwissenschaftlichen Forschung. Ergänzend werden auch Tagungsbände und Qualifikationsarbeiten (Dissertationen, Habilitationsschriften) publiziert.

In the course of the "spatial turn" of the social sciences and humanities, the number of scientific researches in this field has increased significantly. With the series "RaumFragen: Stadt – Region – Landschaft" scientists are offered a forum to present innovative approaches in anthropogeography and social space research. The series focuses on fundamental questions of the social understanding of space. The aim is to integrate different theoretical approaches of anthropogeographical and social-scientific urban and regional research. Spatial references should be on a micro- and mesoscale level in particular. The series comprises theoretical and theory-based empirical work. These include monographs and anthologies, but also introductions to some aspects of urban and regional geographical and social science research. In addition, conference proceedings and qualification papers (dissertations, postdoctoral theses) are also published.

Hans-Jürgen Bieling · Thomas Diez ·
Riccarda Flemmer · Andrea Futterer
Editors

Transnational Infrastructures and the Transformation of Global Orders

Springer VS

Editors
Hans-Jürgen Bieling
Institut für Politikwissenschaft
Eberhard Karls Universität Tübingen
Tübingen, Germany

Thomas Diez
Institut für Politikwissenschaft
Eberhard Karls Universität Tübingen
Tübingen, Germany

Riccarda Flemmer
Institut für Politikwissenschaft
Eberhard Karls Universität Tübingen
Tübingen, Germany

Andrea Futterer
Institut für Politikwissenschaft
Eberhard Karls Universität Tübingen
Tübingen, Germany

ISSN 2625-6991 ISSN 2625-7009 (electronic)
RaumFragen: Stadt – Region – Landschaft
ISBN 978-3-031-74845-5 ISBN 978-3-031-74846-2 (eBook)
https://doi.org/10.1007/978-3-031-74846-2

This Springer VS imprint is published by the registered company Springer Nature Switzerland AG
The registered company address is: Gewerbestrasse 11, 6330 Cham, Switzerland

Contents

Introduction: Transnational Infrastructures and Global Order(s)

Hans-Jürgen Bieling, Thomas Diez, Riccarda Flemmer and Andrea Futterer

Abstract

This introductory chapter reflects on the framework for analysing ordering effects of transnational infrastructures. It outlines the role such infrastructures play in global politics, and indicates ways to conceptualise this relationship based on existing literature and the contributions to this volume. Furthermore, the introduction gives an overview of how this volume is organised along the central lines of research, focusing on new forms of communication, socioeconomic and ecological development, and political authority.

Keywords

Transnationalism · Infrastructures · Global order · Change · Power · Globalisation

H.-J. Bieling · T. Diez · R. Flemmer · A. Futterer (✉)
Institut für Politikwissenschaft, Universität Tübingen, Berlin, Germany
e-mail: andrea.futterer@uni-tuebingen.de

H.-J Bieling
e-mail: hans-juergen.bieling@uni-tuebingen.de

T. Diez
e-mail: thomas.diez@uni-tuebingen.de

R. Flemmer
e-mail: riccarda.flemmer@uni-tuebingen.de

H.-J. Bieling et al. (eds.), *Transnational Infrastructures and the Transformation of Global Orders*, RaumFragen: Stadt – Region – Landschaft,
https://doi.org/10.1007/978-3-031-74846-2_1

1 Transnational Infrastructures in a Transformed Global Context

Transnational infrastructures represent a crucial—yet often overlooked—prerequisite of processes of political, social, and economic globalisation and the (re)ordering processes that such processes entail. Thus, transnational infrastructures have long been regarded as a core pillar of an increasing international interdependence that deepens the ties between individuals, societies and states on a regional and global scale. These interrelated and transnational systems of transport, energy, or communication shape the way in which our societies evolve. The interconnectivity of networks by cables, pipes and ports has facilitated communication and trade across long distances—often with the expectation that this would contribute to a more peaceful world.

At the same time, today's multiple crises call to mind not only the importance of infrastructures, but also the fact that they are vulnerable and highly contested. Climate change has revealed the inadequacy of many of our current infrastructure systems, demonstrating their negative environmental impact and their susceptibility to climate events. This, in turn, raises questions about the future organisation of energy production and consumption. In order to achieve a viable future, it is clear that investments in renewable energies are crucial. The funding for related infrastructure projects requires the involvement of foreign aid in the form of international investment. Furthermore, the Covid-19 pandemic has caused disruptions to global production and value chains, which challenge the resilience of current and future transport routes.

The war in Ukraine threatens the energy security of states, resulting in the suspension of major infrastructural projects and in the necessity to rethink energy systems and consumption patterns. What is more, the dispute over Russian gas pipelines and the Huthi attack on shipping routes through the Red Sea have demonstrated that transnational infrastructures and their production, operation and utilisation, are more than neutral technologies. Instead, infrastructures are always contested, can be instrumentalised, and may ultimately change domestic and international or even global power relations. Embedded in broader social networks and processes, infrastructures can facilitate the emergence and rise of certain political actors and the decline of others; they influence the distribution of power and material assets; they express or have an impact on regional and global norms; and they contribute to changing patterns of practice. In other words, transnational infrastructures are closely linked to the development of global orders. Accordingly, infrastructural change has ordering effects of different kinds, it can stabilize such orders as well as foster their reconfiguration.

Political and academic debates reflect this relevance of infrastructures. Since the early 2010s, a number of disciplines, including Anthropology, History, Media and Urban Studies, have seen an "infrastructural turn" (Anand et al. 2018; Blok et al., 2016; Bridges, 2023; Hesmondhalgh, 2021), grounded in a shift toward seeing infrastructures not as neutral physical devices but taking them seriously as material factors in interplay with conceptual debates and symbolic discourses. However, the effects of infrastructure on orders that exceed the state have only just begun to initiate research, with often disparate and contradictory claims. Scholars have investigated infrastructures by paying attention to their security aspects, particularly with regard to critical infrastructures (Langenohl, 2020). From a geoeconomic perspective, work has focused on the so-called "weaponization" of interdependence between states (Farrell & Newman, 2019; Gertz and Evers, 2020). Others have analysed the role of new communication technologies (Plantin and Punathambekar, 2019) and their impact on diplomacy (Duncombe, 2017; Kampf et al., 2015). Studies have also considered the (dis)enabling consequences of infrastructures for non-state actors to participate in international politics and global finance (Bernards & Campbell-Verduyn, 2019; De Goede, 2021; Petry, 2021; Westermeier, 2020). Additional work has emerged on the impact of material infrastructures on landscapes (Kühne, 2018); migration and territorial borders (Gill, 2022); renewable energy provision (Paraschiv et al., 2014); and patterns of regionalization (Glass et al., 2019). Yet most of these authors have not taken the infrastructural turn on board fully and have treated infrastructures as mere instruments in the hands of powerful actors or as mediums for enhancing connectivity. As a result, the production, operation and effects of infrastructures in international relations remain underexplored and underconceptualised (Bueger et al., 2023; Mayer & Acuto, 2015).

This volume contributes to filling this gap. Its contributions examine the relationship between infrastructure and processes of global (dis)ordering in an explicit, systematic and interdisciplinary manner. They engage with the overarching question, whether, to what extent and by which means transnational infrastructures generate particular effects that impact the transformation of global orders. Coming from a diverse set of academic backgrounds, they also contribute to an emerging dialogue between different disciplines, argumentative claims, and conceptual debates.

2 Conceptualising the Infrastructure-Order(s)-Nexus

The main purpose of this section is to conceptualise orders and infrastructure to provide the basis for studying their mutual impact and development in the infrastructure-order(s)-nexus. Let us start with the concept of order. At the most basic level, order denotes a relatively stable or "routinised" arrangement of actors and their relations with each other (Bull 1977, p. 4; Rosenau, 1992, p. 5). Thus, a first core element of orders are patterns of practice that define and sustain an order. For Hedley Bull (1977), these are the institutions (in a broader, sociological sense) that form the backbone of order. These patterns of practice reflect the norms on which an order is built. While such norms often remain implicit and unwritten, orders may also function on or require explicitly formulated norms in treaties, constitutions, or other forms of laws and agreements. Yet any order is also characterised by uneven power relations based on the distribution of material assets.

Thus, we define orders as *constellations of patterns of practice*, *institutionalised norms*, and *distributions of material assets* among actors. Analysing orders thus involves the study of each of these three dimensions.

In this volume, we are specifically interested in global order(s). Our understanding of "global" is broad and does not imply that the orders that we are interested in are of truly global or universal scope. Instead, we use the term "global" to distinguish domestic orders from those that exceed individual states, including regional or functional orders which are interconnected and may sometimes compete over or lead to universal arrangements (Acharya, 2018, pp. 9–10). This does not exclude references to domestic orders in the contributions to this volume. Yet the nexus of infrastructures and order(s) in a domestic setting has been far more extensively studied than the nexus between infrastructures and orders beyond single state territories. Furthermore, given the lack of a centralised formal hierarchy outside of states, orders and ordering processes follow their own logic once we leave the domestic realm. Yet while others have used the concept of "international order(s)", our preference for "global order(s)" indicates that our interest is not only in orders between and among states, but involves a variety of actors such as transnational corporations or civil society organisations. Indeed, one of the questions that the contributions to this volume address is the extent to which the importance of non-state actors in the patterns of practice, norms and distribution of material assets has shifted over time (see also e.g. Rosenau, 1992; Stephen & Zürn, 2019).

Two further clarifications are necessary to prevent misunderstandings. The first is that while orders, following our definition, are "relatively stable", this does not mean that they are static. Without any stability in the patterns of practice, norms, and distribution of material assets, we cannot observe any kind of order. Yet at the same time, orders always need to be re-produced and re-enacted. They need continuous efforts of ordering. These ordering processes always entail, often subtle, shifts and movements, which then may at some point build up to more visible cracks and what we then, often in hindsight, identify as a change of order. Any such change, however, cannot be reduced to a single moment and involves continuities. Thus, scholars have pointed to the fact that what we often identify as the "Westphalian" order cannot be reduced to the Treaty of Westphalia but involved a much longer transitional process (e.g. Teschke, 2003). Similar debates put a question mark on or at least qualify the supposed ruptures of 1918 (Bromber et al., 2018), 1945 (Patel & Kaiser, 2018) or 1989 (Lawson et al., 2010). This also means that orders are always contested. There are competing and contesting practices and norms and struggles over the distribution of assets. Change emerges from those contestations of order, even though contestation may also lead to the reification of particular norms and practices (Wiener 2014).

Second, our definition of orders follows what is often referred to as the "analytical", "descriptive" or "empirical" and not a "normative" understanding of order (Acharya, 2014; Rosenau, 1992, pp. 9–11). While any society, whether on the state, regional or global level, needs a particular order to function, it is an entirely different matter how we evaluate such an order, its functions, and its defining practices, norms and distribution of material assets. We therefore do not see value in order as such. Indeed, we consider all orders to be normatively ambiguous. They require careful consideration of their normative implications. In addition, orders are always infused with power: they make some actors legitimate participants and exclude others; they advantage some actors and disadvantage others; they support practices that are beneficial to some and in specific circumstances yet have negative consequences to others and in other contexts. To see order and justice in tension is therefore misleading—order and justice are intertwined, and orders tend to come along with specific forms of justice and injustice. This does not mean that the contributions to this volume do not take very strong, and often critical stances towards the global orders they analyse. Yet this underlines that any order has significant normative downsides, which we need to expose and address, even if we prefer some global orders over others on normative grounds.

Let us now turn to our definition of infrastructures. We start from an understanding of infrastructures as socio-technical systems or networks (Edwards, 2003; Mayntz, 1988). Generally, we follow the definition by Brian Larkin (2013, p. 328), according to whom:

> Infrastructures are built networks that facilitate the flow of goods, people, or ideas and allow for their exchange over space. As physical forms they shape the nature of a network, the speed and direction of its movement, its temporalities, and its vulnerability to breakdown. They comprise the architecture for circulation, literally providing the undergirding of modern societies, and they generate the ambient environment of everyday life.

This implies that the technical and social aspects of infrastructures are interwoven and mutually dependent. While for the purposes of this volume, we do not follow others who have expanded the concept of infrastructure to immaterial aspects such as language or culture, we at the same time argue that infrastructures cannot be reduced to their physical, technological existence but evolve within and with a societal context. The ways infrastructures are planned, produced, operated and used are significant for social relations—and vice versa. Dirk van Laak (2018) thus calls infrastructures the "lifelines of our society" and Eva Barlösius (2019) speaks of "social order services".

In this sense, ordering effects are characteristic for all kind of infrastructures, as they produce patterns of interaction that stabilize expectations in future behaviour, create or reproduce norms, and structure power relations. Since we are interested in global ordering, we focus primarily on infrastructures that exceed the boundaries of the state and conceptualize them as multi-layered and multi-faceted systems that involve the influence and utilization by different actors—states, corporations, civil society—and whose components are located on various scales—global, regional, national, and local.

The development of infrastructural networks—be it in transport, energy, education, finance, communication, migration, or any other field—is the historical product of social processes that articulate certain, sometimes conflicting, demands on the design of these systems (Abels & Bieling, 2024). Thus, they evolve over time (temporal dimension) and within particular spaces (spatial dimension). At the same time, infrastructures influence the political and social orders from which they emerge. This circular relationship reflects in four dimensions of political conflict over infrastructures as socio-technical systems.

1. In the early stages of *planning and deliberation*, specific narratives or visions around a potential creation or upgrading of infrastructures are competing. At this stage, alliances can be formed, composed of social groups and political organizations, including governments and administrations, political parties, non-governmental organizations (NGOs), and the media. This has ordering effects as the competing alliances provide alternative views on the purpose and political priorities, benefits and societal costs of the infrastructures under consideration
2. The *financing and production* of infrastructures is based on the capacity of actors to engage in such an undertaking and of the demands articulated by influential social groups. It has ordering effects on aspects such as the provision of energy and mobility, training and education, the distribution of production sites, nodes of transport or communication, the use of specific technologies, the transformation of the ecological environment, the organization of labour, etc.
3. The *operation* of infrastructures is linked to questions of control over central nodes within the system and over regulation. This has ordering effects as it provides actors with the ability to set standards and norms related to the access to infrastructures. It impacts the use and distribution of resources deciding on the inclusion and exclusion of individuals or other entities from the system
4. The *utilisation* of infrastructures largely depends on their accessibility and embeddedness in social practices and discourses. In turn, how infrastructures are used has ordering effects on societal processes. Together with political regulation it determines the effectiveness of infrastructures and their transformative impact on (sustainable) production, everyday life and transnational interactions

The way in which infrastructures operate is thus not solely determined by their technology and materiality, but also by specific regulatory standards and societal adaption processes (Turner & Johnson, 2017). The connection of these four aspects is what makes transnational infrastructures large-scale socio-technical networks. They are constantly evolving as they are shaped and constructed from below (everyday practices), above (state and private production and governance), and horizontally (dynamic interaction of infrastructures).

As a variety of actors is involved in these processes, we are certain to witness conflicts over infrastructures. As Daniel Drezner (2019, p. 287) argues, "any technological change is also an exercise in redistribution". Thus, we assume that actors from the state, private businesses, or civil society have (often opposing) interests on what kind of infrastructures need to be produced and how these should be run and used. More specifically, we can observe how social and ecological targets are overshadowed by national and business interests when we look at large-scale infrastructure initiatives like the Chinese Belt and Road Initiative (BRI), the US-led Partnership for Global Infrastructure and

Investment (PGII), and the EU's Global Gateway (Flint & Zhu, 2019; Leonard, 2021). This "geoeconomization" of how infrastructure investments are provided (Abels & Bieling, 2023) expresses itself in the major powers' non-altruistic willingness to contribute to these initiatives. They seek to gain from such exchanges and create dependencies.

Such strategic concerns are certainly characteristic in the current global constellation. However, it would be insufficient to analyse the infrastructure-order(s)-nexus only in this way. As indicated, the ordering effects of infrastructures, their impact on power constellations between different kinds of actors—nation-states, transnational corporations (TNCs), civil society organizations, etc.—and the hierarchies between them are often indirect and complex. They can be produced by individual or collective agency and intentional utilization as much as by indirect, uncontrolled and unintended—material and discursive—implications, most likely a combination of both. Despite all strategic action, most ordering effects remain to a certain extent contingent. This is even more so, as the making and provision of infrastructures is often related to specific kinds of transnational or global crises or challenges—ecological crises, pandemics, wars, poor investment, vulnerable transport and communication, poverty and unemployment, insufficient education or medical services, etc.—the precise meaning of which remains contested and open to change.

Our definitions of global order(s) and transnational infrastructures has demonstrated the many ways in which they are interlinked. They work together in providing subjects with agency and legitimacy; they allow certain practices to appear and become routinised; they facilitate and uphold particular norms; and they work towards the distribution of material assets. Sometimes, powerful actors instrumentalise infrastructures to pursue such outcomes. At other times, it is infrastructures that make actors powerful in the first instance, spark the emergence of new practices, norms and redistributions. Scholarship has so far often focused on isolated instances of the infrastructure-order(s)-nexus. Our aim is to move towards a more systematic exploration across cases that differ both spatially and temporally.

3 Structure of the Volume

This volume thus approaches the infrastructure-order(s)-nexus from a perspective that is sensitive to the crises-driven and multi-scalar nature of ongoing (re)ordering processes. Furthermore, we are convinced that an interdisciplinary dialogue will help to generate new empirical and conceptual inspirations and insights. This openness is not to dilute the focus of this volume: we are interested in the global ordering effects of transnational infrastructures and, by analysing these, take into account historical, legal, technical, political, and social dimensions.

In the first part on "Infrastructures and the Remaking of Global Orders", three chapters explore the interplay between infrastructures and the reconfiguration of global orders, each offering an insight into this process, reflecting on international society, statehood, capitalism, and global power dynamics. In "Infrastructural Development and the Ordering of International Society", *Thomas Diez* examines how infrastructures shape and sometimes challenge established international orders. He does so by focusing on what he calls international society, investigating how one of its core institutions, diplomacy, is influenced by developments in communication technology. *Jutta Bakonyi* and *May Darwich*, in "Capitalism and Infrastructural Ordering: (Re)Crafting of Statehood and Territorial Power", delve into how capitalism is both enabled by and embedded within the development and expansion of infrastructures. They illustrate this by showing how recent infrastructural booms in the Global South challenge traditional state-centric notions of territoriality and statehood, revealing processes of (re)crafting polities and societies. *Hans-Jürgen Bieling's* "Infrastructure Conflicts in a New Geoeconomic Order—a Political Economy Perspective", focuses on the interconnection between globalization-relevant infrastructures and the emerging new geoeconomic global order. By clarifying the critical role of infrastructures in transnational value chains, Bieling focuses on potential conflicts arising over their control. He illustrates these dynamics by looking at competing infrastructure projects by China, the US and the EU.

The two chapters in the second part on "New Forms of Communication" address the infrastructure-order(s)-nexus by investigating changes in technology and communication with regards to the (re)organisation of public spheres, global justice, and environmental sustainability. In "Dimensions of Infrastructures and the Digital Transformation of the Public Sphere", *Florian Muhle* explores how the digitalisation of public communication—more precisely the establishment of social media platforms—is linked to infrastructural changes of the public sphere. Muhle then links his findings to claims and concepts for regulating the public sphere. *Anne Burkhardt's* "Infrastructural Perspectives on Artificial Intelligence—On the Implications of AI Infrastructures for Global (In)Justice" examines the role of AI infrastructures in perpetuating or mitigating global inequalities. She highlights their impact on the access to resources and opportunities, thereby shaping global power dynamics and raising ethical considerations about justice.

The chapters in the third part on "Socioeconomic and Ecological Development" examine how infrastructures impact global orders through addressing historical, environmental, and socio-economic challenges. *Karin Polit and Lokesh Ohri's* chapter, "The Ambivalence of Infrastructures: The Complex Interplay of Development and Conservation in the Garhwal Himalayas", explores the dual role of infrastructure in promoting development while challenging conservation efforts. *Bernd Grewe's* "The Political Economy of Transport Infrastructure and Energy Crisis: A Regional Study in 19th Century Germany", highlights how transport infrastructures affected energy supply during historical energy crises, focusing on the interaction between local and transnational systems. In "Open Veins or Lifelines of Society? Infrastructures and the Order of Global Resource Extractivism in Latin America", *Riccarda Flemmer* examines how infrastructures support resource extraction, perpetuating global inequalities and providing leverage for opposition. *Heidi Megerle's* "Blue-green Infrastructure as an Innovative Approach to Sustainable Development", discusses integrating blue-green infrastructure to address sustainability targets. In "Landscape Conflicts within Germany's Energy Transition", *Corinna Jenal and Olaf Kühne* investigate social conflicts in Germany's efforts to shift to renewable energy, emphasising the role of the state and the importance of constructive debate.

The fourth and final part, "Power Relations", explores how infrastructures influence and reshape power dynamics on a global scale through contexts such as space and state-business relations, urban environments, and migration policies. In "Outer Space Infrastructures and Global Order: How the Control over Satellite Constellations Reshapes State-Business Relations", *Joscha Abels* explores the evolving landscape of space infrastructure, where major satellite systems are increasingly owned and operated by private corporations. Abels analyses how states strive to maintain authority over critical space infrastructure amidst the rising power of transnational corporations in the global economy. In "Spaces and Scales of a Street: Shifting Social Orders and Urban Transformation, as Seen From Marseille", *Claire Bullen* and *Matteo Stefani* provide a grounded analysis of how global power relations manifest in everyday urban spaces and social orders, using a street in Marseille as a microcosm. *Bani Gill's* "Infrastructures of Migration Regulation: Policing Migrant 'Illegality' and Deportation in India", investigates how infrastructural systems are used to regulate migration, highlighting the power mechanisms involved in policing and deporting migrants, and the implications for state control and human rights.

Taken together, these chapters offer a kaleidoscope of how global orders and infrastructures are intertwined. They show how infrastructures have enabled particular orders and how actors at times have instrumentalised them to pursue their ordering practices across different scales. They all take a critical stance towards the ordering processes and their power implications. The picture that emerges from them, rather than seeing transnational infrastructures and global ordering processes in a one-directional and one-dimensional relationship, highlights the complex nature of their nexus, its historical contingency and normative ambiguity.

Acknowledgements This volume originated from the project "Infrastructures and Global Ordering" (IGLO), made possible through the support of the Exploration Fund of the University of Tübingen. The fund is financed by the Federal Ministry of Education and Research (BMBF) and the Baden-Württemberg Ministry of Science, as part of the Excellence Strategy of the German Federal and State Governments.

References

Abels, J., & Bieling, H.-J. (2024). Drivers and limits of the geoeconomic turn in EU infrastructure policy. *Politics and Governance*, *12*, Article 8127.

Abels, J., & Bieling, H.-J. (2023). Infrastructures of globalization: Shifts in global order and Europe's strategic choices. *Competition & Change, 27*(3/4), 516–533.

Acharya, A. (2014). Global international relations (IR) and regional worlds: A new agenda for international studies, *International Studies Quarterly, 58*(4), 647–659.

Acharya, A. (2018). *Constructing global order: Agency and change in world politics.* Cambridge University Press.

Amin, A. (2014). Lively infrastructure. *Theory, Culture & Society, 31*(7–8), 137–161.

Anand, N., Gupta, A., & Appel, H. (Eds.). (2018). *The promise of infrastructure*. Duke University Press.

Barlösius, E. (2019). *Infrastrukturen als soziale Ordnungsdienste. Ein Beitrag zur Gesellschaftsdiagnose.* Campus.

Bernards, N., & Campbell-Verduyn, M. (2019). Understanding technological change in global finance through infrastructures. *Review of International Political Economy, 26*(5), 773–789.

Blok, A., Nakazora, M., & Winthereik, B. R. (2016). Infrastructuring environments. *Science as Culture, 25*(1), 1–22.

Bridges, M. (2023). The infrastructural turn in historical scholarship. *Modern American History, 6*(1), 103–120.

Bromber, K. et al. (Eds.) (2018). The long end of the first world war: Ruptures, continuities and memories. Campus.

Bueger, C., Liebetrau, T., & Stockbruegger, J. (2023). Theorizing infrastructure in global politics. *International Studies Quarterly, 67*(4), 1–10.

Bull, H. (1977). *The Anarchial Society. A Study of Order in World Politics*. London: Macmillan.

De Goede, M. (2021). Finance/security infrastructures. *Review of International Political Economy, 28*(2), 351–368.

Drezner, D. W. (2019). Technological change and international relations. *International Relations, 33*(2), 286–303.

Duncombe, C. (2017). Twitter and transformative diplomacy. Social media and Iran-US relations. *International Affairs, 93*(3), 545–562.

Edwards, P. N. (2003). Infrastructure and modernity. Force, time and social organization in the history of sociotechnical systems. In T. J. Misa, P. Brey, & A. Feenberg (Eds.), *Modernity and Technology* (pp. 185–225). MIT Press.

Farrell, H., & Newman, A. L. (2019). Weaponized interdependence: How global economic networks shape state coercion. *International Security, 44*(1), 42–79.

Flint, C., & Zhu, C. (2019). The geopolitics of connectivity, cooperation, and hegemonic competition The Belt and Road Initiative. *Geoforum, 99*, 95–101.

Gertz, G., & Evers, M. M. (2020). Geoeconomic competition. Will state capitalism win? *Washington Quarterly, 43*(2), 117–136.

Gill, B. (2022). Dead papers. Migrant 'illegality', city brokers, and the dilemma of exit for unauthorised African migrants in Delhi. *Journal of Ethnic and Migration Studies, 48*(9), 1961–1979.

Glass, M. R., Addie, J.-P.D., & Nelles, J. (2019). Regional infrastructures, infrastructural regionalism. *Regional Studies, 53*(12), 1651–1656.

Hesmondhalgh, D. (2021). The infrastructural turn in media and internet research. In P. McDonald (Ed.), *The Routledge Companion to Media Industries* (pp. 132–142). Routledge.

Kampf, R., Manor, I., & Segev, E. (2015). Digital diplomacy 2.0? A cross-national comparison of public engagement in Facebook and Twitter. *The Hague Journal of Diplomacy, 10*(4), 331–362.

Kühne, O. (2018). *Landscape and power in geographical space as a social-aesthetic construct.* Springer.

Langenohl, A. (2020). Articulating sovereignty within the infrastructural imagination: The case of the securitisation of finance as 'critical infrastructure.' *Politikon, 47*(1), 4–23.

Larkin, B. (2013). The politics and poetics of infrastructure. *Annual Review of Anthropology, 42*, 327–343.

Lawson, G., Armbruster, C., & Cox, M. (Eds.). (2010). *The global 1989: Continuity and change in world politics*. Cambrigde University Press.
Leonard, M. (2021). *The age of unpeace. How connectivity causes conflict.* Bantam Press.
Mayer, M., & Acuto, M. (2015). The global governance of large technical systems. *Millennium, 43*(2), 660–683.
Mayntz, R. (1988). Zur Entwicklung technischer Infrastruktursysteme. In R. Mayntz et al. (Eds.), *Differenzierung und Verselbständigung. Zur Entwicklung gesellschaftlicher Teilsysteme* (pp. 233–259). Campus.
Paraschiv, F., Erni, D., & Pietsch, R. (2014). The impact of renewable energies on EEX day-ahead electricity prices. *Energy Policy, 73*, 196–210.
Patel, K. K., & Kaiser, W. (2018). Continuity and change in European cooperation during the twentieth century. *Contemporary European History, 27*(2), 165–182.
Petry, J. (2021). From national marketplaces to global providers of financial infrastructures. Exchanges, infrastructures and structural power in global finance. *New Political Economy, 26*(4), 574–597.
Plantin, J.-C., & Punathambekar, A. (2019). Digital media infrastructures: Pipes, platforms, and politics. *Media, Culture & Society, 41*(2), 163–174.
Rosenau, J. N. (1992). Governance, order, and change in world politics. In J. N. Rosenau & E.-O. Czempiel (Eds.), *Governance without government: Order and change in world politics* (pp. 1–29). Cambridge University Press.
Stephen, M. D., & Zürn, M. (Eds.). (2019). *Contested world orders: Rising powers, non-governmental organizations, and the politics of authority beyond the nation-state*. Oxford University Press.
Teschke, B. (2003). *The myth of 1648: Class, geopolitics, and the making of modern international relations*. Verso.
Turner, C., & Johnson, D. (2017). *Global infrastructure networks. The trans-national strategy and policy interface*. Edward Elgar.
Van Laak, D. (2018). *Alles im Fluss. Die Lebensadern unserer Gesellschaft*. S. Fischer.
Wiener, A. (2014). *A Theory of Contestation*. Berlin, Heidelberg: Springer.
Westermeier, C. (2020). Money is data. The platformization of financial transactions. *Information, Communication & Society, 23*(14), 2047–2063.

Hans-Jürgen Bieling is Professor of Political Economy at the Institute of Political Science, University of Tübingen. His research focusses on transformations in the global and European political economy, in terms of finance, labour markets and social security systems, governmental strategies and forms of political participation. Some of his research was published in Review of International Political Economy, New Political Economy, Competition & Change, Globalizations, Journal of European Public Policy, Journal of Common Market Studies, Transfer: European Review of Labour and Research or Politics & Governance. More recently, he works on the transformative role of—globalisation-relevant—infrastructures, also as PI of the Project "EUInfra: Strategies of the EU in the global competition for economic expansion and geoeconomic control", funded by the DFG.

Thomas Diez is Professor of Political Science and International Relations at the University of Tübingen and a former President of the European International Studies Association (EISA). He previously held positions at the Copenhagen Peace Research Institute and the University of Birmingham and has taught in Copenhagen, Aarhus, Munich and Victoria (BC). Among his publications are *The Routledge Handbook on Critical European Studies* (co-editor, Routledge, 2021), *The*

EU and Global Climate Justice (co-author, Routledge, 2021); *The EU, Promoting Regional Integration, and Conflict Resolution* (co-editor, Palgrave 2017), *The Securitisation of Climate Change* (co-author, Palgrave, 2016), as well as many articles in journals including *Review of International Studies*, *International Affairs*, *International Organization* and *Cooperation and Conflict*.

Riccarda Flemmer is Junior-Professor for "Political Struggles in the Global South" at the Institute of Political Science at the University of Tübingen. She previously worked as a researcher at the German Institute for Global and Area Studies (GIGA) and the University of Hamburg. She is council member of the Amazonia Section at the Latin American Studies Association (LASA), member of the Advisory Board of the Heidelberg Institute for International Conflict Research's (HIIK) annual Conflict Barometer and part of the focal group on 'Ethnographic Methods' of the Deutsche Vereinigung für Politikwissenschaft (DVPW) as well as part of the Environmental Justice Network (EnJust), the Political Ecology Network (POLLEN) and the Red de Estudios sobre las Resistencias Indígenas (RERI). Her research interests include indigenous peoples' rights, environmental conflicts, Rights of Nature and the ontological politics of human-nature relations.

Andrea Futterer is a postdoctoral researcher and lecturer at the Institute of Political Science at the University of Tübingen. Her research interests are social security systems, especially healthcare, the EU and infrastructures. Andrea Futterer is currently coordinating the research project "Infrastructures and Global Ordering". From 2020 to 2023, she was a researcher in the BMBF-funded research project "Common Public Goods. The Political Organization of Infrastructure Provision in the Regulatory State".

Part I

Infrastructures and the Re-making of Global Orders

Infrastructural Development and the Ordering of International Society

Thomas Diez

Abstract

This chapter argues that infrastructures have enabled particular kinds of international order in specific historical and regional circumstances, and their use, as well as the emergence of new technologies, have in turn undermined established orders. I suggest five different influences of infrastructure on ordering processes: infrastructures allow constituent units to be formed; they change the interaction capacity among those units; they affect prevailing societal discourses and thus the formation of norms; they have an impact on the patterns of practices among units; and they change the ways in which secondary institutions operate. Current debates about the instrumentalisation of infrastructure or its "weaponisation" are thus too limited. I show how infrastructure is not only used by actors to advance their goals; the actors themselves owe their very existence to infrastructural developments. Infrastructural changes thus need to be seen as a site of struggles over the order not only of international but also domestic societies.

Keywords

International society · International order · Infrastructure · Solidarization · International organisations · Political struggle

T. Diez (✉)
Institut für Politikwissenschaft, Universität Tübingen, Tübingen, Germany
e-mail: thomas.diez@uni-tuebingen.de

H.-J. Bieling et al. (eds.), *Transnational Infrastructures and the Transformation of Global Orders*, RaumFragen: Stadt – Region – Landschaft,
https://doi.org/10.1007/978-3-031-74846-2_2

1 Introduction

China's Belt and Road Initiative and the EU's Global Gateway have highlighted the ways in which international actors use infrastructure to project their power within and beyond their own regions. An essential part of these projections is the shaping of a particular order in terms of the allocation of material assets, the institutionalisation of particular norms and the shaping of specific practices, as defined in the Introduction to this volume. Thus, the linkage between infrastructures and international ordering have been put into the limelight of public debates in the 2000s.

I argue in this chapter that this linkage is nothing new and that infrastructure has always been both the backbone and a menace to international orders. The linkage between them goes far beyond the instrumentalization of infrastructure—or even what some have called its "weaponisation" (Farrell & Newman, 2019). Instead, infrastructures have enabled particular kinds of international order in specific historical and regional circumstances, and their use, as well as the emergence of new technologies, have in turn undermined established orders.

In line with the general approach of this volume, I use a narrow conceptualisation of infrastructure as 'built networks that facilitate the flow of goods, people, or ideas and allow for their exchange over space' (Larkin, 2013, p. 328). As Larkin notes, such infrastructures 'literally provid[e] the undergirding of modern societies' (Larkin, 2013, p. 328). This, I argue, also applies to what I call the international society, or the society of states. Understanding the international not merely as a system but as a society of collective actors such as states focuses our attention on the institutions of that society, which in turn make up the core of its order. Central among these institutions is diplomacy, and it is easy to see how the development of infrastructure based on different forms of communication technology has influenced diplomacy over the centuries. This is just one example of the nexus between infrastructure and international order.

As I will show, infrastructure not only influences the practices with which states engage with each other; it has also allowed states to emerge as the prime constituent units of the international society. Yet infrastructural developments have allowed actors such as civil society organisations, international organisations and transnational corporations to contest states as the prime units of political organisation. When analysing the impact of infrastructure on international orders, we thus must not only look at the patterns of interaction but also at the very constitution of the main subjects of that order.

As a starting point, I introduce the concept of international society and its relation with the concept of order in Sect. 2. Section 3 discusses the role of institutions and their relevance for the ordering processes in international society. Section 4 then shows how infrastructures have been both the backbone and a menace to international orders in history—how they have enabled and undermined ordering practices. I conclude with some reflections on what this means for our current debates about the infrastructure-order-nexus, in which I plead for less presentism and a recognition of the ever-changing nature of infrastructures and thus of ordering processes, its inherent ambiguities and its contestations.

2 The Order(s) of International Society

The study of order in the discipline of International Relations is closely linked to the concept of international society, most famously in the work of Hedley Bull (1977). Bull's study of 'order in world politics' rests on the idea that states do not only form a system in which mechanistic relations emerge from the fact that states are functionally so deeply intertwined that the actions of one have effects on another even if such effects were not intended. Traditionally, the international has been described in such systemic terms, particularly in realism. One can see the systems logic at work in the idea that over time, states will form a balance of power, and that violations of this principle will automatically lead to the reassertion of such a balance, most likely through war. Readers will recognise this sort of reasoning in John Mearsheimer's argument that NATO expansion is the cause of Russia's invasion of Ukraine (Mearsheimer, 2022).

Bull, in contrast, argues that relations between states are not purely mechanistic and cannot be understood in terms of universal, transhistorical rules. Instead, he maintains that states 'form a society in the sense that they conceive themselves to be bound by a common set of rules in their relations with one another, and share in the working of common institutions' (Bull, 1977, p. 13). In contrast to societies within states, the society of states is not hierarchically organised: it is an 'anarchical society'. The shared interests of the states in this society are to secure their existence and predominant status. Thus, this society only knows rudimentary norms, most importantly sovereignty and non-intervention. Yet these norms are forceful nonetheless: they have led to an aversion to recognise secessionist entities in the United Nations, to reinstating the decision-making authority of states over civil society actors in climate regime negotiations, or to limit the possibilities of enforcing human rights globally.

It is important to emphasize that the international society thus conceived is a society of states, not individuals. Scholars have traditionally distinguished between international and world society, or more recently between an inter-state society on the one hand, and transnational and inter-human societies on the other (Buzan, 2004). In particular, international society is not some ideal of peace and harmony: as any other society, it is always changing, always contested, and always full of power implications. Consequently, any order within this society is never stable. While we may be able to observe a prevailing order at a given moment in time, across time we should rather speak of ordering processes that never cease to end. And these ordering processes do not necessarily lead to a more peaceful or egalitarian society: they always imply the imposition of power relations; they exclude as much as they include; they marginalise as they integrate; they stratify relations among states and between states and other actors (Keene, 2014).

The way I understand order departs from Bull's work, in which order is a value to be upheld against potential threats because it is the foundation for peace. Bull had a strong preference for a pluralist conception of international society in which the sovereignty of states is prior to any other claims. This led him to juxtapose the order of such an international society to a conception of justice that he relates to world societal claims of human rights or other universalist claims. Bull sees such universalisms as a threat to order, at least as long as state leaders do not share them (Bull, 1971; Wheeler & Dunne, 1996). Yet such a static and statist conceptualisation of order (and justice) is strangely ahistorical (given Bull's preference for historical rather than social scientific analysis) and belittles the negative aspects of a pluralist order. It ignores that there are in fact different orders, across history but also contemporaneously, and sometimes even overlapping. For instance, scholars have juxtaposed Bull's conception of a pluralist order to a solidarist one in which states take into account world societal claims such as human rights or climate justice (Ahrens & Diez, 2015; Bain, 2014; Wheeler, 1992). The post-Cold War liberal international order may be described as a more solidarist one, while its demise is testament to the simultaneous persistence of contending orders as well as to its many shortcomings in terms of global justice (Buzan, 2021; Diez & von Lucke, 2023).

Ordering processes in international society comprise three dimensions. First, they lead to a particular distribution of material assets. Stratification thus is an inherent aspect if ordering processes. They assign privileged roles such as "great powers" in relation to material assets and shape the flow of economic benefits from trade and other forms of exchange and extraction. Second, ordering processes are about shaping patterns of practice in the interactions between members of any, including international society. Third, they forge the institutionalisation of norms that prescribe what is appropriate behaviour in a society. These latter two dimensions are clearly related to each other, as the interactions between members of a society will be shaped by the norms and vice versa, and it is these two dimensions that I will focus on in my reflections on how infrastructure influences order in international society.

Last but not least, scholars have rightly pointed out that international societies historically have had other constituent units than states, such as clans or empires, and that other units, such as regions or functionally defined organisations, may in the future become constitutive, even if the label international society may then no longer be appropriate (Buzan & Little, 2000; Buzan & Schouenborg, 2018). An important aspect of studying the order of international society thus concerns not only the dimensions outlined above but also the more fundamental question of what allowed states to become the main organising unit of societies on a global scale and whether they will continue to maintain this status.

3 Institutions and Ordering Processes in International Society

Order in international society is maintained through international institutions. Scholars distinguish between institutions in a broader sense, defined as patterns of practice, and often referred to as "primary institutions", and institutions in a narrower sense, or "secondary institutions", such as international organisations or regimes, which turn the norms emerging from patterns of practice into formalised rules (Buzan, 2006; Spandler, 2015). In the definition of order that we use in this volume, these primary and secondary institutions appear as two of the core dimensions of order, patterns of practice and institutionalised norms. Rather than maintaining order, which would be difficult to distinguish from the order itself, primary and secondary institutions are thus part of the order itself. This leaves out the distribution of material assets, and International Society scholarship has thus been criticised for ignoring economic aspects, although material assets are not necessarily economic in nature (Buzan, 2005).

The relationship between primary and secondary institutions is a matter of debate. While the labels suggest that primary institutions precede secondary institutions, the development of international organizations and regimes also often changes the broader patterns of practice. Thus, the established labels are slightly misleading, and one should think of a reciprocal relationship between institutions more narrowly and more widely conceived (Friedner Parrat, 2017).

Also debated is what the core primary institutions are. One problem in this context is how to empirically identify "patterns of practice", which will always be a matter of judgement. Another problem is the distinction between single norms and institutions as practices related to a set of norms. Some have thus included "sovereignty" (Wight, 1991) or "environmental stewardship" (Falkner & Buzan, 2019) in their list of (potential) primary institutions, but I suggest that, in the interest of not excessively expanding the notion of primary institutions, we ought to consider both as (potential) norms rather than institutions as they do not seem to bundle norms in a set of practices to maintain norms. A third problem is that many authors suggest that with decolonisation, we have seen the emergence of a single, global international society. Yet this ignores that there are competing visions of this society (e.g. along the pluralist—solidarist dimension) and thus multiple international societies (Flockhart, 2016); that we cannot assume a static, everlasting order but competing ordering processes; and that even if we assume a global international society, we would find several regional international societies nested within it, developing norms and institutions that often are in tensions with those of the ideal typical international society that we find in Bull, for example (Diez & Whitman, 2002; Karmazin, 2014).

Yet the five primary institutions originally identified by Bull (1977) are on most people's lists. They include diplomacy, international law, great power management, balance of power, and war. Of these, diplomacy and international law are likely to meet intuitive approval: states routinely engage in diplomatic relations, invoke law and build legal institutions to organise their relations with each other. As my discussion of the impact of infrastructure on these institutions within the scope of this article will be merely illustrative, I will focus on diplomacy and international law as the two institutions that seem largely undisputed. As core dimensions of international ordering processes, they serve as important instruments for states to communicate with each other, for norms and rules to be developed, negotiated and interpreted, for compliance with norms to be monitored, for actions to be legitimised, etc. To fulfil these functions, states form secondary institutions that codify broader norms into concrete rules and decision-making procedures and, in their more formalised versions, provide an administrative apparatus. Thus, change and contestation may operate at the level of primary or secondary institutions to affect the order as a whole.

Change and contestation may alter practices, norms and rules within institutions or fundamentally challenge them. If they are fundamentally challenged, this often implies a change in the constituent subjects of international society. One of the reasons why Bull's five institutions form a sort of consensus view is that they have, in their variations, been core to state practices over a long time, and have served states to instal and defend sovereignty, prevent the rise of global hegemons or a world government, and defend their status against contenders. This does not mean that they have not changed. Yet the debates about an increasingly solidarist international society in the 1990s and 2000s have, at least in retrospect, clarified two core things:

First, the "solidarisation" led to an amendment of norms and rules within institutions but not to their abandonment. Think of the severely limited scope within which the International Criminal Court (ICC) may act or intervention under the Responsibility to Protect (R2P) was envisioned. Likewise, non-state actors were integrated into international society by giving them legal standing or incorporating them into decision-making processes, but again, this was heavily circumscribed and never questioned the dominance of states.

Second, moves towards more solidarism were always contested and implied the imposition of a particular "purpose" of global governance (Ashley, 1989). Yet the strongest contenders, at least from the perspective of the mid-2020s, were not transnational civil society activists but states who wanted to maintain or revert to the pluralist order of international society. Whether the US under Trump, China or Russia, or many countries of the Global South: their objection to the post-Cold War liberal international order did not ask for more radical changes, but for the reinsertion of the core practices and institutionalised norms of a pluralist society, with state sovereignty at its heart, even if Russia, most obviously, violated that very core principle numerous times through its military invasions of other states.

All of this is not to say that more radical change may not happen in the future, and that infrastructure may play a crucial role in this change. As I proceed now to discuss the impact of infrastructure on these institutions, I explicitly argue that in the long run, infrastructural developments will be the most likely source of more radical change. Yet even the impact of infrastructure is more likely to make practices and rules evolve within existing frameworks. In the short- to medium-term, it, therefore, seems more likely that the development of international order will move within the spectrum of becoming more pluralist or more solidarist (Watson, 1997) rather than moving towards a radically different order.

4 The Role of Infrastructure

As both the state practices that form primary institutions and the workings of secondary institutions depend on infrastructure, the argument that infrastructure has core effects on these institutions and thus on ordering processes should make immediate sense. In his seminal treatment of the rise and possible change of territoriality as a core organising principle of international order, John Ruggie (1993), for instance, refers to technological and infrastructural changes as one of four main, interconnected driving forces for changes in the international order.

While infrastructural effects include the distribution of material resources, I will largely bracket resources and refer to other contributions in this volume (see, e.g. Bieling 2024). I suggest five different influences of infrastructure on ordering processes:

1. Infrastructures allow constituent units to be formed
2. They change the interaction capacity among those units
3. They affect prevailing societal discourses and thus the formation of norms
4. They have an impact on the patterns of practices among units
5. They change the ways in which secondary institutions operate

Whereas influences 1–3 may be considered laying the groundworks for influences 4 and 5, the latter may also be affected by infrastructure directly, especially if changes are not of the radical kind.

Infrastructures Allow Constituent Units to Be Formed

International society theorists see the emergence of the international society linked to the formation of the modern territorial state and the diffusion of this model from a European core to global reach (Bull & Watson, 1985). Leaving aside the Eurocentrism of this narrative (Zarakol, 2022), its account largely omits the role of infrastructure in making the modern territorial, and later nation state possible. Yet as Michael Mann (1984, 1993), among others, has demonstrated, infrastructure played a crucial role in establishing state control over territory and developing national identities. For Mann, the power of the state rests on two sources, ideology and infrastructure, and he defines "infrastructural power" as 'the capacity of the state to actually penetrate civil society, and to implement logistically political decisions throughout the realm' (Mann, 1984, p. 189). This capacity builds on a centralised state bureaucracy providing, maintaining and controlling core infrastructures from (rail)roads to rivers, electricity grids, printing machines and distribution mechanisms, etc.

Yet for the state to utilise such infrastructure resources to control territory and penetrate societies, it also needed the technology that allowed infrastructural projects to be carried out. No modern bureaucracy would have been possible without the development of the printing machine and telecommunication technologies. The surveillance of borders relies on cameras, roads networks and yet again communication facilities. A sense of a territorially bounded nation is promoted by the ability to build national grids of electricity, motorways, railways and television transmissions.

Thus, the rise of the modern territorial state as the primary form of political organisation relied on the availability of an infrastructure that made it possible to communicate and circulate goods and people within a confined space, and to control that space. Even during the high time of the nation state in the early 1900s, this control was never complete: people could travel further than their states' borders, but to do so, they needed to invest considerable energy and financial resources. Likewise, it was possible to receive foreign radio or TV channels in the mid-1900s, but only if one had the necessary technological know-how.

There is no 1:1 relationship between infrastructures and constituent units of an international society. The same infrastructures that enabled the formation of the territorial state also made empires possible. Still, our predominant form of political organisation would look very different if it was not for the existence of printing machines, roadworks, railroads or telecommunication channels, which allowed the standardisation of language, the control of territorial borders, and the communication of hierarchically organised bureaucracies.

Drawing on Anthony Giddens' concept of structuration, Paul Edwards has captured the co-constitutive nature of infrastructure and actors by calling it "infrastructuration" (Edwards, 2019). The development of the constituent units of international society is one such process of infrastructuration. Changing infrastructural technologies provides new opportunities for the formation of such units, or for shifts in their relative importance. The rise of mass travel, global trade, the internet and social media, among others, have all challenged the nation state as the predominant form of political organisation and our narratives of national identities. They have also been used by novel forms of actors such as the European Union to promote a different, regional kind of international order. Yet as Mann (1997) has pointed out, we should not be too quick to judge their impact—exactly because their effect is not a one-way stream, and our ideologies are still very much tied to the state and its national imagination. Thus on the one hand, new infrastructures may make 'people more "cocky", experimental and improvisational' and thus 'more democratic and less fixed and hierarchical' (Connolly, 2002), leading to the formation of new kinds of political organisations. Yet on the other hand, it is still unclear what and where 'the place' may be 'that might, if not supplant loyalty to the state, compete with it so that sometimes a new "we" finds itself bestowing allegiance on constituencies and aspirations in ways that contest the state's monopoly over political allegiance' (Connolly, 1995, p. 159). But chances are that in the long run, international society will no longer be built on states as we know them today, to a large part because infrastructural technology has made the formation of new constituent units possible.

Infrastructures Change the Interaction Capacity Among Those Units

Ordering processes depend on the forms and degrees to which it is possible for the units in a society to interact with each other. Indeed, the institutions of international society are patterns not of any kind of action, but of interaction. In various works with different co-authors, Buzan has therefore highlighted the role that interaction capacity plays for the development of order in international societies. In his definition, '[i]nteraction capacity refers to the amount of transportation, communication and organisational capacity within the system: how much in the way of information, goods and people can be moved over what distances, at what speeds and at what cost' (Buzan, 2010, p. 11). For Buzan, the 'evolution of technology continuously raises the absolute capability for interaction available within the system' (Buzan et al., 1993, p. 69). Interaction capacity cannot be controlled by individual units alone; it is a structural component of the system, and as such provides an ordering function in society (Buzan et al., 1993, p. 71). Like Edwards, Buzan emphasises the mutual constitution of technological (i.e. infrastructural) and institutional developments.

Enhanced interaction capacity enables swifter communication and has a profound impact on the possibilities to control communication. In the classic pluralist state order, diplomacy required the possibility to communicate at long distances between states as the main constituent units of international society. Yet at the same time, such diplomacy relied on limited speed so that responses could be considered and decided upon. It also relied on the exclusion of civil society actors to reduce outside pressure on states. Higher degrees of interaction capacity have led to an acceleration of communication, which on the one hand allowed the formation of intensified structures of global governance, as crises became known much more quickly globally. They also led to a better possibility to respond by providing assistance and intervening across long distances. At the same time, this has increased the number of issues to be dealt with and resulted in a considerable overload of diplomacy, now operating under a much higher degree of time pressure and under more public scrutiny (Kleiner, 2008).

In this context, Buzan et al., following Rosenau, suggest that in systems of high interaction capacity, units may change, and so states may come under pressure from 'a better educated, more aware, more critical, more engaged, and more networked global citizenry' (Buzan et al., 1993, p. 78). Yet state actors have also made use of new infrastructural technology and have engaged, for instance, in "Twitter diplomacy" (Duncombe, 2018). The results are ambiguous. More possibilities to engage and react have not always meant more cooperation, but also new forms of hegemony and exerting pressure. This would require a longer discussion which I cannot pursue in the context of this chapter. The main point though is that infrastructural developments change the interaction capacity of a system in which societies are operating, and this has profound effects on the constituent units of that society and their institutions.

Infrastructures Affect Prevailing Societal Discourses and Thus the Formation of Norms
For Buzan et al. (1993, p. 79), interaction capacity is not only about technology, but also involves the 'societal capabilities across the system'. This societal aspect of interaction however depends a great deal on how the actors within a society construct their world(s), the challenges they face and potential solutions. Ruggie (1993) captured this in his concept of "societal epistemes": the ways in which societies operated with different discursive constructions of time and space, identities and differences.

Infrastructures significantly influence such prevailing discourses in societies, and thus societies' possibilities to imagine particular institutions in their ordering practices. These influences work partly through the imagination of the main units of political organisation. The formation of the nation state was thus not only dependent on the availability of a certain technological infrastructure but also on the imagination of the nation that this infrastructure allowed (Anderson, 1983): the emergence of a discourse of national cultural homogeneity through schooling, museums, or even censuses, all of which relied on the possibility to move information within relatively closed territorial spaces and thus on mobilisation as much as on immobilisation. The further development of transport and communication infrastructure has significantly changed the understanding of who we are and how the world ought to be organised—think of nomadic versus state societies, or conceptions of the "Grand Tour" through Europe in the eighteenth century versus the maps of Interrail and budget airline travels today (Manka, 2024).

Yet infrastructures also influence the way we conceive relations between units and shape expectations of involvement. Mass media events such as the 1985 Live Aid concert contributed to the 'globalisation of compassion' (O'Sullivan, 2021) while perpetuating the stratification of international (and world) society (Grant, 2015). They not only shaped the imagination of the global but also expectations about state engagement to alleviate food crises and that non-state actors play a legitimate role in these efforts. Forty years later, infrastructures have allowed media communication to globalise even further, and at the same time to significantly diversify. Global imaginations have thus become more like a patchwork, and for better or worse, this has multiplied the ways in which a more diverse range of actors in international society actors, including non-governmental organisations and companies, are expected to engage with each other.

Infrastructures Have an Impact on the Patterns of Practices Among Units

Thus, both through technological interaction capacity and prevailing societal discourses, infrastructure changes the institutions of international society in their broader sense as patterns of practices among constituent units. I have already mentioned the impact on diplomacy. Classic diplomacy relies on limited communication between states through controllable channels and heavily regulated, formalised and routinised practices. The classic diplomat operated between being a bureaucrat, a hero and a mediator (Neumann 2005), and s/he practised these roles through a specific infrastructure. Practices such as the recognition of diplomats and the extraterritoriality of embassies, the summoning of ambassadors, accreditation of diplomats and the privileges of their passports, diplomatic correspondence and dress codes—all operate within a space of communication that is heavily regulated and reliant on technologically limited communication.

Yet the availability of ever-increasing communication channels has changed these practices significantly. It is not only individual state leaders and diplomats who use social media. The latter has also had a major impact on public diplomacy. It has become much easier to reach and influence the debates in another state, and as a consequence, it has become more difficult to maintain a closed debate within authoritarian states but also allowed misinformation campaigns undermining democracies (Erpul, 2023).

Similarly, practices of international law have changed on the back of infrastructural changes (Perritt, 1997). The persecution of crimes against humanity has become easier as the internet has opened up new sources of investigation and made more traces of crimes available. At the same time, the reimagination of global responsibilities has led to a demand that such crimes are persecuted. Both have facilitated the solidarisation of international law through the formation of the ICC or the formulation of the R2P. Yet this is only one policy area in which international law has been changing. Another one is environmental law, where the internet and social media have changed the possibilities of civil society actors to organise and take states to court on the back of international treaties and agreements.

While these changes are significant, it is important to stress that, as I have argued in Sect. 3, they have not led to a wholesale abandoning of diplomacy and international law. Instead, practices have been expanded to new actors, from NGOs to celebrities, and sources, from media reports to tweets. As Corneliu Bjola and Ilan Manor (Bjola & Manor, 2022, p. 471) argue in relation to diplomacy, 'physical and virtual engagements are expected to integrate, complement and empower each other'.

Infrastructures Change the Ways in Which Secondary Institutions Operate

Technological infrastructures not only change primary institutions but also secondary institutions. Improved transport links make it easier for developmental organisations to get aid into different areas. New communication technologies allow bureaucracies to stay in touch with partner offices in other regions and different states, obtain information from a variety of sources and check compliance (Ecker-Ehrhardt, 2023). Where a physical meeting used to be complex to arrange, virtual meetings have become easy ways to continue conversations between bigger conferences. The possibilities of generating and storing data have expanded so much that future modelling has become easier, while the selection of relevant data has become a challenge.

The broader infrastructural impact on primary institutions is thus reflected in the concrete work of secondary institutions. The ICC, for instance, uses a series of technological advancements in its proceedings, from software to store case-relevant data to videoconferencing, from digital public diplomacy to tools to facilitate contacts with government bureaucracies, other courts, international and non-governmental organisations (Corrie, 2015).

These changes in the operation of secondary institutions are part of and influence ordering processes. They lead to new centralisations and fragmentations of knowledge among different actors. States struggle with international organisations over who has which decision-making power, while the distribution of knowledge generated by communication and data infrastructure often leads to informal authority. In some instances, the involvement in secondary institutions has become more dispersed, in others more centralised. While they go in different directions and require further analysis, the main point in the context of this article is that these changes are all intertwined with the development of infrastructure, where technological infrastructure allows new forms of communication, while actors use infrastructure to support their own position.

5 Conclusion

The aim of this chapter was to demonstrate that infrastructural developments are a major source of change in the ordering processes of international societies. I have argued that infrastructural innovations have allowed the territorial state as the main unit of political organisation to rise, and have enabled challengers to the state to appear. Infrastructure is a core aspect of the interaction capacity of a system and affects the predominant societal discourses and self-understandings. Infrastructure changes the patterns of practice amongst states and other actors as much as it has an impact on the way secondary institutions operate. All of these changes affect ordering processes: they change the nature of the constitutive units of international society, its main primary institutions, its institutionalised norms, and the distribution of material assets between actors within a society (even though I largely bracketed this latter point).

Current debates about the instrumentalisation of infrastructure or its "weaponisation" are thus too limited. Infrastructure is not only used by actors to advance their goals; the actors themselves owe their very existence to infrastructural developments. Approaching infrastructural change with a focus on its management overlooks the degree to which such change will alter the fundamental ways in which international society works, and fails to acknowledge the degree to which our present constellation of orders has emerged on the basis of the development of infrastructural technology.

Infrastructure thus has always been the backbone and a menace to international order: sea passages and the advancement of ship technology have allowed empires to rise and destroyed previously existing "international" societies; communication and transport infrastructures have allowed the nation state to emerge and are now threatening its predominant status; they have underpinned traditional diplomacy and are now heralding its change. It would be a fallacy to assume we can control these changes. Instead, we need to see them as struggles about our future in which a return to national autonomy seems unlikely, even if the 2020s have seen a major trend towards bringing infrastructures back into the fold of the state.

"Infrastructuring", as my explorations in this short piece have shown, is a complex process of technological development and what actors make of it, to paraphrase Wendt (Wendt, 1992). That makes it all the more important to engage in further research on how infrastructural developments are linked to ordering practices in different historical, regional and policy contexts.

References

Ahrens, B., & Diez, T. (2015). Solidarisation and its limits. *Global Discourse, 5*, 341–355. https://doi.org/10.1080/23269995.2015.1053189

Anderson, B. (1983). *Imagined communities—Reflections on the origins and spread of nationalism.* Verso.

Ashley, R. K. (1989). Imposing international purpose. In E. O. Czempiel & J. N. Rosenau (Eds.), *Global changes and theoretical challenges. Approaches to world politics for the 1990s* (pp. 251–290). Lexington Books.

Bain, W. (2014). The pluralist-solidarist debate in the english school. In C. Navari & D. Green (Eds.), *Guide to the english school in international studies* (pp. 159–169). Wiley-Blackwell.

Bjola, C., & Manor, I. (2022). The rise of hybrid diplomacy: From digital adaptation to digital adoption. *International Affairs, 98*, 471–491. https://doi.org/10.1093/ia/iiac005

Bull, H. (1971). Order vs. justice in international society. *Political Studies, 19*, 269–283. https://doi.org/10.1111/j.1467-9248.1971.tb00674.x

Bull, H. (1977). *The anarchical society.* Macmillan.

Bull, H., & Watson, A. (1985). *The expansion of international society.* Oxford University Press (Repr. as paperback).

Buzan, B. (2004). *From international to world society?* Cambridge University Press.

Buzan, B. (2005). International political economy and globalization. In A. J. Bellamy (Ed.), *International society and its critics* (pp. 115–134). Oxford University Press.

Buzan, B. (2006). An english school perspective on 'What kind of world order?' *Cooperation and Conflict, 41*, 364–369. https://doi.org/10.1177/0010836706069603

Buzan, B. (2010). Culture and international society. *International Affairs, 86*, 1–25. https://doi.org/10.1111/j.1468-2346.2010.00866.x

Buzan, B. (2021). Will the liberal international order survive? An english school perspective. In Y. Chu & Y. Zheng (Eds.), *The decline of the Western-centric world and the emerging New Global Order. Contending views* (pp. 166–185). Routledge.

Buzan, B., Jones, C., & Little, R. (1993). *The logic of anarchy: Neorealism to structural realism.* Columbia University Press.

Buzan, B., & Little, R. (2000). *International systems in world history.* Oxford University Press.

Buzan, B., & Schouenborg, L. (2018). *Global international society: A new framework for analysis.* Cambridge University Press.

Connolly, W. E. (1995). *The ethos of pluralization.* Minneapolis: University of Minnesota Press. New edition, Vol. 1.

Connolly, W. E. (2002). *Neuropolitics.* University of Minnesota Press.

Corrie, K. L. (2015). The International criminal court: Using technology in network diplomacy. In C. Bjola & M. Holmes (Eds.), *Digital Diplomacy* (pp. 145–163). Routledge.

Diez, T., & von Lucke, F. (2023). Global justice and EU climate policy in a contested liberal international order. *International Affairs, 99*, 2221–2239.

Diez, T., & Whitman, R. G. (2002). Analysing European integration: Reflecting on the english school—Scenarios for an encounter. *Journal of Common Market Studies, 40*, 43–67.

Duncombe, C. (2018). Twitter and the challenges of digital diplomacy. *SAIS Review of International Affairs, 38*(2), 91–100. https://doi.org/10.1353/sais.2018.0019

Ecker-Ehrhardt, M. (2023). The digital adaptation of international bureaucracies. In C. Bjola & I. Manor (Eds.), *The Oxford Handbook of Digital Diplomacy* (pp. 348–366). Oxford University Press.

Edwards, P. N. (2019). Infrastructuration: On habits, norms and routines as elements of infrastructure. In M. Kornberger, G. C. Bowker, J. Elyachar, A. Mennicken, P. Miller, & J. Randa Nucho et al. (Eds.), *Thinking infrastructures* (pp. 355–366). Emerald Publishing Limited. https://doi.org/10.1108/S0733-558X20190000062022

Erpul, O. (2023). Digital diplomacy and international society in the age of populism. In P. W. Hare, J. L. Manfredi-Sánchez, & K. Weisbrode (Eds.), *The Palgrave Handbook of Diplomatic Reform and Innovation* (pp. 143–166). Springer International Publishing. https://doi.org/10.1007/978-3-031-10971-3_7

Falkner, R., & Buzan, B. (2019). The emergence of environmental stewardship as a primary institution of global international society. *European Journal of International Relations, 25*, 131–155. https://doi.org/10.1177/1354066117741948

Farrell, H., & Newman, A. L. (2019). Weaponized interdependence: How global economic networks shape state coercion. *International Security, 44*(1), 42–79. https://doi.org/10.1162/isec_a_00351

Flockhart, T. (2016). The coming multi-order world. *Contemporary Security Policy, 37*, 3–30. https://doi.org/10.1080/13523260.2016.1150053

Friedner Parrat, C. (2017). On the evolution of primary institutions of international society. *International Studies Quarterly, 61*(3), 623–630. https://doi.org/10.1093/isq/sqx039

Grant, J. (2015). Live Aid/8: Perpetuating the superiority myth. *Critical Arts, 29*(3), 310–326. https://doi.org/10.1080/02560046.2015.1059547

Karmazin, A. (2014). Introduction: English school investigations at the regional level. In A. Karmazin, F. Costa-Buranelli, Y. Zhang, F. Merke, & K. Kaczmarska (Eds.), *Regions in International Society. The English School at the sub-global level* (pp. 1–21). Masarykova Univerzita.

Keene, E. (2014). The standard of 'civilisation', the expansion thesis and the 19th-century international social space. *Millennium—Journal of International Studies, 42*, 651–673. https://doi.org/10.1177/0305829814541319

Kleiner, J. (2008). The inertia of diplomacy. *Diplomacy & Statecraft, 19*, 321–349. https://doi.org/10.1080/09592290802096380

Larkin, B. (2013). The politics and poetics of infrastructure. *Annual Review of Anthropology, 42*, 327–343. https://doi.org/10.1146/annurev-anthro-092412-155522

Manka, M. (2024). Creating informal European integration by travelling? Swedish and Finnish travel reminiscences of Interrail travel 1972–1993. *Scandinavian Journal of History,* 1–21. https://doi.org/10.1080/03468755.2024.2324933

Mann, M. (1984). The autonomous power of the state: Its origins, mechanisms and results. *European Journal of Sociology/Archives Européennes De Sociologie/Europäisches Archiv Für Soziologie, 25*, 185–213.

Mann, M. (1993). Nation-states in Europe and other continents: Diversifying, developing, not dying. *Daedalus, 122*(3), 115–140.

Mann, M. (1997). Has globalization ended the rise and rise of the nation-state? *Review of International Political Economy, 4*, 472–496. https://doi.org/10.1080/096922997347715

Mearsheimer, J. J. (2022). The causes and consequences of the Ukraine War. *Horizons, 21*, 12–27.

O'Sullivan, K. (2021). *The NGO moment: The globalisation of compassion from Biafra to live aid.* Cambridge University Press.

Perritt, H. H. Jr. (1997). The internet is changing international law. Symposium on the internet and legal theory. *Chicago-Kent Law Review*, *73*(4), 997–1054.

Ruggie, J. G. (1993). Territoriality and beyond: Problematizing modernity in international relations. *International Organization, 47*, 139–174. https://doi.org/10.1017/S0020818300004732

Spandler, K. (2015). The political international society. *Review of International Studies, 41*, 601–622. https://doi.org/10.1017/S026021051400045X

Watson, A. (1997). *The limits of independence.* Routledge. https://doi.org/10.4324/9780203448069

Wendt, A. (1992). Anarchy is what states make of it: The social construction of power politics. *International Organization, 46*, 391–425. https://doi.org/10.1017/S0020818300027764

Wheeler, N. J. (1992). Pluralist or solidarist conceptions of international society: Bull and Vincent on humanitarian intervention. *Millennium—Journal of International Studies, 21*, 463–487. https://doi.org/10.1177/03058298920210030201

Wheeler, N. J., & Dunne, T. (1996). Hedley Bull's pluralism of the intellect and solidarism of the will. *International Affairs, 72*, 91–107.

Wight, M. (1991). *International theory: The three traditions.* Leicester: Leicester University Press. Edited by G. Wight & B. Porter.

Zarakol, A. (2022). *Before the west: The rise and fall of eastern world orders.* Cambridge University Press.

Thomas Diez is Professor of Political Science and International Relations at the University of Tübingen and a former President of the European International Studies Association (EISA). He previously held positions at the Copenhagen Peace Research Institute and the University of Birmingham and has taught in Copenhagen, Aarhus, Munich and Victoria (BC). Among his publications are *The Routledge Handbook on Critical European Studies* (co-editor, Routledge, 2021), *The EU and Global Climate Justice* (co-author, Routledge, 2021); *The EU, Promoting Regional Integration, and Conflict Resolution* (co-editor, Palgrave 2017), *The Securitisation of Climate Change* (co-author, Palgrave, 2016), as well as many articles in journals including *Review of International Studies, International Affairs, International Organization* and *Cooperation and Conflict.*

Capitalism and Infrastructural Ordering: (Re)Crafting of Statehood and Territorial Power

Jutta Bakonyi and May Darwich

Abstract

This chapter examines how capitalism is enabled by and anchored in the development and expansion of infrastructures. We show that infrastructures are more than just materials that enable movement. They facilitate the expansion of capitalist relations and provide crucial ordering mechanisms as they connect, direct and interrupt and hence shape how movements between people, things and societies unfold. We show how infrastructures are carving out state spaces from the wider capitalist relations, and that their dynamic evolves in the dialectic tension between materiality and mobility. While infrastructures enable the expansion and consolidation of statehood, and thus constitute boundaries through interruptions of movement, contemporary acceleration of mobilities also challenges and transforms these boundaries and spatial fixtures. Especially recent infrastructural booms in the Global South reveal how infrastructural dynamics challenge state-centred notions of territoriality and statehood, in what is revealed as a continuous process of crafting and recrafting of polities and societies.

This chapter is a spin-off from Bakonyi & Darwich, 2024. While some arguments may overlap, the current focus on the (international) political economy of infrastructures, and content, therefore, changed significantly.

J. Bakonyi (✉)
School of Government and International Affairs, Durham University, Durham, UK
e-mail: jutta.bakonyi@durham.ac.uk

M. Darwich
Department of Political Science and International Studies, University of Birmingham, Birmingham, UK
e-mail: m.darwich@bham.ac.uk

H.-J. Bieling et al. (eds.), *Transnational Infrastructures and the Transformation of Global Orders*, RaumFragen: Stadt – Region – Landschaft,
https://doi.org/10.1007/978-3-031-74846-2_3

Keywords

Capitalism · Infrastructure · Statehood · Territoriality · Mobility

> The wealth of those societies in which the capitalist mode of production prevails presents itself as "an immense accumulation of commodities" (Karl Marx)
>
> If you want to understand capitalism, you should visit IKEA (Marten Keetz 1989)

At the end of the 1980s, when Jutta was living in Hamburg (Germany), IKEA came to town. These were also the years when she started engaging with Karl Marx in reading groups organised by one of the many Marxist groups of that time. Jutta remembers vividly the discussions with her friend Marten when they first visited the newly opened store. IKEA seemed then paradigmatic for the way capitalist societies display their wealth. They were fascinated by the sheer size of the store and the modular design of their commodities. Mostly, however, both were impressed by the way consumers were channelled through the store's corridors while provided with paper and pencil to note down the things they would later pick up in the warehouse. The faces of these consumers displayed both stress and lust, attesting to the libidinal aspects of modern consumerism. The discussion soon turned to Wolfgang Pohrt's critique of modern consumer culture, and his observations of a declining use-value of commodities in societies, where production evolves as an end in itself and life is reduced to consumption (Pohrt, 1976, pp. 18–19). Three decades later, in 2013, May experienced a similar fascination when the first IKEA store opened in Cairo wrapped in its iconic blue and yellow brand colours. As this modern consumerism expands to the Middle East, the store continues to change consumer culture across the globe. In Egypt too, people became increasingly occupied with the purchase of such commodities, which also advanced into a sign of modernity for the upper and middle classes in the Global South.

Today, Amazon, more than IKEA, is a typical model for the workings of capitalism. Both IKEA and Amazon provide examples of the way infrastructure developments change spatial experiences in capitalist societies, and as we argue below, exemplify how infrastructures transform state-society relations and shape political understandings of territoriality. IKEA and Amazon are usually located on the outskirts of urban centres, at main highway junctions to which they are directly linked. Their business models rely on smooth movement and seamless infrastructural connectivity. While IKEA integrated shop and warehouse into one spatial system, Amazon took advantage of information and communication technologies to relocate its shop into the virtual world. Amazon became a gigantic distribution centre, which, unlike a shop or warehouse, does not primarily display or store goods but channels their flows and 'direct[s] their motion instead' (Birtchnell et al. 2015, p. 5). IKEA still needs to be accessible to consumers, while Amazon operates physically detached from the buyers, a detachment that is, as we will argue below, among the effects of contemporary infrastructural reordering. Both companies expanded their activities across borders,[1] although Amazon's expansion is again unparalleled, starting from an e-platform for books in the USA to an e-platform and distribution centre for nearly everything, delivered directly at the consumer's home and, at least for Prime customers, also at an extraordinary pace. The spatial expansion of the company, the diversification of goods Amazon offers, their speedy turn-around, and their focus on distribution attest to the shift from industrial capitalism to 'supply-chain-capitalism' (Tsing, 2009) and the logistics revolution in which this shift is embedded.

The remainder of this article shows how capitalism and infrastructural development are inextricably related, as capitalist modes of societal reproduction require mobility and continuous circulation enabled by infrastructural fixtures. We explore that infrastructural developments not only allow capitalist expansions but also transform capitalist modes of reproduction, which in turn change the conventional understanding of territoriality and statehood. We first discuss how capitalism is itself enabled by and anchored in the development and expansion of infrastructures, defined by Larkin (2013) as materials that enable the movement of other materials. We then attend to the link between infrastructure and statehood, analysing how infrastructures carve out states from wider societal relations as they enable, interrupt, direct and order movements between societies and people. The third section discusses the challenges that contemporary infrastructure developments pose to state-centred notions of territoriality, including state frontiers, where material and spatial fixes are themselves continuously transformed.

1 Infrastructural Anchorage and Transformation of Capitalism

In *The Capital* (MEW 23, 1988), Karl Marx outlined, in enormous analytical and empirical detail over hundreds of pages, how capitalism works. In this argument, capitalism constitutes a historically specific social system, centred around the production and exchange of commodities. For Marx, commodities materialise the dialectic tension between use-value (what we need) and exchange-value (what we receive in exchanging/selling the commodity), the latter based on the transformation of living labour into a commodity. Therefore, labour too has a use-value, the human capacity to produce goods and to insert value into things; and it has an exchange-value, realized in wages. These wages, however, are below the value that labourers insert into the commodity during the production processes, thus allowing the capitalist to extract a surplus.

Capitalism is characterised by the generalisation of the commodity form, the commodification of labour power, and the development of money as a medium of exchange.

[1] In 2019, IKEA has 422 shops across Europe, Australia, the Middle East, East-Asia, and the Americas becoming the world's largest home furniture provider. https://www.mike-barker.com/writing/ikea-visualisation-notes (accessed 16 May 2024).

For Marx, capitalism is not merely an economic system, but a historic specific modality of social organisation. The only objective of capital is the *accumulation of capital*, i.e., to make more money out of money. Commodification (transforming everything into a commodity) and commercialisation (making money out of the exchange of these commodities) drive the insatiable capitalist dynamic, which unfolds beyond the control of the people who created it (MEW 23, pp. 164, 168; Postone, 1993, p. 31). In its continuous expansion, capitalism devours every non-capitalist social form and subsumes it to its logic. Capital, therefore, is a universalizing and a global force and constitutes the so far 'only historical social system that has become truly global in scale and scope' (Arrighi, 2006, p. 201). This does not mean that capitalism takes the same form everywhere. On the contrary, capitalist relations develop dynamics in their encounters with existing inter-societal inequalities (Rosenberg 2013, 208–9) and local contexts. The societal modalities of capitalism are, therefore, always historically and locally specific.

In analysing the intricate dynamics of capitalism, Marx also acknowledged the importance of circulation. While labour inserts value into the commodity during the production process, it is within the sphere of circulation that the exchange value is realized, and the commodity is transformed into money. Meanwhile, money flows in the opposite direction of the commodity, from the consumer to producer to resource extractor. The reality of circulation is, of course, more complex, as many things move through many different places. Capital, therefore, 'is a category of movement, of expansion; it is a dynamic category, "value in motion"' (Postone, 1993, p. 269).

Mobility is a central feature of capitalism, where circulation is immersed in its reproduction and required at every stage of the commodity chain, including 'extraction, production, consumption, and waste disposal' (Ciccantell & Bunker, 1998, p. 6). Raw materials, electricity, water, and labour are moved to factories, commodities are transported to retailers, and garbage is produced at every stage of the process, segregated, and shipped away to be disposed of or recycled, thus, inserted with value and transformed into a commodity. As capitalist modes of societal reproduction require mobility and facilitate continuous circulation, the advance of capitalism goes hand in hand with the development of infrastructures. Infrastructures not only enable capitalist expansion across space and time but they also contribute to the reconfiguration of both space and time (Postone, 1993), what humans increasingly experience as 'time–space compression' (Harvey, 1989, p. 240).

The second half of the nineteenth century, for example, witnessed a global wave of engineering with ports, canals, roads, and trains facilitating the infrastructural integration of empires. The advent of the steamship and train introduced a new rhythm of life that no longer aligned with the rhythm of nature, overcoming day/night shifts, seasons, tides, currents, and winds. Railways gave rise to a 'railway time' and led to the designation of standard times and time zones in the 1880s and 1890s (Joyce, 2003, p. 14). Infrastructural advances were embedded in Europe's imperial expansion. They integrated societies and local histories into a new universal 'world-historical framework' (Giddens, 1990, p. 20), which constituted humanity as the subject of history (Koselleck, 2004, p. 194) and temporalized this history as directional, irreversible, and progressive (Koselleck, 2004, p. 256). The 19th-century infrastructural boom, therefore, shaped how space and time were experienced, and gave rise to a new epistemology embedded in 'ideologies of progress', modernisation, and development (Buzan & Lawson, 2015, pp. 97–126). These ideas drove the infrastructural boom of the postcolonial world in the 1960s and 70 s and continue to structure current infrastructural (mega-)projects (Cupers & Meier, 2020).

A recent wave of time–space-compressions started to take shape from the 1970s onward in the context of new information and communication infrastructures and, not to be underestimated, with the invention and global spread of a simple steel box, i.e., the container (Levinson, 2016). Containers tremendously increased the quantity and velocity of material flows and initiated a new round of spatial standardization as ports, roads, trains, and ships became compatible with intermodal transport. Such, large-scale infrastructural transformations were accompanied by the transnational reorganisation of production (Gereffi, 1994, p. 219) and initiated the collapse of the spatial separation of resourcing (extraction), production, circulation, consumption, and waste management into 'lean' and 'just-in-time' production systems that hold goods in motion throughout the whole process (Bäumer Escobar et al., 2023). The integration of production and circulation has a large impact on the organisation of labour, as lived labour needs to become mobile as well, and workforces are mobilised to enable globalized production, among others to ensure the logistics for the new mobility requirements. Similar to the international shipping industry's practice of using flags of convenience, multinational companies try to take advantage of national differences in wages, safety standards, and labour rights (Ziadah, 2023, p. 51).

The expanded imperative of mobility went hand in hand with a 'weeping overhaul of capitalist circulatory systems' (Danyluk, 2017, p. 634). It also contributed to the growth of multinational corporations taking advantage of spatially dispersed and accelerated activities.[2] Above all, it transformed logistics, that is the management of circulation, into a global industry (Cowen, 2014; Roberts, 2010, pp. 75–96). The importance of logistics in modern capitalism is visible in the port and shipping industry. In the Global North, containerisation and modernisation of port infrastructures have reached their peak. Global interest in infrastructure investments has, therefore, moved towards the Global South, especially after China announced its Belt and Road Initiative in 2013. Global logistics and port operating companies have competed to develop maritime port infrastructures. With around 80 per cent of global goods moving across seas, ports constitute critical nodes in global supply chains. Again, over 80 per cent of global container trade is handled by commercial port operators (ADB, 2010, p. 78), and over 50 per cent of this trade is dominated by a handful of companies (Ziadah, 2023, p. 51), including

[2] The predecessors of multinational corporations emerged during colonialism, such as the English East India Company (EIC) and the Dutch East India Company (VOC) founded in 1600 and 1602 respectively (Gelderblom, de Jong, & Jonker, 2013).

PSA International (former Port of Singapore Authority), Hutchinson Port Holdings (Hong Kong), APM Terminals (Møller-Maersk group, Denmark), COSCO Shipping Ports (China), Dubai Ports World (United Arab Emirates), and International Container Terminal Services Inc. (Philippines). The countries of origin of these companies—some of which are state-owned, others are composed of public–private partnerships or are entirely private—point to globally shifting power relations. The politico-economic rise of South and East Asia is not only rooted in their enormous industrial dynamism, visible in the pace and size in which mega-factories and industrial cities are built from scratch (Arboleda, 2020, p. 7) but also in their enormous capacity to manage mobilities. In any case, Europe has lost its political and epistemic gravity, is provincialized (Chakrabarty, 2000), and 'downgraded into one among several other world provinces' (Arboleda, 2020, p. 8). Such developments illustrate a new round of capitalist expansion in the Global South as it reshapes economic, political, and societal realities across the globe.

Infrastructures craft dense webs of interactions while creating new types of agencies. Infrastructural (mega-) projects across Africa, Asia, and Latin America increase the velocity and range of circulations while they densify connections and interactions within and between cities, countries, regions, and continents. While these projects facilitate mobility, they also initiate spatio-political transformations at an enormous scale and speed (Schindler et al., 2019, p. 2). The next section will attend to these spatial forms, focussing on the role of infrastructure in the (re-)configuration of both statehood and territoriality.

2 Infrastructures and State-Centric Spatial Ordering

Infrastructures play a crucial role in facilitating capitalism's spatial expansion, and while they enable and accelerate mobilities they also shape the social dynamism that capitalism develops. While infrastructures make movement possible, they have solid moorings and 'spatial fixes' (Harvey, 2003). On the one hand, infrastructures expand global connectivity, accelerate mobilities, and densify interdependencies, and on the other hand, they produce ordering patterns by separating and erecting boundaries. We will show this infrastructural (re)crafting of polities and discuss how the current infrastructural advances transcend many of the spatial fixes that infrastructures once helped to set up.

From a material perspective, the building of European empires can be read as a series of infrastructural megaprojects that served a dual purpose: extracting resources and moving them to Europe. Infrastructures were crucial to moving goods, violence, people, labour, and knowledge (military personnel, engineers, and administrators) necessary for the extractivist endeavours and for putting the resources (including human labour) in the service of the colonial project (Headrick, 1981; Smith, 2021). Imperialists built their power upon already existing connections which they violently moulded around their needs.[3] In India, for example, colonial infrastructure destroyed existing industries and shifted the country's commercial focus from production towards extraction of raw materials. In Tanzania, the German railway replaced a porter-based long-distance trade network and introduced a racially differentiated system of free labour (Karuka, 2019, p. 40). Colonial advances of European powers went hand in hand with the development of dense infrastructural networks across the metropole, allowing governments to roll out coercive and administrative power across a designated territory. Infrastructural power in the colonies was not geared towards territorial penetration but towards the maximisation of resource extraction and revenue generation for the metropole. Infrastructural designs in many colonies reflect the outward-facing imperative of resource extraction. At independence, most coastal African countries, for example, had but one strategic port connected through a main highway to resource-rich regions (Cooper, 2002, p. 4). This outward-facing and extractive logic continued to shape the administrative practice and political power in many postcolonial African states (see also Dorman, 2018, p. 313).

The infrastructural design in the metropole followed a different path. In the United Kingdom, for example, Guldi (2012) showed how the first large-scale road project in the nineteenth century was geared towards the conquest of Scotland. Engineers and surveyors cooperated closely with militaries to curb Scottish resistance. When soldiers were later replaced by ordinary labourers, the military organisation of the workforce was upheld, with groups of labourers dedicated to specific tasks working in parallel at different locations and according to set times. Eventually, governments in the Global North rolled out infrastructures to control the population, crafting a 'unified territorial reach' (Mann, 1984, pp. 189, 199) that culminates in the perceived unity of territory and people characteristic of the modern nation-state. Depictions of the state as a 'cage' (Mann, 1986) or 'container' (Giddens, 1985) directly speak to this very material dimension of state power.

Infrastructures significantly reordered socio-spatial relations. Roads, for example, were planned as 'lines across varied landscapes' and then built 'in as direct a fashion as possible' (Guldi, 2012, p. 30). These infrastructural standardizations are, as Scott (1998) argues, making the world legible in state-centric ways. For Scott, infrastructures not only provide the state with a physical structure to penetrate society and curb resistance but also diffuse a state-centred (govern)mentality. This diffusion takes place through governmental techniques that reduce space diversity through abstraction (maps and metrics), simplification (standards and grids), and universalisation (quantification and statistics), and these calculative and instrumental logics are inserted into the social. Infrastructural logics, therefore, align with the generalization of the commodity form, the mobility of

[3] Due to the focus on the West, academia often ignores how pre-colonial infrastructural assemblages were crucial for the imperial advances of Europe.

capital, and a sociality mediated by the market. Standards, metrics, and rules that were set up during the infrastructural crafting, paved the way for accelerated capitalist circulation.

For capitalism to function, it requires extra-economic support in the form of infrastructure building and market regulations, both often provided by the state. Infrastructures then diffuse 'state simplifications' (Scott, 1996) as they render messy social relations manageable while configuring the social in ways that align with the market. While states were (violently) carved out from the unequal and often overlapping intersocietal relations that capitalist expansions simultaneously forge and transform, it now seems that these entities become the drivers of relations between each other. States are rigidified through immobilization and interruptions of movements (Holloway, 1994, pp. 27, 31), which lead to the emergence of governmental mobility regimes that produce 'international' flows of people, goods, animals, plants, and water as they determine what is allowed to move within and across state borders.

Inspired by the work of Strang (2021), we drew elsewhere analogies between states and modern water dams (Bakonyi & Darwich, 2024). A dam, due to its (often massive) concrete barrier, appears as a monolithic and static entity, but is composed of many things, such as walls, machines, pumps, tunnels, switches, cables, people, animals, pipes, legal arrangements, and texts. Far from being static, these things are assembled to channel, contain (store), redirect, and repurpose the flows of water subordinating it to an extractive and instrumental logic. The drift of the channelled water is, for example, used to produce electricity, and some water is redirected for agriculture and human consumption, or transformed into lakes which are used for leisure activities and tourism. The dam itself is composed of multiple movements to, from and through the dam. If these movements were before multiple and messy, they now appear as 'ordered and organised, calculated, and rendered unambiguous' (Mitchell, 1991, p. 13). Mitchel's quote refers to states, but their resemblance with dams is not accidental, as states are composed of multiple overlapping infrastructural assemblages that create ordering effects by directing movements and subordinating them to a state-centric logic.

3 Infrastructures and (Re)Crafting Statehood

While infrastructures are a constitutive element in establishing and consolidating states, they also reconfigure, challenge, and transform these political units. Infrastructural booms throughout the late twentieth and beginning twenty-first centuries have started to challenge the image of the state as a sovereign, political container, illustrated in the rise of new spatial metaphors that point to transnational connectivity, such as networks or nodes. Some of these metaphors were used as theoretical devises for the analysis of, for example, global cities (Sassen, 1991, 1996), understood as cities that manage to position themselves as infrastructural connectors (or nodes) in the global economy facilitating, managing, and governing interurban flows and mobilities. These global cities operate with an increasing degree of independence from the state (Abu-Lughod, 1999; Curtis, 2016; Sassen, 1991).

Zones emerged as another important component of these spatial transformations. Free zones are designated areas, where goods can be stored and re-shipped without payment of customs (Alansary and Al-Ansari, 2023). Free zones were established to mitigate the tension between capital's drive to transcend all boundaries and states' tendency towards enclosure. Zoning became the prime spatial technology for the sweeping overhaul, rapid expansion, and unequal densification of capitalist circulatory systems (Easterling, 2014; Ong, 2004). Contemporary port developments along the coast of Africa illustrate zoning dynamics. Modernisation of these ports have initiated a series of infrastructure projects, such as transport corridors, roads, pipelines, railways, electricity, and communication networks that are connecting ports to wider hinterlands, where 'new towns' are 'built up from scratch' and existing cities are entirely revamped as 'self-contained enclaves' (Noorloos & Kloosterboer 2018, p. 1223). Ports are not only used for the transhipment of goods, but (spatially) differentiated in terminals with distinct functions, each linked to different supply chains and integrated in various logistics systems with warehouses, production sites, intermodal transport spaces, dry ports, and freezones. Such nodal arrangements change the way territoriality is perceived and experienced, moving away from the bounded space of the territorial state to the many networked places and multiple scales. This does not necessarily mean the end of the state, but it points to a shift in the modality of statehood and in the way governments are experienced. Ong (2000, 2004), in her analyses of zoning technologies in East Asia, demonstrated how states relegate governing functions to foreign corporations, and gradually relinquish sovereignty to remain competitive on the global market. This shift has, however, an impact on the definition of citizenship making, where productivity becomes a criterion for the provision of rights and services.

The modernization and transformation of ports into spatially dispersed nodal sites happen alongside a relocation from urban centres to the outskirts of cities, similar to IKEA and Amazon. In this way, ports disentangle themselves from the cities and the urban lifeworlds they once created. Many of the container ports and terminals become ghostly spectres (Cupers, Meier, and Mahajan 2023), to be watched by city residents from a distance, often hidden away behind walls, surrounded by layers of security, and saturated in secrecy. The ghostly spectre is further underscored by flexible, autonomous, and smart technologies that radically transform labour processes, where capital increases significantly while radically diminishing human labour (Arboleda, 2020, pp. 3–5). Once bustling hubs filled with the sounds of manual labour, shouting dockworkers, and the creaking of wooden crates, the modernization of ports turned these spaces into mechanized, streamlined, and (nearly) lifeless spaces.

Since the 1970s, many states, especially in Global North have privatized ports, in what may seem a state delegation of control over mobility. A closer look, also in current port developments in the Global South, reveals that the private–public partnerships in infrastructure development come in many combinations. Governments have historically been the major investors in infrastructure and continue to play a major role as they mobilize space through planning, investment, and policy (Chua et al., 2018, p. 622). Two of the top global five port operators, the Chinese company COSCO and the UAE-based Dubai Port World (DP World) are either state-owned or closely aligned with a government. Governments may use infrastructures to improve their position in the international hierarchy of states (Ziadah, 2023, pp. 53–54) or use them to infuse their control in places far distanced from 'home'. How the infrastructure boom rearranges territory and transforms understandings of statehood remains an empirical question that can currently be studied in real-time across the Global South.

Scholarly work on infrastructure, however, remains state-centric; either they analyse what happens inside the state container or attend to global imaginaries projected by hegemonic powers. We argue that a multi-spatial and multi-temporal analysis of actors, materials, and movements engaged in infrastructure development would increase scholarly understanding of the socio-political and spatial transformations that infrastructures engender. As infrastructural power unfolds, it transforms predominant scales, increasing, for example, the ability of local political elites and economic entrepreneurs to directly engage and cooperate with actors elsewhere. China's massive infrastructuring along the BRI, for example, empowers some corporate and regional actors but also stimulates competition in ways that can fracture national cohesion. Goodfellow (2020), for example, explores how the BRIs 'hit the ground' and found that infrastructure developments were less influenced by geopolitical visions than by daily encounters, negotiations, and the bargaining power of a large range of actors from different countries. Infrastructural development, therefore, can be empirically studied as a multi-sited and temporally layered (rather than linear) process. We show elsewhere how, through infrastructural crafting, spaces are transformed, meaning is remade, and understandings of politico-economic processes change in the context of densified connectivity and accelerated mobility (Bakonyi & Darwich, 2024).

One solution for the dialectic tension between materials and movements, can be found in modular designs. This is most apparent in the mobilisation of spatial fixes on the frontiers of modernity. Some of these spatial fixes are no longer geared towards permanence and territorial control. Instead, they emanate liminality, as they use modular designs comprising easily transportable and moveable elements that can be speedily erected, disassembled, re-packaged, and moved to new places. Forms of such modular zoning can be found at building sites and in labour camps (Murray, 2017), they structure on off-shore oil rigs (Appel, 2012, p. 693) and wind parks (Moehlecke, Thrall, and Wellhausen 2023). Above all, modular designs are found at the 'military humanitarian frontiers' (Weizman, 2007) such as designated areas for international peace- and statebuilding experts (Bakonyi, 2022), refugee camps, and immigration detention centres (Mainwaring & Cook, 2018; Mountz et al., 2012).

4 Conclusion

The contemporary infrastructure boom reveals an ongoing re-ordering of state-society relations. Infrastructures, as we have shown, shape the dynamics of capitalist relations and the forms that political power takes. They bring to the fore the imperative of mobility and its intertwinement with solid moorings and point to the dialectic tensions between movements and fixtures, connections and disruptions, and material and ideational crafting. Recent infrastructure booms have transformed understandings of space and scale while blurring political boundaries that we have long taken for granted. They give rise to new governing arrangements that rescale and blur entrenched scalar distinctions and challenge the doxa of (binary) spatial metaphors, such as local versus global, bottom-up versus top-down, inside versus outside (Swyngedouw, 1996). Infrastructures, above all, open ontological and epistemological assumptions about the world, its spatiality, and relationality, and invite multi-scalar and multi-locational analysis of flows and fixes that render units and scales legible. The state, in this reading, is not irrelevant but continues to change its form adapting to, and simultaneously, driving the reorganisation of capitalist modes of reproduction.

Acknowledgements *Research in this piece was made possible by a grant from the Carnegie Corporation of New York. The statements made and views expressed are solely the responsibility of the authors. The research is part of the project:* Port Infrastructure, International Politics, and Everyday Life in the Horn of Africa.

References

Abu-Lughod, J. L. (1999). *New York, Chicago, Los Angeles: America's global cities.* Minnesota University Press.

ADB (2010). Reforms and the regulatory framework of African ports. *In African Development Report 2010* (pp. 76–106). African Development Bank. https://www.afdb.org/fileadmin/uploads/afdb/Documents/Publications/African%20Development%20Report%202010_CH%203.pdf

Alansary, O. S.-a., & Al-Ansari, T. (2023). Defining 'free zones': A systematic review of literature. *Heliyon, 9*(4). https://doi.org/10.1016/j.heliyon.2023.e15344

Appel, H. (2012). Offshore work: Oil, modularity, and the how of capitalism in Equatorial Guinea. *American Ethnologist, 39*(4), 692–709.

Arboleda, M. (2020). *Planetary Mine. Territories of extraction under late capitalism.* Verso.

Arrighi, G. (2006). Spatial and other 'fixes' of historical capital. In C. Chase-Dunn & S. J. Babones (Eds.), *Global social change: Historical and comparative perspectives* (pp. 201–212). Johns Hopkins University Press.

Bakonyi, J. (2022). Modular sovereignty and infrastructural power: The elusive materiality of international statebuilding. *Security Dialogue, 53*(3), 256–278. https://journals.sagepub.com/doi/full/10.1177/09670106211051943

Bakonyi, J., & Darwich, M. (2024). Infrastructure and international relations: A critical reflection on materials and mobilities. *International Studies Review, 26*(4). https://doi.org/10.1093/isr/viae046

Bäumer Escobar, V., Schober, E., Sibilia, E., Poulimenakos, G., & Høyer Leivestad, H. (2023). The crisis of movement: Making and remaking global supply chains in container ports. *Anthropologica (Ottawa), 65*(1). https://doi.org/10.18357/anthropologica65120232609

Birtchnell, T., Savitzky, S., & Urry, J. (2015). Moving cargos. In T. Birtchnell, S. Savitzky, & J. Urry (Eds.), *Cargomobilities: Moving materials in a global age* (pp. 1–16). Routledge.

Buzan, B., & Lawson, G. (2015). *The global transformation: History, modernity and the making of international relations.* Cambridge University Press.

Chakrabarty, D. (2000). *Provincializing Europe: Postcolonial thought and historical difference.* Princeton University Press.

Chua, C., Danyluk, M., Cowen, D., & Khalili, L. (2018). Turbulent circulation: Building a critical engagement with logistics. *Environment and Planning d: Society and Space, 36*(4), 617–629.

Ciccantell, P. S., & Bunker, S. G. (1998). Introduction: Space and transport in the world-system. In P. S. Ciccantell & S. G. Bunker (Eds.), *Space and transport in the world-system* (pp. 1–15). Greenwood Press.

Cooper, F. (2002). *Africa since 1940: The past of the present.* Cambridge University Press.

Cowen, D. (2014). *The deadly life of logistics. Mapping violence in global trade.* University of Minnesota Press.

Cupers, K., & Meier, P. (2020). Infrastructure between statehood and selfhood: The trans-African highway. *Journal of the Society of Architectural Historians, 79*(1), 61–81.

Cupers, K., Meier, P., & Mahajan, N. (2023). *Port against archipelago in Lamu, Kenya.* Workshop Paper presented at Port Infrastructures in the Middle East and Horn of Africa, Birmingham, UK.

Curtis, S. (2016). *Global cities and global order.* Oxford University Press.

Danyluk, M. (2017). Capital's logistical fix: Accumulation, globalization, and the survival of capitalism. *Environment and Planning d: Society and Space, 36*(4), 630–647.

Dorman, S. R. (2018). Beyond the gatekeeper state? Studying Africa's states and state systems in the twenty-first century. *Third World Thematics: A TWQ Journal, 3*(3), 311–324.

Easterling, K. (2014). *Extrastatecraft. The power of infrastructure space.* Verso.

Gelderblom, O., de Jong, A., & Jonker, J. (2013). The formative years of the modern corporation: The Dutch East India Company VOC, 1602–1623. *The Journal of Economic History, 73*(4), 1050–1076.

Gereffi, G. (1994). The international economy and economic development. In N. J. Smelser & R. Swedberg (Eds.), *The Handbook of Economic Sociology* (pp. 206–233). Princeton University Press.

Giddens, A. (1985). *The nation-state and violence.* Polity.

Giddens, A. (1990). *The consequences of modernity.* Polity.

Goodfellow, T. (2020). Finance, infrastructure and urban capital: The political economy of African 'gap-filling.' *Review of African Political Economy, 47*(164), 256–274.

Guldi, J. (2012). *Roads to power: Britain invents the infrastructure state.* Harvard University Press.

Harvey, D. (1989). *The condition of postmodernity. An enquiry into the origins of cultural change.* Blackwell.

Harvey, D. (2003). *The new imperialism.* Oxford University Press.

Headrick, D. R. (1981). *The tools of empire: Technology and European imperialism in the eineteenth century.* Oxford University Press.

Holloway, J. (1994). Global capital and the national state. *Capital & Class, 18*(1), 23–49.

Joyce, P. (2003). *The rule of freedom: Liberalism and the modern city.* Verso.

Karuka, M. (2019). *Empire's tracks: Indigenous nations, Chinese workers and the transcontinental railway.* UC Press.

Koselleck, R. (2004). *Futures past: On the semantics of historical time.* Columbia University Press.

Larkin, B. (2013). The politics and poetics of infrastructure. *Annual Review of Anthropology, 42*, 327–343.
Levinson, M. (2016). *The Box. How the shipping container made the world smaller and the world economy bigger* (Revised, 2 ed.). Princeton University Press.
Mainwaring, C., & Cook, M. L. (2018). Immigration detention: An Anglo model. *Migration Studies, 7*(4), 455–476.
Mann, M. (1984). The autonomous power of the state: Its origins, mechanisms and results. *European Journal of Sociology/archives Européennes De Sociologie/europäisches Archiv Für Soziologie, 25*(2), 185–213.
Mann, M. (1986). *The sources of social power.* Cambridge University Press.
MEW 23, M. K. (1988). *Das Kapital. Kritik der politischen Ökonomie Bd.1: Der Produktionsprozeß des Kapitals.* Dietz.
Mitchell, T. (1991). *Colonising Egypt:* University of California Press.
Moehlecke, C., Thrall, C., & Wellhausen, R. L. (2023). Global value chains as a constraint on sovereignty: Evidence from investor–state dispute settlement. *International Studies Quarterly, 67*(1).
Mountz, A., Coddington, K., Catania, R. T., & Loyd, J. M. (2012). Conceptualizing detention: Mobility, containment, bordering, and exclusion. *Progress in Human Geography, 37*(4), 522–541.
Murray, M. J. (2017). *The urbanism of exception. The dynamics of global city building in the twenty-first century.* Cambridge University Press.
Noorloos, Fv., & Kloosterboer, M. (2018). Africa's new cities: The contested future of urbanisation. *Urban Studies, 55*(6), 1223–1241.
Ong, A. (2000). Graduated sovereignty in south-east Asia. *Theory, Culture & Society, 17*(4), 55–75.
Ong, A. (2004). The Chinese axis: Zoning technologies and variegated sovereignty. *Journal of East Asian Studies, 4*, 69–96.
Pohrt, W. (1976). *Theorie des Gebrauchswerts. Oder ueber die Vergänglichkeit der historischen Voraussetzungen, unter denen allein das Kapital Gebrauchswert setzt.* Syndikat.
Postone, M. (1993). *Time, labor, and social domination.* Cambridge University Press.
Roberts, A. (2010). *The logic of discipline global capitalism and the architecture of government.* Oxford University Press.
Rosenberg, J. (2013). Kenneth Waltz and Leon Trotsky: Anarchy in the mirror of 'uneven and combined development. *International Politics, 50/2,* 183–230.
Sassen, S. (1991). *The global city: New York, London, Tokyo.* Princeton University Press.
Sassen, S. (1996). Spatialities and temporalities of the global: Elements for a theoretisation. In A. Appadurai (Ed.), *Modernity at large: Cultural dimensions of globalization* (pp. 260–278). University of Minnesota Press.
Schindler, S., Fadaee, S., & Brockington, D. (2019). Contemporary megaprojects: An introduction. *Environment and Society, 10*(1), 1–8.
Scott, J. C. (1996). State simplifications: Nature, space and people. *Nomos, 38*, 42–85.
Scott, J. C. (1998). *Seeing like a state. How certain schemes to improve the human condition have failed.* Yale University Press.
Smith, N. W. S. (2021). *Colonial chaos in the southern Red Sea: A history of violence from 1830 to the twentieth century.* Cambridge University Press.
Strang, V. (2021). Materialising the state: The meaning of water infrastructure. In A. Dundon & R. Vokes (Eds.), *Shifting states: New perspectives on security, infrastructure and political affect* (pp. 43–61). Bloomsbury Press.

Swyngedouw, E. (1996). The city as a hybrid: On nature, society, and cyborg urbanisation. *Capitalism, Nature, Socialism, 7*(25), 65–80.
Tsing, A. (2009). Supply chains and the human condition. *Rethinking Marxism, 21*(2), 148–176.
Weizman, E. (2007). *Hollow land: Israel's architecture of occupation.* Verso.
Ziadah, R. (2023). Logistic landscapes. Corporate power and capital in the maritime industry. *Socialist Register, 59*, 47–63.

Jutta Bakonyi is Professor in Development and Conflict at the University of Durham, United Kingdom. Her main research focus is on violence, and she has published extensively on actors and dynamics of wars, statehood, orders of violence beyond the state, peacekeeping, and humanitarian interventions. Currently she works on the material side of politics, with a particular focus on infrastructures. Her recent book on 'Precarious Urbanism: Displacement, Belonging and the Reconstruction of Somali Cities' (co-authored with Pete Chonka) explores the nexus of displacement and urbanisation in the Horn of Africa and shows the growth of cities is experienced by urban in-migrants.

May Darwich is Associate Professor in International Relations of the Middle East at the University of Birmingham, United Kingdom. She is the author of Threats and Alliances in the Middle East: Saudi and Syrian Policies in a Turbulent Region (Cambridge University Press, 2019). Her research attempts to bring Middle East cases to debates within IR theory with research interests including threat perception and alliance politics, identity, and foreign policy. Her current research also focuses on cross-regional interlinks between the Middle East and Africa through the lens of port infrastructures. She is PI of the project 'Port Infrastructure, International Politics, and Everyday life: From the Arabian Gulf to the Horn of Africa', funded by Carnegie Corporation NY. Some of her recent research has appeared in internationally renowned journals, namely *Foreign Policy Analysis, Journal of Global Security Studies, Democratization, Mediterranean Politics, International Studies Perspectives.*

Infrastructure Conflicts in a New Geoeconomic Order—a Political Economy Perspective

Hans-Jürgen Bieling

Abstract

This chapter focuses on the interconnection of structural global power shifts and the reorganisation of globalisation-relevant infrastructures. It argues that in an emerging geoeconomic order, the control of transnational value chains—and by extension, infrastructure policy—is increasingly perceived as decisive. To substantiate this argument, the paper first examines the justification for considering the current global order as a new geoeconomic paradigm distinct from neoliberal globalization. It then clarifies what infrastructures are and illustrates their significance for transnational value chains. Furthermore, it highlights the potential conflicts associated with the control of these value chains. It will be shown how the geostrategic orientation of states and transnational corporations is reflected in competing infrastructure strategies. Despite the intensified geoeconomic competition, it would be however one-sided to neglect that transnational infrastructures also create new forms of cooperation and potentially generate public or common goods.

Keywords

Transnational infrastructures · Geoeconomics · Global value chains · Belt and Road initiative · Global Gateway

H.-J. Bieling (✉)
Institut für Politikwissenschaft, Universität Tübingen, Tübingen, Germany
e-mail: hans-juergen.bieling@uni-tuebingen.de

H.-J. Bieling et al. (eds.), *Transnational Infrastructures and the Transformation of Global Orders*, RaumFragen: Stadt – Region – Landschaft,
https://doi.org/10.1007/978-3-031-74846-2_4

1 Introduction: Transnational Infrastructures and Global Order(s)

The global political economy is currently undergoing a period of significant turbulence, marked by a rise in interstate conflicts driven by complex and multifaceted causes. In response to various crises—including economic and energy crises, climate change, the Covid-19 pandemic, and Russia's war against Ukraine—there has been an increasing demand for state intervention. This demand persists even when it presents challenges to the market or neoliberal economic order and discriminates against companies in other countries or regions. Moreover, large sections of the population now tolerate or even advocate for state interventionism. In any case, interstate conflicts are becoming more acute as the negative aspects of globalisation become more apparent and are perceived as threats, with security issues and geostrategic considerations gaining prominence.

The global financial crisis of 2007/08 served as a pivotal starting point or catalyst for these developments. The crisis' trajectory and management, which involved significant burdens and costs, contributed to intensifying and accelerating global and social transformations (Tooze, 2018). Two aspects are particularly prominent in the academic discussion: first, the transformation of global economic structures, emphasising the growing importance of China and the Asian economic area, and the increasing conflicts with the United States and the European Union (Bieling, 2019; Hung, 2022; Leonard, 2021); second, the conflictual reorganisation of globalisation-relevant infrastructures (Abels & Bieling, 2024a). While China has been actively promoting this reorganisation through the Belt and Road Initiative (BRI), the US and the EU have recently positioned themselves with the Partnership for Global Infrastructure and Investment (PGII) and the Global Gateway.

This chapter seeks to clarify the relationship between the transformation of global economic structures and the reorganisation of globalisation-relevant infrastructures. The argument posits that understanding the control of transnational value chains provides a lens through which these interconnections can be viewed. Control of these value chains is the central focus of geoeconomic strategies, primarily contested in the arena of international technology competition and infrastructure policy, leading to a changed global order.

The chapter is structured as follows: the second section outlines the justification for considering the current geoeconomic global order as different from the old order of neoliberal globalisation. The third section then turns to the relevance of transnational infrastructures, clarifying what infrastructures are and discussing their importance for transnational value chains. The fourth section addresses the potential conflicts associated with the control of these value chains by both states and transnational corporations, illustrating how their geostrategic orientations are reflected in competing infrastructure policy strategies. Finally, the fifth section argues that while geoeconomic concerns are prominent, it would be short-sighted to conclude that they will inevitably triumph. After all, transnational infrastructures also foster new forms of cooperation and potentially generate public or common goods.

2 After Neoliberal Globalisation: Contours of a New Geoeconomic Global Order

For some time now, the momentum of globalisation has noticeably slowed down. In both public and academic discussions, terms like "end of globalisation", "de-globalisation" or "slowbalisation" have become increasingly prominent. While some terms and characterisatios may exaggerate this trend, reports and statistics from international organisations provide evidence that globalisation has stalled and is even partially retreating. This phenomenon can be examined through three primary dimensions.

The first dimension relates to the development of international trade compared to global value added (see Fig. 1). This ratio has grown almost continuously in the decades following the Second World War. Notably, during the period from the early 1980s to the global financial crisis, a time characterised by neoliberal deregulation and privatisation, i.e., a strategically driven expansion of market relations, cross-border trade virtually exploded. Although the financial crisis did not reverse this process and global trade—as a percentage of global GDP—remained at a very high level of around 60%, it partially declined in some sectors, such as fossil fuels.

The second dimension concerns international production. A significant portion of international trade occurs within transnational corporations and established supply or value chains, which heavily depend on Foreign Direct Investments (FDIs). Similar to trade, FDIs have experienced stagnation. The share of global value chains (GVCs) to cross-border trade is slightly declining (see Fig. 2). This may be temporarily influenced by stock price development, as FDIs predominantly consist of mergers and acquisitions. Additionally, companies are increasingly aware of the vulnerabilities and risks associated

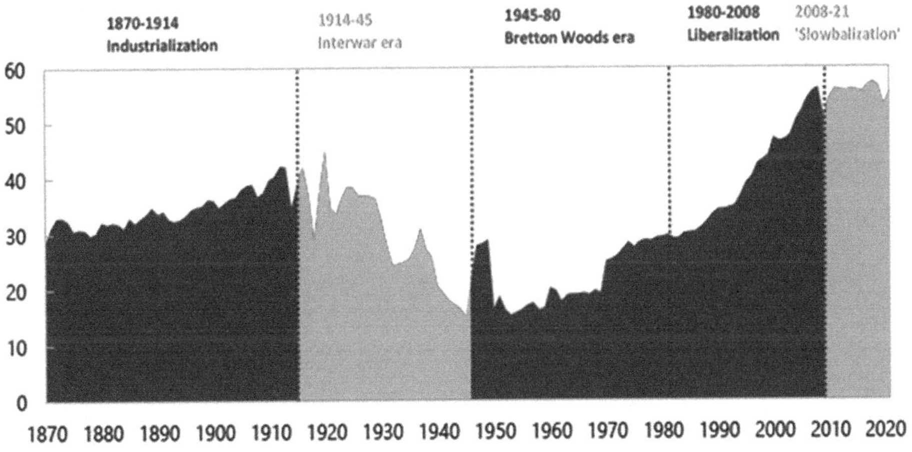

Fig. 1 Trade Openness, Sum of exports and imports as a percentage of GDP. (Aiyar et al., 2023, p. 6)

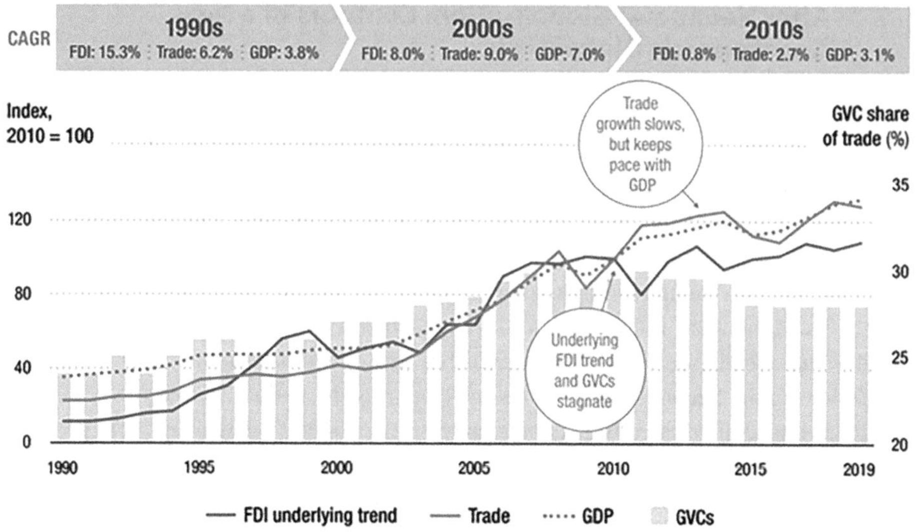

Fig. 2 International Production and Global Value Chains. (UNCTAD, 2020, p. 123)

with globalised value creation and are selectively scaling back their transnational production networks to regain control.

The third dimension concerns changes in global finance. After the financial crisis, cross-border capital flows significantly declined (see Fig. 3). Despite a recovery following the Covid-19 pandemic, driven by positive stock prices development, transnational financial transactions have structurally slowed. Factors contributing to this slowdown include muted expectations from many financial institutions in the context of a partial re-regulation of financial markets, and the cumulative crises leading up to the Covid-19 pandemic, which have made many actors increasingly perceive the risks as unacceptable.

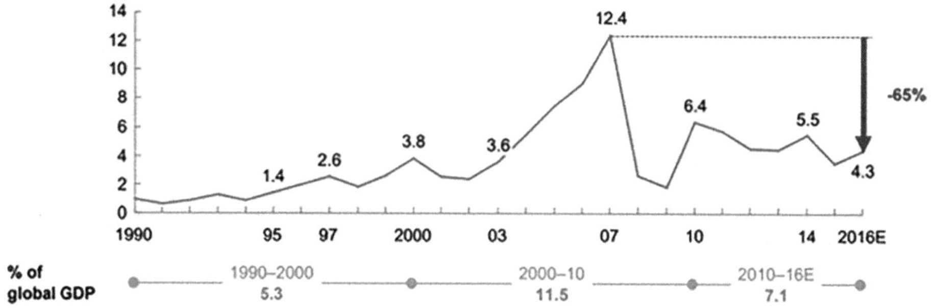

Fig. 3 Cross-border capital flows. (McKinsey Global Institute, 2017, p. 1, based on IMF statistics)

These three dimensions—trade, production networks, and financial transactions—point to a structurally altered, rather than temporarily disrupted, mode of globalisation. Since the global financial crisis approximately 15 years ago, the regulatory parameters of cross-border economic relations have changed. From the 1980s until the financial crisis, the main goal was to reorganise the global economy by intensifying cross-border competition, limiting politically motivated market corrections, and comprehensively protecting property rights (Gill, 1998). However, new or additional criteria have sinced emerged. Questions of power and security are increasingly addressed in shaping global economic relations. Accordingly, governments mobilise instruments of economic protection and political control, leading to a gradual de-liberalisation of the global economy. Given the "securitisation of economic policy" and the "economisation of strategic policy", some observers note a transition from a neoliberal order to a new geoeconomic order (Roberts et al., 2019), especially as these processes are becoming more embedded in the rules, norms, and practices of international organisations and regimes.

In public and academic discourse, this trend is reflected, among other things, in the frequent use of the terms "geopolitics" and "geoeconomics". However, the interchangeable use of these two concepts often obscures their analytical distinction. This conflation is somewhat understandable, as both concepts reference territory or space. Nonetheless, it is crucial to distinguish between them for a precise analysis.

Within geopolitical discussions, there is a difference between older and newer concepts (Kuus, 2010). Recent geopolitical concepts critically distance themselves from the older attempts to derive political processes and strategies from natural spatial determinants. Instead, they reverse the relationship between space and politics and emphasize the political shaping of spatial conditions. They thus develop a social constructivist approach to geopolitical issues, positing that space is simply not given. Rather, numerous economic, political, and civil society actors strive to influence the nature of space through discourses, laws, and everyday decisions and practices.

Concepts of geoeconomics align with the social constructivist understanding of geopolitics. However, it is essential to distinguish between state-centric perspectives, which primarily discuss geoeconomic strategies in terms of interstate rivalry (Luttwak, 1990), and contributions from critical geoeconomics. The latter focuses on the complex power relations manifest in the spatial control of economic relations. In this context, the conception of "spatio-temporal fixes" developed by David Harvey (2003, pp. 114–24) is analytically insightful. Corresponding to the double meaning of the word "to fix", this concept addresses two aspects: first, the structural embeddedness of capitalist development in specific socio-cultural, institutional, and political contexts; and second, the stabilisation and repair of inherently unstable capitalist accumulation. This includes the macroeconomic management through economic stimulus or infrastructure programmes, as well as the repair or securing of value chains.

Geoeconomic control strategies reflect not only state interests, but also private capitalist ones. The articulation of these interests in specific political projects is an empirical question. In principle, the arsenal of instruments that can be used for geoeconomic purposes is comprehensive. On one hand, numerous measures—such as asymmetric tariffs, market access restrictions, investment controls, embargoes, and withholding of crucial resources or intermediate products—aim to increase a country's power to control economic areas or to put other states and companies under pressure through forms of discipline and surveillance. This aspect is central to the "weaponization" debate (Farrell & Newman, 2019), which highlights the asymmetric nature of economic interdependencies and the possibility of forcing others to behave in line with one's interests by controlling crucial nodes of infrastructure networks. When this occurs, the strategic aspects of geoeconomics—using infrastructure for geopolitical purposes—come to the fore. However, it is an oversimplification to limit the geoeconomic discussion to this aspect alone. There are many instruments—such as low-cost loans, investment and trade agreements, extensive economic diplomacy, strategic partnerships, etc.—aimed at promoting specific industries and value chains. In other words, to the extent that control of space supports and secures capitalist valorisation, geoeconomics also encompasses productive aspects (Abels & Bieling, 2024a).

The new geoeconomic order is characterized by the increased significance of the aforementioned instruments. It represents a constellation where competitive control of economic spaces has been pushed to the centre of the state and private capitalist activities. The discussion revolves around both the leadership roles in crucial sectors—such as semiconductors, data communication, or energy systems—which justify extensive industrial policy programmes, and on transnational infrastructures, indispensable for the aforementioned key sectors and, more generally, for the reliable operation of numerous value chains. Understanding the new patterns of conflict and cooperation necessitates considering the structural relations between the US and China. However, other actors, notably the EU, also play a significant role. Additionally, it is essential to consider that the strategic positions and specific activities of state actors are negotiated in conjunction with the involved corporations and their associations (Babić et al., 2022), as well as under the influence of civil society actors.

3 Transnational Infrastructures and Logistics

Control over global value chains is closely linked to the ways transnational infrastructures operate, which underwent significant reorganisation in the context of the "revolution in logistics" (Cowen, 2014, pp. 23–52). This multi-stage transformation began with the shift from logistics as an essentially military art to a business concept in the post-war decades. While military considerations and strategies persisted, they became increasingly subordinate to the capitalist optimisation of value chains. This process was further accentuated by a twofold change in the 1960s: the increasing importance of logistic companies responsible for value chain management alongside scientific advancements in logistics, reflected in the establishment of numerous research institutes, lively research activity, and ever new concepts and practices. In this context, the focus of logistics also changed: it was no longer concerned only with questions of cost minimisation but—from a systemic perspective—on logistics as an integrated dimension of optimised production processes.

Since the 1990s, the concept of "just-in-time" production has gained prominence. Rather than maintaining costly stockpiles, most companies have been adopting a strategy of promptly supplying preliminary products for further processing. This shift was politically encouraged by deregulation and liberalisation in the logistics sector. Deregulation primarily affected labour relations, while liberalisation pertained to the cross-border activities of logistics companies. To minimise friction and conflict, international standards were also defined to accompany the modularisation of logistics, with container shipping being a notable example. Despite these advancements, numerous risks remained, including natural disasters, epidemics, accidents, and forms of piracy or sabotage. These risks continued to favour processes of securitisation, resulting in military or police protection of value chains (Bieling, 2023).

At this juncture, it becomes evident that logistics systems are inextricably linked to the functioning of infrastructures. If, from an economic perspective, logistics is defined as "the management of firms' acquiring and distributing activities over space" (Cowen, 2014, p. 42), then infrastructures are socio-technical systems or networks that facilitate this process. The concept of networks is here particularly instructive since networks are comprised of nodes and edges, lines or channels of connectivity. Examples include ports and sea or waterways, railway stations and tracks, public utilities and electricity grids, car parks and roads, universities and media of knowledge communication, cloud systems and the internet, banks and payment systems, and so on. Brian Larkin (2013, p. 328) refers to the comprehensive and substantial character of infrastructures, defining them as "built networks that facilitate the flow of goods, people, or ideas and allow for their exchange over space."

This peculiarity of infrastructures—the fact that they are matter that at the same time establishes relations between other matter, data, and people—is amplified by some paradoxical characteristics. For example, critical geographer David Harvey (2003, pp. 98–100) stresses the tension between the mobility infrastructures provide and their immobility:

> Fluid movement over space can be achieved only by fixing certain physical infrastructures in space. Railways, roads, airports, port facilities, cable networks, fibre-optic systems, electricity grids, water and sewage systems, pipelines etc., constitute 'fixed capital embedded in the land' [... and] act as a significant drag upon geographical transformations and the relocation of capitalist activity.

Capitalist activities often trigger infrastructural conflicts. However, infrastructures are not solely utilised for profit production and capital accumulation. As the "lifelines" of modern society (van Laak, 2018), they also serve social, cultural, or ecological purposes. The relevance of these purposes depends on the capacity of various actors to inscribe their interests or motives into the respective infrastructures. Such inscriptions can occur at different phases, including planning, financing, production, regulation, and utilisation, determining the extent to which the respective infrastructural objectives, motives, and functions are realised (Bieling & Abels, 2024b, pp. 5–6).

The socio-technical character of infrastructures includes different dimensions, referring to the processes of infrastructure policy design and manifesting in the specific forms of infrastructure utilisation. Due to their durability and costly construction and operation (Bieling & Möhring-Hesse, 2023), infrastructures function as "ordering services" that permanently structure societies (Barlösius, 2019). Nevertheless, infrastructures may change over time, for instance, when they enter a stage of decay if new investments and necessary work fail to materialise, or when their functionality changes due to layering, i.e., when new infrastructures—such as the internet and processes of digitisation—cause a transformation of extant infrastructures.

4 Infrastructure Strategies After 2008—New Features and Dynamics

Following the financial crisis of 2008/09, trans- and international conflicts have been on the rise. As geoeconomic competition intensifies, the infrastructures of globalisation have increasingly taken centre stage (Bieling, 2023). At times, the issue at hand is the threat to international trade routes. Examples include the blockade of the Suez Canal by the container ship 'Ever Given', the closure of important ports as part of the Chinese zero-Covid strategy, or the Houthi attacks in the Gulf of Aden. In other instances, the issue is the lack of international energy supply, manifesting in the control over oil and gas pipelines, the construction of LNG port terminals, the reorganisation of electricity grids, the development of a hydrogen infrastructure, and so forth. Control over international payment systems (e.g. SWIFT) or high-tech infrastructures such as internet communication, cloud systems, navigation systems (GPS, Galileo) or 5G networks also holds considerable potential for conflict (Abels & Bieling, 2023). This development is further fuelled by the large-scale, geoeconomically motivated infrastructure strategies of China, the US and the EU.

4.1 China: Belt and Road Initiative (BRI)

Infrastructure policy activities have historically been significant for major powers, including during periods of colonialism or systemic competition following the Second World War. However, in recent times, they have emerged as a prominent feature within a distinct context. One key driver behind this shift is the growing involvement of countries of the Global South, particularly China, in infrastructure policy (Hönke et al., 2024). This has spurred processes of transnational development and geoeconomic competition.

The Belt and Road Initiative (BRI) exemplifies China's strategy to secure its own capitalist development model by constructing new transport routes (rail networks, roads, raw material pipelines, ports, and sea routes) as well as communication and supply networks, including the so-called "Digital Silk Road" and the "Health Silk Road". The significance and mode of operation of the BRI is largely derived from the dynamics and crisis processes of what is known as "Sino-capitalism" (McNally, 2012). This type of capitalism is characterised by a complex network of capitalist structures, informal networks (guanxi), and developmental state control of key sectors (financial markets, internet, high technology, construction, etc.), with financial support programmes and state-owned enterprises (SOEs) playing an important role. Furthermore, Sino-capitalism is predicated on an export-oriented growth model. This includes numerous technologically advanced products while requiring the import of energy, raw materials, and both primary and intermediate products.

Until the global financial crisis, China's "Going Global" policy encouraged export orientation (Züfle, 2023, pp. 46–9). However, the crisis initiated a certain reorientation, with comprehensive economic stimulus programmes launched to compensate for the decline in exports and reduce over-capacities, thereby strengthening the Chinese domestic market. Furthermore, a relative decoupling from the US economy and a simultaneous intensification of economic relations with other Asian and African countries were sought to reduce external dependencies. This aim of a "dual circulation economy" was later heralded by Xi Jinping, whereby "external circulation", i.e. world market integration, became subordinated to the "internal circulation", i.e. the requirements of capitalist accumulation dynamics in China itself. According to Mark Leonard (2021, pp. 153–4).

> the purpose of dual circulation is to make China more self-reliant. After previously basing Chinas development on export-led growth, policymakers are trying to diversify the country's supply chains so that it can access technology and know-how without being bullied by the United States [...].

The BRI also reflects China's aspiration for autonomy and independence. It represents a comprehensive connectivity programme that responds to economic crisis trends and internal contradictions of the Chinese development model (Sum, 2019, pp. 3–6). This initiative is steered by the Chinese developmental state, beginning with the negotiation of memoranda of understanding (MOUs), frequently in international forums such as the 17+1 or 16+1 Forum for Europe or the Forum for China-Africa Cooperation (FOCAC). Subsequently, specific projects are implemented in collaboration with the Ministry of Foreign Affairs or the Ministry of Trade, in conjunction with financial vehicles and Chinese SOEs (Züfle, 2023, pp. 83–94; Mohan & Tan-Mullins, 2019, p. 1372).

It is estimated that between 600 billion and 2.3 trillion US dollars were mobilised for the BRI from 2013 to 2021. These loans are primarily provided by Chinese financial institutions, including the China Investment Corporation (CIC), the China Development Bank (CDB), and the Export and Import Bank of China (ExIm). These institutions focus on loans for investment projects in Asia, Africa, and Latin America (Huotari, 2018, pp. 135–7; Mohan & Tan-Mullins, 2019, p. 1374). Furthermore, international development banks, such as the Asian Infrastructure Investment Bank (AIIB), established in 2014, the New Development Bank (NDB), and the Silk Road Fund, support infrastructure projects initiated as part of the BRI.

The financing system outlined here has implications for the individual projects within the framework of the BRI. Contrary to the loan conditions of the International Monetary Fund (IMF) or the World Bank, China emphasises the principles of national sovereignty and territorial integrity, i.e. non-interference, to simultaneously place the implementation of the infrastructure projects in the hands of Chinese companies with their predominantly Chinese workforce. In economic terms, this implies that a significant proportion of the loans granted to other countries and regions remain within China (Mohan & Tan-Mullins, 2019, p. 1374). While this reduces the risk of corruption and ensures quick and professional project implementation, it does not necessarily provide immediate development impetus for the recipient countries. Only after a transitional period, infrastructural ownership is transferred to local companies, with the Chinese players withdrawing, provided that this is technologically and operationally possible. The exact procedure is laid down in BOT (Build, Operate and Transfer) contracts with the recipient countries.

At an earlier point in time, Chinese policymakers were successful in presenting the BRI as a product of inclusive cooperation under the banner of "peaceful rise and harmonious world" (Sum, 2019, pp. 8–9). However, the geoeconomic aspects of the initiative have become more prominent, mostly due to the more nationalistic rhetoric under Xi Jinping, but also to the intensifying global competition with the US and the EU. In this context, China is refining the strategic aspects of its international infrastructure policy, contingent on the requirements of its development model. Cooperation remains precarious, with gowing scepticism not only in the US and the EU but also among developing countries facing significant challenges in financing the BRI.

4.2 U.S.: Partnership for Global Infrastructure and Investment (PGII)

More recently, the US has also become more active in infrastructure policy within and outside its territory. On the one hand, the government has responded to a considerable backlog of demand. As a result of privatisation and financialization processes, investment in infrastructure has been insufficient in many areas. On the other hand, there was a growing fear that without an increase in infrastructure spending, the country could easily fall behind in geoeconomic competition with China. The Biden administration has launched several initiatives in recent years to address this dual problem (Abels & Bieling, 2024a, pp. 10–12).

The "Build Back Better" agenda, a comprehensive public investment programme with the aim of social, infrastructural, and ecological modernisation, was launched in 2020 and 2021. The infrastructural policy elements were primarily bundled in the "American

Jobs Plan", which proposed to allocate more than 600 billion of the initial 2.3 trillion US dollars into expanding US transport infrastructure and approximately 100 billion US dollars into energy infrastructure development. A significant portion of the funds was also intended for "social infrastructure", including the care system, public housing, water supply, and public schools. However, the funding of this latter area met with resistance from industry associations (Business Roundtable, 2021) and Congress, leading to a reduced investment volume in the final "Infrastructure Investment and Jobs Act". This act totaled 1.2 trillion dollars and focused primarily on expanding technical infrastructure, such as the transport, energy, and telecommunications sectors. The ecological components of the Build Back Better Agenda also remained controversial. They were ultimately transferred to the "Inflation Reduction Act", passed in 2022, which comprised about 900 billion euros and was strongly characterised by industrial policy components and geoeconomic motivation (Bernoth & Meyer, 2023).

Notwithstanding the intricate nature of the negotiation processes, US infrastructure policy on the globalisation-relevant domains like transport, energy supply, and data communication, enjoys the support of a broad coalition of political and economic actors (Scherrer, 2022). In the context of the geoeconomic competition with China, it seems crucial to enhance the production and export capabilities of US companies through the implementation of effective and productive infrastructures. This consensus on a comprehensive, state-sponsored modernisation of infrastructural conditions also transcends national boundaries. In recent years, a more clearly defined transnational agenda has become discernible. The US government encouraged its Western counterparts to develop a global infrastructure strategy that could rival the BRI. With this objective in mind, the G7 countries unveiled the Build Back Better World (B3W) initiative in June 2021. The objective was to finance and implement projects globally through coordination. The B3W initiative prioritised investment in low- and middle-income countries, with a particular focus on Latin America, the Caribbean, Africa, and the Indo-Pacific region (The White House, 2021). In these regions, the US and its Western partners are seeking to establish investment partnerships with other countries to curtail China's financial and political influence. The investments are primarily aimed at the priority areas of climate protection, health security, digital technology, and gender equality.

These priorities have since been further concretised. In addition, following the domestic political failure of Biden's Build Back Better agenda, the B3W was renamed the 'Partnership for Global Infrastructure and Investment' (PGII). The planned investment volume of 600 billion US dollars for the years 2022 to 2027 is undoubtedly considerable, although it falls short of the global investment requirement estimated by the OECD, which is 6.9 trillion US dollars per year. Furthermore, the PGII is characterised by two problematic features:

The first is the fragmentation of the "Western" approach. This can already be seen in the provision of financial resources. Of the 600 billion US dollars, 200 billion will be provided by the US, 65 billion by Japan, 40 billion by the UK, and 300 billion by the European Union. Although the consensus on the joint development of transnational infrastructure and the coordination of infrastructure policy activities will reduce some friction, national—namely geoeconomic—interests are also likely to diverge at times. This is already reflected in the fact that some European countries—for example, Bulgaria, Croatia, the Czech Republic, Greece, Hungary, Poland, Romania, Slovakia, Slovenia and, until recently, Italy—are involved in the BRI cooperation, while others view the PGII primarily as a counter-project to the BRI. Integrating key PGII partners such as South Korea and Japan, which are major infrastructure players in East Asia, remains uncertain.

Second, the financing modalities are problematic. The US and its Western partners are following the World Bank's "Billions to Trillions" (BTT) agenda, which aims to provide a relatively modest amount of public money in the form of subsidised loans, guarantees, and public equity to attract private capital. This "market-driven" approach reflects public financial constraints, in which political authorities strive to lure in private capital. Whether it works, so that the 600 billion US dollars will be achieved, remains an open question (Hameiri & Jones, 2023). In case it does, private investors will get a say in planned projects potentially weakening the US and G7 practices compared to China's approach, where the government and the national and international development banks control the infrastructure strategy.

4.3 European Union: Global Gateway

In the context of the PGII, the European Union also attempted to refine its infrastructure policy profile at the end of 2021. In the 1990s and 2000s, it had already been engaged in infrastructure policy. However, its primary objective was to enhance the functionality of the internal market. This was achieved by liberalising network-based infrastructures, including rail transport, postal and telecommunications services, and electricity and gas networks (Bieling & Deckwirth, 2008). Moreover, the EU, with the support of transnational corporations (TNCs) and their associations promoted the development of trans-European networks (TENs). Later, the neighbouring regions in Eastern Europe and the Mediterranean were also included in the TEN strategy as part of the European Neighbourhood Policy (Paci, 2020). Furthermore, in 2018, the EU launched a geographically broader connectivity initiative aiming at the Indo-Pacific region (EC-HR, 2018), resulting in partnership agreements with Japan and India.

The Global Gateway initiative builds on these previous activities (Heldt, 2023), bringing numerous outward-looking EU infrastructure projects together under a new branding. Between 2021 to 2027, the initiative aims to mobilise approximately 300 billion euros, primarily with private capital, to implement infrastructure and connectivity projects worldwide, mainly in Africa, Latin America, and Asia (European Commission, 2021). The activities focus on the promotion of digitalisation, energy supply and transport, as well as on the areas of health, education, and research. The latter areas indicate that the

Global Gateway is also intended to help close the global infrastructure policy gap and implement the Sustainable Development Goals (SDGs). However, in the public presentation of the initiative, the geoeconomic and geopolitical competition with China has been often taking centre stage.

Geoeconomic considerations are particularly important in the expansion or modernisation of energy networks, such as the supply of climate-friendly hydrogen, or high-tech infrastructures (Abels & Bieling, 2024b), like the development of navigation systems (Galileo), the broad-based supply of 5G mobile communications technology, and the establishment of a European cloud system (Gaia-X). These examples illustrate that infrastructure policy projects are also supported by industrial policy programmes. The upgrading of industrial policy through the Important Projects of Common European Interest (IPEIs) and the strengthening of national and European development banks (Mertens & Thiemann, 2018), including the European Investment Bank (EIB) and the European Bank for Reconstruction and Development (EBRD), point in this direction. The development banks provide funding to modernise the industrial and infrastructure base, and mobilise private capital, as exemplified by the European Fund for Strategic Investment (EFSI), established in 2015 and often referred to as the "Juncker Fund", and the Connecting Europe Facility (CEF), both merged into "InvestEU" in 2021.

The financing of Global Gateway also adheres to this approach. The 300 billion euros that will be made available in the years 2021–2027 are composed of several packages (European Commission, 2021, pp. 8–11). The first package, amounting up to 135 billion euros, is largely based on the European Fund for Sustainable Development (EFSD), the financial arm of the Neighbourhood, Development and International Cooperation Instrument (NDICI)—Global Europe. In this context, 40 billion euros in guarantees will be provided in cooperation with the EIB to tap into further private sources of finance. A second package is to comprise a further 145 billion euros, which will be financed primarily by the European and national development banks. Thirdly, 18 billion euros will be made available in the form of grants through the EU's external support programmes. Finally, there are existing instruments such as the Instrument for Pre-Accession (IPA) III, Interreg, InvestEU, and Horizon Europe, which also leverage private capital.

This indicates that the financing model of Global Gateway is similar to the US one. It combines grants and loans from national and European public institutions to mobilise private capital. National development aid programmes are also included. However, the concrete procedures and implementation steps are still largely open and are negotiated within the framework of a specific governance structure. The identification, negotiation, and implementation of Global Gateway projects will be decided by a so-called "Team Europe", which brings together the national governments, European and national financial institutions as well as companies and civil society organisations under the leadership of a Global Gateway Board, responsible to the Commission Presidency and the High Representative. Through their umbrella organisation, Business Europe (2021), European companies have advocated for the establishment of a "Business Advisory Group on the

Global Gateway" and the exclusion of non-European companies from participation if their countries do not adhere to open procurement procedures comparable to those of the EU.

To date, Global Gateway has established a consensus on infrastructure investment priorities, including the construction of fibre optic cables, transport corridors, and clean power transmission lines. Additionally, it has approved the expansion of specific trade corridors in Africa, Latin America, and Asia. However, it is premature to provide detailed information regarding the concrete implementation, operation, and utilisation of the new infrastructures. A European consensus emphasises that infrastructure projects, in the spirit of good governance and sustainable development, must adhere to specific conditionalities, promoting democracy, transparency, partnership, operational and social security, climate neutrality and private sector investment (European Commission, 2021, p. 3). This consensus will likely be maintained in the subsequent operation and utilisation of the infrastructures.

5 Outlook: Beyond Geoeconomics and "Weaponization"

The strategies outlined above by states and regional integration organisations such as the EU indicate a renewed interest in infrastructure policy. In the context of a global landscape that has undergone significant transformation, they are increasingly focusing on infrastructure as a field of action to control transnational value chains. Other motives, such as improved investment conditions and higher profits, or a climate-friendly or socially oriented reorganization of models of capitalist development, also play a role. However, they are often secondary to geopolitical and geoeconomic considerations. The re-emergence of such considerations is not a completely new phenomenon. The recurrent threat to so-called "critical infrastructure", particularly in the US and in the EU, was already the subject of intense debate in the 2000s. The material-discursive practices (Aradau, 2010), often reflecting processes of "securitization", showed an increasing public awareness of the central and highly political role of many infrastructures. In recent years, governments drove forward these practices in a more targeted and instrumental manner. The focus was increasingly on the dynamics of "weaponization" (Farrell/ Newman 2019), a concept that has moved quickly from the academic sphere into public debate, and is also reflected in official documents and strategy papers. The European Economic Security Strategy of 2023 makes this point explicitly.

> The Commission and the High Representative have identified the following broad and non-exhaustive categories of risks to economic security namely risks related to: (1) resilience of supply chains; (2) physical and cyber security of critical infrastructure; (3) technology security and technology leakage; and (4) weaponisation of economic dependencies or economic coercion. These risks can occur along the entire value chain, from knowledge creation and basic research to commercialisation and manufacturing at scale. (European Commission, 2023, p. 5)

The risks and fears enumerated here are not mere speculation. At least partially, they are substantiated by specific events and conflicts with major powers. Frequently mentioned are Russia and China, but sometimes also the US. The focus is on access to important raw materials, the supply of semiconductors and medical products or energy supplies, or foreign control of technological expertise, data, and payment flows. In this sense, the weaponisation debate has a rational core.

Nevertheless, a "weaponization of everything" (Galeotti, 2022) exaggerates the extent to which social relations and infrastructures can be weaponized. It also ignores the economic and political costs of weaponization and the very nature of infrastructures which are not solely or primarily created to exert pressure on other countries and companies. Rather, their general function, as previously emphasised in Larkin's (2013) definition, is to facilitate processes of social and transnational connectivity. These "productive" aspects must be continually borne in mind. Even though infrastructures may also give rise to violent relationships and generate social or ecological harm, they are indispensable for the provision of global common or public goods. Such goods are characterised by two principles (Samuelson, 1954): they rule out any rivalry between users (principle of non-rivalry), as they are not or hardly depleted in use; and they are accessible to everybody, no-one excluded (principle of non-exclusion).

On closer examination, however, these two criteria only apply to a few selected goods, such as sunlight or air, which are provided by nature. The majority of public goods are 'impure', meaning they require specific access rules and are often subject to user fees, as they are not abundant but need to be produced and maintained through infrastructure policy. The SDGs adopted by the United Nations illustrate this point, as their achievement depends on the implementation of suitable infrastructure policy programmes. Therefore, even amid the transition to a new geopolitical and economic global order, the multiple productive potential of transnational infrastructures remains relevant. This potential encompasses the promotion of capitalist accumulation dynamics, including the circulation of goods and capital, and the generation of profitable investments, which remains relevant. However, it also extends to the realisation of ecological, social, and democratic goals. The prioritisation of these objectives is not solely determined by the global order but is also significantly influenced by domestic conflicts and political negotiations.

Acknowledgements The author of this chapter thanks Chiara Mattioli for her assistance in preparing the final manuscript.

References

Abels, J., & Bieling, H.-J. (2023). Infrastructures of globalization: Shifts in global order and Europe's strategic choices. *Competition & Change, 27*(3/4), 516–533.

Abels, J., & Bieling, H.-J. (2024a). The geoeconomics of infrastructures: Viewing globalization and global rivalry through a lens of infrastructural competition. *Globalizations, 21*(4), 722–739.

Abels, J., & Bieling, H.-J. (2024b) Drivers and limits of the geoeconomic turn in EU infrastructure policy. *Politics and Governance, 12*, Article 8127.

Aiyar, S., Chen, J., Ebeke, C., Garcia-Saltos, R., & et al. (2023). Geoeconomic fragmentation and the future of multilateralism. Staff Discussion Note SDN/2023/001. International Monetary Fund, Washington, DC.

Aradau, C. (2010). Security that matters: Critical infrastructure and objects of protection. *Security Dialogue, 41*(5), 491–514.

Babić, M., Adam, D., & Liu, I. T. (Eds.). (2022). *The political economy of geoeconomics: Europe in a changing world.* Palgrave Macmillan.

Barlösius, E. (2019). *Infrastrukturen als soziale Ordnungsdienste. Ein Beitrag zur Gesellschaftsdiagnose.* Campus.

Bernoth, K., & Meyer, J. (2023). US inflation reduction act demands quick strategic action from the EU. *DIW Weekly Report, 13*(6), 54–60.

Betz, J., Bieling, H.-J., Futterer, A., Möhring-Hesse, M., & Nagel, M. (Eds.) (2023). *Konflikte um Infrastrukturen: öffentliche Debatten und politische Konzepte.* Transcript.

Bieling, H.-J., & Deckwirth, C. (2008). Privatising public infrastructure within the EU: The interaction between supranational institutions, transnational forces and national governments. *Transfer: European Review of Labour and Research, 14*(2), 237–257.

Bieling, H.-J., & Möhring-Hesse M. (2023). Einleitung: Infrastrukturkonflikte. In J. Betz, H.-J. Bieling, A. Futterer, M. Möhring-Hesse & M. Nagel (Eds.), *Konflikte um Infrastrukturen: Öffentliche Debatten und politische Konzepte* (pp. 9–26). Transcript.

Bieling, H.-J. (2019). Globalisierungskonflikte: Die strategische Positionierung und Rolle der EU in der neuen Triade-Konkurrenz. *PROKLA. Zeitschrift Für Kritische Sozialwissenschaft, 49*(1), 59–78.

Bieling, H.-J. (2023). Die EU—eine geostrategische Macht im Werden? Strategien und Initiativen zur Kontrolle transnationaler Wertschöpfungsketten. *WSI Mitteilungen, 76*(6), 415–423.

Business Europe (2021). Recommendations for the EU Global Gateway initiative. https://www.businesseurope.eu/publications/businesseurope-recommendations-eu-global-gatewayinitiative

Business Roundtable (2021). Business roundtable statement on Build Back Better framework. https://www.businessroundtable.org/business-roundtable-statement-on-build-back-better-framework

Cowen, D. (2014). *The deadly life of logistics. Mapping violence in global trade.* University of Minnesota Press.

EC-HR (2018). European Commission and High Representative of the Union for Foreign Affairs and Security Policy: Connecting Europe and Asia: Building blocks for an EU strategy. JOIN(2018) 31 final.

European Commission (2021). The Global Gateway. JOIN(2021) 30 final.

European Commission (2023). Joint communication to the European Parliament, the European Council and the Council on "European Economic Security Strategy". JOIN(2023) 20 final.

Farrell, H., & Newman, A. L. (2019). Weaponized interdependence: How global economic networks shape state coercion. *International Security, 44*(1), 42–79.

Foundational Economy Collective (2018). *Foundational economy: The infrastructure of everyday life.* Manchester University Press.

Galeotti, M. (2022). *The weaponisation of everything: A field guide to the new way of war.* Yale University Press.

Gill, S. (1998). New constitutionalism, democratisation and global political economy. *Global Change, Peace & Security, 10*(1), 23–38.

Hameiri, S., & Jones, L. (2023). Why the West's alternative to China's international infrastructure financing is failing. *European Journal of International Relations*, online first, 1–28.

Harvey, D. (2003). *The new imperialism.* Oxford University Press.
Heldt, E. C. (2023). Europe's global gateway: A new instrument of geopolitics. *Politics and Governance, 11*(4), 223–234.
Huotari, M. (2018). Learning geo-economics: China's experimental path towards financial and monetary leadership. In M. Wigell & S. Scholvin, Sören (Eds.), *Geo-Economics and Power Politics in the 21st Century* (pp. 128–144). Routledge.
Hönke, J., Cezne, E., & Yank, Y. (Eds.). (2024). *Africa's global infrastructures. South-South transformations in practice.* Hurst & Company.
Hung, H. (2022). *Clash of empires: From 'Chimerica' to the 'New Cold War.'* Cambridge University Press.
Kuus, M. (2010). Critical geopolitics. In R. E. Denemark (Ed.), *The International Studies Encyclopedia* (Vol. II, pp. 683–701). Wiley-Blackwell.
Larkin, B. (2013). The politics and poetics of infrastructure. *Annual Review of Anthropology, 42*, 327–343.
Leonard, M. (2021). *The age of unpeace. How connectivity causes conflict.* Bantam Press.
Luttwak, E. N. (1990). From geopolitics to geo-economics: Logic of conflict, grammar of commerce. *The National Interest, 20*, 17–23.
McKinsey Global Institute (2017). Executive Summary: The new dynamics of financial globalization. https://www.mckinsey.com/~/media/mckinsey/industries/financial%20services/our%20insights/the%20new%20dynamics%20of%20financial%20globalization/mgi-financial-globalization-executive-summary-aug-2017.pdf
McNally, C. A. (2012). Sino-capitalism: China's reemergence and the international political economy. *World Politics, 64*(4), 741–776.
Mertens, D., & Thiemann, M. (2018). Market-based but state-led: The role of public development banks in shaping market-based finance in the European Union. *Competition & Change, 22*(2), 184–204.
Mohan, G., & Tan-Mullins, M. (2019). The geopolitics of South-South infrastructure development: Chinese-financed energy projects in the global South. *Urban Studies, 56*(7), 1368–1385.
Paci, S. (2020). The international dimension of the EU infrastructure strategy. In C. Secchi & A. Belladonna (Eds.), *Infrastructure in a Changing World. Trends and Challenges* (pp. 93–102). ISPI.
Roberts, A., Moraes, H. C., & Ferguson, V. (2019). Toward a geoeconomic order in international trade and investment. *Journal of International Economic Law, 22*(4), 655–676.
Samuelson, P. A. (1954). The pure theory of public expenditures. *Review of Economics and Statistics, 36*(4), 387–389.
Scherrer, C. (2022). Biden's foreign economic policy: Crossbreed of Obama and Trump? *International Review of Public Policy, 4*(1), 129–138.
Sum, N.-L. (2019). The intertwined geopolitics and geoeconomics of hopes/fears: China's triple economic bubbles and the 'One Belt One Road' imaginary. *Territory, Politics, Governance, 7*(4), 528–552.
The White House (2021). Fact sheet: President Biden and G7 leaders launch Build Back Better World (B3W) partnership. https://www.whitehouse.gov/briefing-room/statements-releases/2021/06/12/fact-sheet-president-biden-and-g7-leaders-launch-build-back-better-world-b3w-partnership/
Tooze, A. (2018). *Crashed: How a decade of financial crises changed the world.* Penguin.
UNCTAD (2020). International production: A decade of transformation ahead. In *World Investment Report 2020: International Production Beyond the Pandemic.* https://unctad.org/system/files/official-document/WIR2020_CH4.pdf
van Laak, D. (2018). *Alles im Fluss. Die Lebensadern unserer Gesellschaft.* S. Fischer.
Züfle, S. (2023). *The political economy of China's belt and road initiative in east Africa.* Springer Nature.

Hans-Jürgen Bieling is Professor of Political Economy at the Institute of Political Science, University of Tübingen. His research focuses on transformations in the global and European political economy, in terms of finance, labour markets and social security systems, governmental strategies and forms of political participation. Some of his research was published in Review of International Political Economy, New Political Economy, Competition & Change, Globalizations, Journal of European Public Policy, Journal of Common Market Studies, Transfer: European Review of Labour and Research or Politics & Governance. More recently, he works on the transformative role of—globalisation-relevant—infrastructures, also as PI of the Project "EUInfra: Strategies of the EU in the global competition for economic expansion and geoeconomic control", funded by the DFG.

Part II

New Forms of Communication

Dimensions of Infrastructures and the Digital Transformation of the Public Sphere

Florian Muhle

Abstract

There is a broad consensus in media and communication studies that the public sphere is undergoing another structural transformation. This transformation is largely attributed to infrastructural changes, often characterised as 'platformisation'. However, what exactly is meant by platformisation and what characterises the infrastructural changes is disputed. On the one hand, this is because infrastructures are conceptually unruly. On the other hand, there is little systematic discussion of the concept of infrastructure within media and communication studies. This chapter aims to change this. After presenting various ways in which infrastructural changes in the public sphere have been referred to in the disciplinary debate, it systematically examines concepts of infrastructure as developed in other disciplines, such as science and technology studies and anthropology. On this basis, four dimensions of infrastructures are identified and the ways in which the infrastructure of the public sphere is changing in these dimensions are briefly outlined. In this way, the chapter develops a heuristic that can serve as a starting point for a more in-depth examination of the (infra)structural transformation of the public sphere from a media and communication studies perspective.

Keywords

Public Sphere · Infrastructural Transformation · Platformisation · Infrastructure Studies · Digitalisation · Public Communication · Social Media

F. Muhle (✉)
Fachbereich Kulturwissenschaften & Kommunikationswissenschaften, Zeppelin Universität, Friedrichshafen, Germany
e-mail: florian.Muhle@zu.de

H.-J. Bieling et al. (eds.), *Transnational Infrastructures and the Transformation of Global Orders*, RaumFragen: Stadt – Region – Landschaft,
https://doi.org/10.1007/978-3-031-74846-2_5

1 Introduction

In communication and media studies, there is no doubt that the public sphere is currently undergoing a new structural transformation that is closely linked to the digitalisation of public communication (Enjolras & Steen-Johnsen, 2017; Habermas, 2022; Santos et al., 2019; Staab & Thiel, 2022). This transformation is characterised not only by processes of simultaneous transnationalisation and fragmentation of public communication, but also by the increasing spread of fake news and the loss of relevance of journalistic media. Many scholars assume changes of the infrastructure of public communication to be a fundamental cause and driver of these processes (Eisenegger, 2021; Fischer & Jarren, 2024; Habermas, 2022; Jarren, 2019; Plantin & Punathambekar, 2018; Schneiders et al., 2023; van Dijck et al., 2018). These changes began with the establishment of the World Wide Web in the 1990s and are currently reflected above all in the inescapable relevance of social media platforms as new intermediaries. Accordingly, the current phase of the transformation of public communication infrastructures is often characterised and problematised as 'platformisation' (Eisenegger & Schäfer, 2023; Fischer & Jarren, 2024; Schneiders et al., 2023; Smyrnaios & Baisnée, 2023).

At the same time, however, there are very different understandings in the debate of what exactly characterises platformisation and the transformation of the infrastructure of the public sphere. Essentially, a distinction can be made here between, on the one hand, primarily *material* or rather *technological* and, on the other hand, primarily *institutional* understandings of infrastructures. Corresponding understandings are usually only formulated very briefly, without reference to competing conceptualisations. Accordingly, what has been largely lacking in the disciplinary discussion to date is a systematic examination of the concept of infrastructure that can not only guide empirical and theoretical research, but also integrate the different understandings circulating in the relevant literature. At the same time, however, in other disciplines such as science and technology studies or anthropology, there is already a long tradition of analysing and conceptualising infrastructures that media and communication studies can learn from.

In view of this, the present chapter aims to develop a systematic and integrative concept of infrastructures by analysing the relevant literature on the topic of infrastructures and connecting it with existing research (traditions) in media and communication studies. In this way, the contours of a research programme dedicated to systematic research into the dimensions and consequences of infrastructural change in the public sphere will become visible. In a first step, exemplary contributions on the contemporary digital transformation of the public sphere are presented to briefly show the extent to which different conceptualisations of infrastructures can be found in the current debate (Sect. 2). Building on this, a general socio-technical concept of infrastructures is developed that contains four different dimensions. In these dimensions, both technical, and institutional, or rather social aspects are important (Sect. 3).

The four dimensions are a) the technical-material dimension and thus the 'built networks' of infrastructures, b) control rules, systems and standards, c) political and economic framework conditions, and d) constellations of actors that use infrastructures and are necessary for their maintenance. In the course of the elaborations, these dimensions are first characterised and then specified with regard to the digital transformation of the public sphere (Sect. 3.1–3.4). In this way, a research heuristic is created and starting points for concrete research are shown. As is emphasised at the end, this is intended to encourage further research in media and communication studies that systematically relates the digital transformation of the public sphere to infrastructural changes that form the basis for observable transformation processes in the structures of public communication (4).

2 (Infra-)Structural Transformation of the Public Sphere in the Current Discussion

When we talk about infrastructure in everyday life, we are usually referring primarily to physical or technical infrastructures. In this sense, "*roads, railways, airports, ports, pipelines, fibre optics cables, data, and logistics centres*" (Knox et al. 2023, p. 1) are referred to as infrastructures, which form "*the arteries of our contemporary world*" (Knox et al. 2023, p. 1). In such an understanding, the printing press, later broadcast technology and today the internet would traditionally be considered the relevant infrastructure for public communication. In such an understanding, infrastructural change thus means a change in the material basis of public communication.

Corresponding perspectives that represent a material understanding of infrastructures in this sense can also be found in the media and communication science debate since the 1990s. In these days the World Wide Web became established as a new medium for public communication, based on the technology of the internet, whose architecture, in contrast to the classic broadcasting system, is designed as a distributed network. While broadcast technologies like radio and TV are restricted to one-way communication, this network structure allows every user to be both a receiver and a sender of communication. As sociologist Emanuel Castells puts it, this change can be characterised as follows:

> The communication system of the industrial society was centered around the mass media, characterised by the mass distribution of a one-way message from one to many. The communication foundation of the network society is the global web of horizontal communication networks that include the multimodal exchange of interactive messages from many to many both synchronous and asynchronous. (Castells, 2019, p. 88).

An overview of the early discussion of the consequences of this transformation of the material basis of public communication is provided by the much-cited article 'The virtual sphere' by Zizi Papacharissi (2002).[1] Without explicitly using the term infrastruc-

[1] At this point, the discussion still refers to web 1.0.

ture, the article shows that and how the technical conditions of communication on the Internet are being recognised as triggers for changes in public communication in the early academic debate about the new media. The debate builds on the observation that "the internet and related technologies have created a new public space for politically oriented conversation" (Papacharissi, 2002, p. 9). The new technology of the Internet is thus identified as the cause of observable or anticipated changes in communication. The only controversy in the literature is which changes should be emphasised, and both possible positive and negative consequences are considered. Positive "democratising effects" (Papacharissi, 2002, p. 10) are seen, for example, in an increase in opportunities for participation and the "ability to connect people from diverse backgrounds" (Papacharissi, 2002, p. 15) around the globe. In this interpretation, the Internet enables the emergence of a democratic 'global village' (McLuhan & Powers, 1989) and thus the emergence of a new democratic global order.[2]

Against this, sceptical positions were quick to emphasise the danger of a fragmentation of the public sphere resulting from the distributed network structure (Papacharissi, 2002, p. 17). Jürgen Habermas takes up this point early on (albeit very briefly at this point), clearly rejecting praise for the democratic potential of the Internet. In his view, the decentralised structure of the internet does not create a new and democratic public sphere. According to Habermas, "the rise of millions of fragmented chat rooms across the world tend instead to lead to the fragmentation of large but politically focussed mass audiences into a huge number of isolated issue publics" (Habermas, 2006, p. 423; FN 3).

While there may be disagreement regarding the consequences, the above-mentioned contributions make it clear that transformations of public communication are primarily conceptualised here as a consequence of transformations in the material basis of communication. Similar understandings can be found in the more recent debate on platformisation. Pfister and Yang (2018), for example, take a critical look at changes to technical infrastructures by platform operators in the name of 'technoliberalism'. These changes, which for instance prioritize engagement (Pfister & Yang, 2018, p. 252) are intended to create certain behaviours and emotions on the side of the platform users. The authors describe this as "a certain kind of ordering of the world" through the establishment of "certain kinds of technical infrastructures" (Pfister & Yang, 2018, p. 260). Similarly, West deals with the establishment of technical infrastructures through social media plat-

[2]A particularly striking example of this positive vision of the consequences of the internet is the 'Declaration of the Independence of Cyberspace' formulated by John Perry Barlow in 1996. In this text, online communication is described as a "great and gathering conversation" in which "a world [emerges] that all may enter without privilege or prejudice accorded by race, economic power, military force, or station of birth" (Barlow 1996). The World Wide Web is understood here as an independent transnational space that is not bound to the borders of states in the physical world and in which equals meet among equals who are not related to each other in structures of superordination and subordination, but in a hierarchy-free network.

forms that allow geoblocking (West, 2022) and thus serve the interests of particular state actors that can realize their own version of the internet based on the provided technical infrastructure.

However, there are also other understandings of what constitutes public sphere's infrastructure. These tend to focus on *institutional* aspects of infrastructures. Such an understanding can be found in some of Habermas' considerations about the public sphere, but also in many current contributions that deal with platformisation. As early as 1990, Habermas wrote in the foreword to the new edition of 'Strukturwandel der Öffentlichkeit' that the infrastructure of the public sphere is characterised by the "forms of organisation, distribution and consumption" (Habermas, 1990, p. 24). In accordance with this, in his most recent 'Reflections and Hypotheses on a Further Structural Transformation of the Political Public Sphere' he writes:

> The technically and organisationally highly complex media system requires a professionalised staff that plays the gatekeeper role (as it has come to be called) for the communicative currents from which the citizens distil public opinions. This staff comprises journalists who work for the news services, the media and the publishing houses—in other words, specialists who perform authorial, editorial, proofreading and managerial functions in the media and publishing business. This staff directs the throughput and, together with the companies that manage production and organise distribution, forms the infrastructure of the public sphere. (Habermas, 2022, p. 157).

This understanding makes it clear that it is not the material basis of the distribution channels that form the infrastructure of the public sphere. It is, in fact, the organisations and professions relevant to the creation and distribution of content that do so. These organisations and professions are the ones who ensure the reproduction of the public sphere system. They use the available material communication channels for this purpose. Van Dijck et al. (2018) make a similar argument in their book 'The Platform Society'. The authors trace the rise of the five big tech companies (Alphabet-Google, Apple, Facebook, Amazon, and Microsoft) and describe their establishment as an infrastructural change, as most global communication flows now run via the platforms operated by these companies. In their analysis, they deliberately neglect to analyse the technical infrastructure of the internet, on which the platforms are also based (van Dijck et al., 2018, p. 8). Instead, they are interested – similarly to Eisenegger (2021), for example – in the institutional change of the public sphere associated with platformisation, which threatens to cause journalists and news media to lose their status as the traditional infrastructure of the public sphere (2018, p. 49ff). In a similar manner, Jarren (2019) describes social media platforms as the new 'communicative infrastructure' of the public sphere, as they have established themselves as intermediaries controlling public communication flows in addition to and in competition with the traditional journalistic media.

Numerous other examples of both the focus on technical and institutional aspects (of change) of infrastructures can be found in the relevant literature on the transformation of the public sphere. However, these will not be discussed further here. Instead, the overview aims to show by way of example that different conceptualisations exist, each of which emphasises different aspects of infrastructures and at the same time largely manages without explicit references to one another. This inevitably results in the fact that sometimes completely different things are meant when talking about infrastructures. Furthermore, there is a clear need for systematisation. This must go hand in hand with a clear explanation of how different understandings should be meaningfully related to each other and placed in relation to each other. The next section achieves this, building on existing concepts of infrastructures as they have long been negotiated in science and technology studies (Star, 1999; Star & Bowker, 2002) or anthropology (Larkin, 2013; Knox et al. 2023).

3 Dimensions of Infrastructures and the Infrastructural Transformation of the Public Sphere

When it comes to defining infrastructures, one problem is that they "are conceptually unruly" (Larkin, 2013, p. 329). As a consequence, the literature, which has been dealing with infrastructures for a long time, still contains diverse and not always compatible definitions. Against this background, the following proposal to distinguish between four dimensions of infrastructures represents a synthesis of different considerations that attempts to integrate key aspects emphasized in the academic discourse on infrastructures.

3.1 Built Networks

The first dimension of infrastructures consists of their built materiality. In this sense, roads, railways, pipelines, power grids or telephone lines form the built dimension of infrastructures. Seen this way, infrastructures appear as "built networks that facilitate the flow of goods, people, or ideas and allow for their exchange over space" (Larkin, 2013, p. 328). It is exactly this dimension that is emphasized in technical understandings of infrastructures outlined above (Sect. 2). Anthropologist Brian Larkin (2013, p. 329) explains this material aspect of infrastructures using the example of computers: "Take, for example, the computer I have used to write this article. What is its infrastructure? Electricity may be the most obvious substratum that allows the computer to operate".

Without an electricity grid that supplies the computer with power, it cannot work. To function for online communication, the computer also needs a connection to the Internet. Power grids and the Internet in its physical form are therefore fundamental aspects of the infrastructure of the digital public sphere. Regarding the transformation of the public sphere, however, the electricity grid appears less important than the Internet, which enables interactive online communication (see Sect. 2). This would be different if one were not concerned with the public sphere but with climate change. In this case, the relevance of the electricity grid as an infrastructure for online communication would be much more relevant, as electricity consumption has increased immensely due to internet technologies and cloud computing (Uchechukwu et al. 2014; Batmunkh, 2022).

This example makes it clear that different infrastructures are interlinked and therefore different 'layers' of infrastructures must be distinguished (Star & Bowker, 2010), some of which build on each other. At the same time, it also becomes clear that it depends on the respective question and research problem as to which layers are to be considered (particularly) relevant for consideration. In this sense, "discussing an infrastructure [...] is a categorical act. It is a moment of tearing into those heterogeneous networks to define which aspect of which network is to be discussed and which parts will be ignored" (Larkin, 2013, p. 330). Researchers should bear this in mind and make explicit which aspects of infrastructures they are focussing on and why.

However, this selectivity does not only apply to different 'technical' layers of infrastructures. This is because the material basis is only one dimension of infrastructures that does not have infrastructure status on its own. This point is also recognised by Larkin (2013), who adds to his perspective on infrastructures as 'built networks' outlined above. In line with technology researcher Susan Leigh Star (Star, 1999), he even explicitly problematises approaches that understand infrastructures as a "system of substrates" (Larkin, 2013, p. 329), which consists of a "built phenomenal world such as pipes, cables, sewers, and wires" (Larkin, 2013, p. 329). For such material forms alone do not constitute infrastructure. For them to enable and facilitate "the flow of goods, people or ideas", rules and standards are also needed to organise this flow.

3.2 Standards, and Control Rules and Systems

If we consider roads and cycle paths, for example, as essential elements and 'built networks' of modern transport infrastructure, it quickly becomes clear that the flow of cars, lorries and bicycles would grind to a halt if there were no logic and associated rules to organise traffic on the road. Without standardised traffic rules, but also without traffic control systems based on these rules, which include traffic lights, signs or painted pavements that regulate the flow of traffic, chaos on the roads would be inevitable. A look at the history of the development of motorised traffic and its regulation shows this. There is no doubt that "the rise of traffic signals is tied to the rapid rise of automotive traffic" (Mcshane, 1999, p. 380). In the USA, for example, the start of mass production of Henry Ford's 'Model T' in 1913 led to regular traffic jams and chaos in major cities due to cars parked on the streets (Mcshane, 1999, 380ff). Accordingly, it was not long before the first traffic lights for motor traffic (modelled on railroad signal systems) were put into service.[3] Without appropriate control systems, there would be much more congestion

[3] This was the case in Cleveland in 1914 (Mcshane, 1999, p. 382).

than usual in cities and on motorways today.[4] Built networks can therefore only fulfil their infrastructural function in conjunction with standards, rules and control systems. Only if the latter are taken into account can it be claimed, as Larkin puts it in continuation of his definition quoted above, that infrastructures "comprise the architecture for circulation" (Larkin, 2013, p. 328). For without corresponding rules and standards, streets, electricity grids or the physical internet could not shape the speed or direction of flows.

In terms of the Internet as the material basis of the digital public sphere, this means that it needs standards and traffic rules, just like the transport infrastructure. A very basic example of this is the TCP/IP protocol, which is the basis for sending and receiving data online and which defines exactly how this is done. Similarly, the http protocol is responsible for the functioning of web browsers and websites and regulates how hypertext is exchanged and transmitted. Without this protocol, it would not be possible to access the interface of social media platforms and view them on our own devices.

However, these basic layers of standardised regulation of communication flows are built upon by further layers. In terms of the structural transformation of the public sphere, the predominantly algorithmic control logics implemented on the platforms are of particular importance, as they determine the criteria according to which content is presented to users (Schneiders et al., 2023; van Dijck & Poell, 2013). This is where technical and institutional aspects of infrastructures come together, as the respective logics function according to specific institutionalised criteria. The algorithmic content selection on platforms, for example, is organised according to completely different criteria than the journalistic content selection (Anderson, 2011; Loosen & Scholl, 2017; Muhle & Wehner, 2017; Steiner, 2020).

In media and communication studies with their long tradition of dealing with news values and issues of gatekeeping (Joye et al., 2016; Harcup and O'Neill 2017; Galtung & Ruge, 1965; Clayman & Reisner, 1998; White, 1950), there is a particular focus on the examination of this aspect of the infrastructure of the public sphere. Research on social media logics in this tradition shows that the algorithmic control of communication is largely responsible for the fragmentation and polarisation of public discourse, as well as for the emergence of a transformed attention economy, in which tendencies towards emotionalization, scandalisation and sensationalism are promoted, thus also creating excellent conditions for the spread of fake news (Boler & Davis, 2021; Munger, 2020).

This makes it clear that the study of standards as well as control rules and systems is essential for dealing with infrastructures (of the public sphere). Media and communication studies already have established concepts, procedures and research traditions for dealing with this infrastructural dimension. These are not associated with a focus

[4] In 2023, there was a total of 877,000 km of traffic jam in Germany alone (https://de.statista.com/statistik/daten/studie/200201/umfrage/gesamte-staulaenge-auf-autobahnen-in-deutschland/ [13/07/2024]). This corresponds to a traffic jam that wraps around the earth 20 times.

on infrastructures from the outset. But an infrastructural perspective makes it clear that selection criteria, forms of gatekeeping and news values are an indispensable part of the control rules of the infrastructure of the public sphere. However, these are not only determined by technical possibilities and necessities as well as institutional logics of platforms or news organisations but are also framed by the general political and economic conditions under which public communication takes place. This is also true for any other form of infrastructure.

3.3 Political and Economic Conditions

Standards and control elements are by no means neutral. They are neither 'originally' linked to the 'built networks' on which goods, people or ideas can move, nor can they be freely determined by infrastructure developers or operators. It is true that standards and control rules often emerge in a quasi-natural way together with the need to regulate and control the flow of traffic, people, goods or information, so that there is initially a multitude of local solutions and rules, which may contradict each other. However, for certain technologies and their associated control elements to achieve the status of infrastructure, they also need to be adopted by society as a whole—and thus eventually become standard (Star & Bowker, 2010). In this sense, infrastructures only become established as such "when either one technological system comes to dominate over others or when independent systems converge into a network" (Larkin, 2013, p. 330; see also Hughes, 1987).

States and (supra)governmental institutions responsible for standardisation and regulation and pursuing certain policies play an important role in the corresponding processes of enforcement of certain systems (Knox et al. 2023, p. 5). These policies have a major influence on the specific control rules and technologies as well as the overall functioning of the infrastructure. Fundamentally, issues of funding and ownership play an important role. While the provision and maintenance of infrastructure has long been a clear responsibility of the state, there has been a significant increase in the privatisation of infrastructure since the 1980s (Kessides, 2005), with noticeable consequences for the functioning and operation of infrastructure. Moreover, decisions about the design of infrastructure are always political, as they help to determine which user groups benefit from it and which do not. For example, it makes a difference whether investments in transport are primarily made in multi-lane roads or whether inner-city transport routes are primarily designed for bicycle use (Emanuel, 2018). Similarly, it makes a difference to access to public communication and the associated opportunities for participation in public discourse whether internet connections are also available in rural areas or whether infrastructure is being cut back (Kos-Łabędowicz, 2017; Rooksby et al., 2002). The *political and economic conditions* and the associated policies inscribed in the design and mode of operation are therefore another central dimension of infrastructures and have long been the subject of extensive research, particularly in science and technology studies (Bowker & Star, 1999; Star, 1990; Winner, 1980).

In media and communication studies, this dimension is most likely to be considered in media systems research (Hallin, 2016; Hallin & Mancini, 2004; Papathanassopoulos & Miconi, 2023). In this branch of research, which plays a very subordinate role compared to research on news values, the aim is to examine and compare different variants of the social institutionalisation of media systems. With regard to Western media systems, for example, a distinction is made between liberal models, democratic corporatist models and polarised pluralist models. These differ in terms of the role of commercial media, the role of the state in the media system and the importance of professional journalism (Hallin, 2016). As a rule, these are national media systems into which 'new media' are also integrated in the course of infrastructure change. For research on the transformation of infrastructure, it is therefore relevant to ask how exactly the new internet-based media—and in particular social media platforms—are integrated into the respective media systems and how the systems themselves, and thus the political and economic conditions of public communication, are changing in connection with this. With regard to the establishment of social media platforms, a complete privatisation of the infrastructure can currently be observed (van Dijck et al., 2018, p. 15). This goes so far that "to some extent, governments and public institutions, for their functioning, have all become predicated on the use of private online infrastructures" (van Dijck et al., 2018, p. 16). At the same time, platforms resist being held accountable for content, such as hate speech or fake news, disseminated through them. While journalistic organisations that disseminate public communication are bound by professional criteria and legal requirements, this does not apply to platforms in many parts of the world. However, this is changing, at least in part, as evidenced by the EU's Digital Services Directive, which is changing the policy and legal framework for online communication. What impact this will have on public information flows and their content, and which political and economic frameworks will prevail will have to be explored in the coming years.

3.4 Actor Constellations and Practices

Finally, the fourth inescapable dimension of infrastructures is the actors and their constellations. On the one hand, they are necessary for the operation and maintenance of infrastructures. On the other hand, they use the infrastructures. In the words of technology researchers Star and Ruhleder: "It [an infrastructure; F.M.] becomes infrastructure in relation to organised practices" (Star & Ruhleder, 1996, p. 113). Roads and traffic lights only serve as infrastructure if bicycles or cars actually use them regularly and expectably. If they are not used, they are merely material forms that are built into the world and deteriorate over time. However, long-term use is only possible if infrastructures are continuously maintained and kept in operation. For this reason, organisations and associated professional groups responsible for the construction, maintenance and operation of infrastructure are always formed around the development of material elements of infrastructure. As Hughes (1987, p. 52) writes, using electricity infrastructures as an example, ‘persons who build electric light and power systems invent and develop not only generators and transmission lines but also such organizational forms as electrical manufacturing and utility holding companies”. By highlighting the need to develop organisations and specific “conventions of practice” and “communities of practice” (Star & Ruhleder, 1996, p. 113), it is emphasised that infrastructures “are not simply in existence, but they are built, installed, maintained, repaired, used, worked around/against, appropriated and so on” (Korn et al., 2019, p. 17). Without organised activities, there is no infrastructure—which is why the groups of actors who use and provide the material elements of infrastructures are also an essential part of infrastructures.

Looking at the change in the infrastructure of the public sphere from this perspective, it is immediately apparent that it is characterised by the emergence of large platforms as powerful new actors that play a central role in public communication and have firmly established themselves as intermediaries alongside and in competition with the journalistic media. In the terms of actor-network theory, they can be understood as new ‘obligatory passage points’ (Callon, 1986; Teurlings, 2013), as large parts of public communication now pass through them. This is precisely why they have become part of the infrastructure (van Dijck et al., 2018, p. 16). However, the platforms have not simply joined the existing actors in the public sphere (journalistic actors, political actors, civil society actors). They have also changed the relationships between these actors. On the one hand, they compete with traditional media providers in terms of distribution channels, thus contributing to the crisis of journalism and its business model. On the other hand, they allow political actors, for example, to address their own audiences without the mediation of journalism.

In addition, platforms have brought other players into the public arena. On the front stage, influencers and content creators are the first to come to mind. On the backstage, algorithms play an important role (see Sect. 3.2), taking on the task of curating content, but also click-workers or content moderators, who largely form the new proletariat of the public sphere under precarious working conditions (Gillespie, 2021).[5] New ‘conventions of practice’ are emerging in their work, as well as in media use, which is increasingly associated with less interest in journalistic offerings among younger people and a focus on younger platforms such as Instagram and TikTok, while Facebook is already declining in importance. How the constellations of actors continue to evolve and perhaps even stabilise will therefore be an important part of research into the changing infrastructure of the public sphere.

[5] A special role is played by so-called socialbots, which appear on the front stage as human platform users, but are in fact computer programmes that are generally used for malicious purposes by political actors (Muhle 2023; Howard et al., 2018).

4 Conclusion

Infrastructures are only infrastructures when the dimensions outlined here come together and interact in a specific way. Infrastructures are therefore always both "things and also the relation between things" (Larkin, 2013, p. 329). In this way, according to Larkin, they "operate as systems" (Larkin, 2013, p. 329)—or in other theoretical terms: as heterogeneous networks (Law, 1992) that connect things as diverse as physical forms, control rules and standards, political and economic frame conditions, and different actor groups. If there are no disruptions and no changes occur in one (or more) dimensions, the existing infrastructure systems are relatively stable and can fulfil their social function of enabling the flow of goods, people, or ideas. However, when changes or crises occur, the whole system changes (Larkin, 2013, 330f; Bowker & Star, 1999). This affects both the individual dimensions and the relationships between them, as well as the social practices enabled by the infrastructures—be it the way people get from home to work in the morning, or the way public communication operates.

Against this background, the task of research interested in the transformation of infrastructures is, in a first step, to analyse how change takes place in relation to each of the infrastructural dimensions. It would then be necessary to analyse how the relationships between elements in these dimensions change as a result, and finally to look at the consequences of the change in the infrastructure system for the social practices based on it. As phenomena in each of the dimensions of infrastructures are complex, diverse and interlinked, it is hardly possible to analyse all aspects and interrelationships in individual studies. Inevitably, some aspects have to be selected and others neglected. Decisions for or against the treatment of certain aspects and elements depend directly on the questions of interest, which determine which phenomena are brought into focus (Larkin, 2013, p. 330). In this sense, the understanding of infrastructures and their essential dimensions presented in this chapter serves as a heuristic that allows for a conscious and reasoned selection of certain aspects or dimensions and is aware of the embedding of these dimensions in the overall system of the infrastructure of interest. For the research on the transformation of the public sphere, relevant aspects were identified for each of the infrastructure dimensions. This could only be done cursorily, in order to draw a picture of possibilities and starting points for research, and to highlight references to existing research in media and communication studies—in the hope of stimulating further research and embedding it systematically in the context of the study of infrastructures.

References

Anderson, C. W. (2011). Deliberative, agonistic, and algorithmic audiences: Journalism's vision of its public in an age of audience transparency. *International Journal of Communication, 5*, 529–547.

Barlow, J. P. (1996). A declaration of the independence of cyberspace. Electronic Frontier Foundation. https://www.eff.org/de/cyberspace-independence

Batmunkh, A. (2022). Carbon footprint of the most popular social media platforms. *Sustainability, 14*(4). https://doi.org/10.3390/su14042195

Boler, M., & Davis, E. (Eds.) (2021). *Affective politics of digital media. Propaganda by other means*. New York: Routledge, Taylor & Francis Group.

Bowker, G. C., & Star, S. L. (1999). *Sorting things out. Classification and its consequences*. MIT Press.

Callon, M. (1986). Some elements of a sociology of translation: domestication of the scallops and the fischermen of St Brieuc Bay. In J. Law (Ed.), *Power, action and belief. A new sociology of knowledge?* (pp. 196–223). London: Routledge and Kegan Paul.

Castells, M. (2019). Communication power: Mass communication, mass self-communication and power relations in the network society. In J. Curran & D. Hesmondhalgh (Eds.), *Mass media and society* (6th ed., pp. 83–97). Bloomsbury Academic.

Clayman, S. E., & Reisner, A. (1998). Gatekeeping in action: Editorial conferences and assessments of newsworthiness. *American Sociological Review, 63*(2), 178–199. https://doi.org/10.2307/2657322

Eisenegger, M. (2021). Dritter, digitaler Strukturwandel der Öffentlichkeit als Folge der Plattformisierung. In M. Eisenegger, M. Prinzing, P. Ettinger, & R. Blum (Eds.), *Digitaler Strukturwandel der Öffentlichkeit* (pp. 17–39). Springer Fachmedien Wiesbaden.

Eisenegger, M., & Schäfer, M. S. (2023). Editorial: Reconceptualizing public sphere(s) in the digital age? On the role and future of public sphere theory. *Communication Theory, 33*(2–3), 61–69. https://doi.org/10.1093/ct/qtad011

Emanuel, M. (2018). Making a bicycle city: Infrastructure and cycling in Copenhagen since 1880. *Urban History, 46*(3), 493–517. https://doi.org/10.1017/S0963926818000573

Enjolras, B., & Steen-Johnsen, K. (2017). The digital transformation of the political public sphere: A sociological perspective. In H. Larsen, J. Rogstad & K. Steen-Johnsen (Eds.), *Institutional change in the public sphere. Views on the Nordic model* (pp. 99–117). Warsaw: De Gruyter Open.

Fischer, R., & Jarren, O. (2024). The platformization of the public sphere and its challenge to democracy. *Philosophy & Social Criticism, 50*(1), 200–215. https://doi.org/10.1177/01914537231203535

Galtung, J., & Ruge, M. H. (1965). The structure of foreign news. *Journal of Peace Research, 2*(1), 64–91. http://www.jstor.org/stable/423011

Gillespie, T. (2021). *Custodians of the internet. Platforms, content moderation, and the hidden decisions that shape social media*. [Paperback edition.]. New Haven, Connecticut: Yale University Press.

Habermas, J. (1990). *Strukturwandel der Öffentlichkeit. Untersuchungen zu einer Kategorie der bürgerlichen Gesellschaft ; mit einem Vorwort zur Neuauflage 1990*. Suhrkamp (Suhrkamp-Taschenbuch Wissenschaft, 891).

Habermas, J. (2006). Political communication in media society: Does democracy still enjoy an epistemic dimension? The impact of normative theory on empirical research. *Communication Theory, 16*(4), 411–426. https://doi.org/10.1111/j.1468-2885.2006.00280.x

Habermas, J. (2022). Reflections and hypotheses on a further structural transformation of the political public sphere. *Theory, Culture & Society, 39*(4), 145–171. https://doi.org/10.1177/02632764221112341

Hallin, D. C. (2016). Typology of media systems. In D. C. Hallin (Ed.), *Oxford Research Encyclopedia of Politics*. Oxford University Press.

Hallin, D. C., & Mancini, P. (2004). *Comparing media systems: Three models of media and politics*. Cambridge University Press.

Harcup, T., & O'Neill, D. (2017). What is news? *Journalism Studies, 18*(12), 1470–1488. https://doi.org/10.1080/1461670X.2016.1150193
Howard, P. N., Woolley, S., & Calo, R. (2018). Algorithms, bots, and political communication in the US 2016 election. The challenge of automated political communication for election law and administration. *Journal of Information Technology & Politics, 15*(2), 81–93. https://doi.org/10.1080/19331681.2018.1448735
Hughes, T. P. (1987). The evolution of large technological systems. In W. E. Bijker, T. P. Hughes, & T. Pinch (Eds.), *The social construction of technological systems. New directions in the sociology and history of technology* (pp. 51–82). MIT Press.
Jarren, O. (2019). Fundamentale Institutionalisierung: Social Media als neue globale Kommunikationsinfrastruktur. *Pub, 64*(2), 163–179. https://doi.org/10.1007/s11616-019-00503-4
Joye, S., Heinrich, A., & Wöhlert, R. (2016). 50 years of Galtung and Ruge: Reflections on their model of news values and its relevance for the study of journalism and communication today. *CM, 11*(38), 5–28. https://doi.org/10.5937/comman11-9514
Kessides, I. N. (2005). Infrastructure privatization and regulation: Promises and perils. *The World Bank Research Observer, 20*(1), 81–108. https://doi.org/10.1093/wbro/lki003
Knox, H., & Gambino, E. (2023). Infrastructure. In F. Stein (Ed.), *The Open Encyclopedia of Anthropology*. https://doi.org/10.29164/23infrastructure
Korn, M., Reißmann, W., Röhl, T., & Sittler, D. (2019). Infrastructuring publics: A research perspective. In M. Korn, W. Reissmann, T. Röhl, & D. Sittler (Eds.), *Infrastructuring publics* (pp. 11–47). Springer VS (Medien der Kooperation Ser).
Kos-Łabędowicz, J. (2017). The issue of digital divide in rural areas of the European Union. *Ekonomiczne Problemy Usług, 126*(1/2), 195–204.
Larkin, B. (2013). The politics and poetics of infrastructure. *Annual Review of Anthropology, 42*(1), 327–343. https://doi.org/10.1146/annurev-anthro-092412-155522
Law, J. (1992). Notes on the theory of the actor-network: Ordering, strategy, and heterogeneity. *Systems Practice, 5*(4), 379–393. https://doi.org/10.1007/BF01059830
Loosen, W., & Scholl, A. (2017). Journalismus und (algorithmische) Wirklichkeitskonstruktion Epistemologische Beobachtungen. *M&k, 65*(2), 348–366. https://doi.org/10.5771/1615-634X-2017-2-348
McLuhan, M., & Powers, B. R. (1989). *The global village. Transformations in world life and media in the 21st century.* [POD-uitgave]. Oxford University Press (Communication and society).
Mcshane, C. (1999). The origins and globalization of traffic control signals. *Journal of Urban History, 25*(3), 379–404. https://doi.org/10.1177/009614429902500304
Muhle, F. (2022). Socialbots at the Gates. Plädoyer für eine holistische Perspektive auf automatisierte Akteure in der Umwelt des Journalismus. *Medien & Kommunikationswissenschaft, 70*(1–2), 40–59. https://doi.org/10.30658/hmc.6.4
Muhle, F., & Wehner, J. (2017). "Online-Audiences"—zur Publikumsvermessung im Internet. *kommunikation@gesellschaft, 18*(2). https://doi.org/10.15460/kommges.2017.18.2.585
Munger, K. (2020). All the news that's fit to click: The economics of clickbait media. *Political Communication, 37*(3), 376–397. https://doi.org/10.1080/10584609.2019.1687626
Özcan, İÇ. (2018). The privatization of roads: An overview of the Turkish case. *Case Studies on Transport Policy, 6*(4), 529–536. https://doi.org/10.1016/j.cstp.2018.07.001
Papacharissi, Z. (2002). The virtual sphere: The internet as a public sphere. *New Media & Society, 4*(1), 9–27. https://doi.org/10.1177/14614440222226244
Papathanassopoulos, S., & Miconi, A. (Eds.). (2023). *The media systems in Europe.* Springer International Publishing (Springer Studies in Media and Political Communication).
Pfister, D. S., & Yang, M. (2018). Five theses on technoliberalism and the networked public sphere. *Communication and the Public, 3*(3), 247–262. https://doi.org/10.1177/2057047318794963

Plantin, J.-C., & Punathambekar, A. (2018). Digital media infrastructures: Pipes, platforms, and politics. *Media Culture Society, 41*(2), 163–174. https://doi.org/10.1177/0163443718818376

Rooksby, E., Weckert, J., & Lucas, R. (2002). The rural digital divide. *Rural Society, 12*(3), 197–210. https://doi.org/10.5172/rsj.12.3.197

Santos, T., Louçã, J., & Coelho, H. (2019). The digital transformation of the public sphere. *Systems Research and Behavioral Science, 36*(6), 778–788. https://doi.org/10.1002/sres.2644

Schneiders, P., Stegmann, D., & Stark, B. (2023). Social cohesion in platformized public spheres: Toward a conceptual framework. *Communication Theory, 33*(2–3), 122–131. https://doi.org/10.1093/ct/qtad002

Smyrnaios, N., & Baisnée, O. (2023). Critically understanding the platformization of the public sphere. *European Journal of Communication, 38*(5), 435–445. https://doi.org/10.1177/02673231231189046

Staab, P., & Thiel, T. (2022). Social media and the digital structural transformation of the public sphere. *Theory, Culture & Society, 39*(4), 129–143. https://doi.org/10.1177/02632764221103527

Star, S. L. (1990). Power, technology and the phenomenology of conventions: On being allergic to onions. *The Sociological Review, 38*(1_suppl), 26–56. https://doi.org/10.1111/j.1467-954X.1990.tb03347.x

Star, S. (1999). The ethnography of infrastructure. *American Behavioral Scientist, 43*(3), 377–391. https://doi.org/10.1177/00027649921955326

Star, S. L., & Bowker, G. C. (2002). How to infrastructure. In L. Lievrouw, & S. Livingstone (Eds.), *Handbook of new media. Social shaping and consequences of ICTs* (pp. 151–162). SAGE Publications.

Star, S. L., & Bowker, G. C. (2010). How to Infrastructure. In L. A. Lievrouw & S. Livingstone (Eds.), *Handbook of New Media: Social Shaping and Social Consequences of ICTs* (pp. 230–245). SAGE Publications Ltd.

Star, S. L., & Ruhleder, K. (1996). Steps toward an ecology of infrastructure: Design and access for large information spaces. *Information Systems Research, 7*(1), 111–134. https://doi.org/10.1287/isre.7.1.111

Steiner, M. (2020). Soft presentation of hard news? A content analysis of political Facebook posts. *MaC, 8*(3), 244–257. https://doi.org/10.17645/mac.v8i3.3152

Teurlings, J. (2013). Unblackboxing production. What media studies can learn from actor-network theory. In J. Teurlings, & M. de Valck (Eds.), *After the break. Television theory today* (pp. 101–116). Amsterdam University Press (Televisual Culture).

Uchechukwu A., Keqiu L., & Yanming S. (2014). Energy consumption in cloud computing data centers. *International Journal of Cloud Computing and Services Science* (IJ-CLOSER), *3*(3). https://doi.org/10.11591/closer.v3i3.6346

van Dijck, J., & Poell, T. (2013). Understanding social media logic. *Media and Communication, 1*(1), 2–14. https://doi.org/10.17645/mac.v1i1.70

van Dijck, J., Poell, T., & de Waal, M. (2018). *The platform society. Public values in a connective world.* Oxford University Press. https://search.ebscohost.com/login.aspx?direct=true&scope=site&db=nlebk&db=nlabk&AN=1901418

West, S. M. (2022). Social media as social infrastructures. In D. Rosen (Ed.), *The social media debate. Unpacking the social, psychological, and cultural effects of social media* (pp. 5–19). Routledge, Taylor & Francis Group (Routledge Debates in Digital Media Studies).

White, D. M. (1950). The "gatekeeper". A case study in the selection of news. *Journalism Quarterly, 27*(4), 383–390. https://doi.org/10.1177/107769905002700403

Winner, L. (1980). Do artifacts have politics? *Daedalus, 109*(1), 121–136. http://www.jstor.org/stable/20024652

Florian Muhle is professor of Communication Studies with a focus on digital communication at Zeppelin University Friedrichshafen. His research interests cover human–machine communication, automation of communication and the digital transformation of the public sphere. Florian is also affiliate at the Virtual Observatory for the Study of Online Networks (VOSON) Lab at the Australian National University in Canberra. He is also a member of the Editorial Board of Bielefeld University Press.

Infrastructural Perspectives on Artificial Intelligence—on the Implications of AI Infrastructures for Global (In)Justice

Anne Burkhardt

Abstract

The paper explores the impact of Artificial Intelligence (AI) on global orders by asking to what extent current practices of AI development, production, and use can be considered globally just. It adopts an infrastructural perspective, addressing both the infrastructures on which AI is built, and AI as a (particularly powerful) infrastructure, capable of transforming almost every sphere of life, as well as traditional infrastructures that used to function without AI. Drawing on insights from decolonial theory, Global South Studies, and Critical Technology Studies, as well as current examples, the article reveals how AI and related infrastructures create and reinforce colonial and patriarchal orders and transform social structures to the detriment of minorities and vulnerable groups. By demonstrating that those who benefit most from AI are not the same as those who are most affected by risk and harm, the paper argues that AI and related infrastructures in their current form cannot be considered globally just, and thus contribute to structural inequality with ordering effects on a global scale.

Keywords

Artificial Intelligence · Infrastructures · Global Justice · Global South · Decolonial Theory · Algorithmic Discrimination · Extraction · Exploitation · Diversity-Aware Design · AI Ethics

A. Burkhardt (✉)
RHET AI Center/Institute for Media Studies, University of Tübingen, Tübingen, Germany
e-mail: anne.burkhardt@uni-tuebingen.de

H.-J. Bieling et al. (eds.), *Transnational Infrastructures and the Transformation of Global Orders*, RaumFragen: Stadt – Region – Landschaft,
https://doi.org/10.1007/978-3-031-74846-2_6

1 Toward an Infrastructural View on AI and Global Justice

Scholars and activists concerned with issues of social justice have drawn attention to the exacerbation of structural power asymmetries associated with the development, production, and use of Artificial Intelligence (AI). Contributions from decolonial theory and activism have particularly highlighted the colonial nature of the AI industry's practices that establish colonial hierarchies, new forms of labour exploitation, and extractionism, mostly in countries of the Global South (Amrute, 2019; Arun, 2019). The decolonial perspective reveals that AI not only deepens social inequalities but also reproduces and reinforces colonial orders, thus posing a problem of global injustice (Burkhardt, 2023, pp. 3–5). But how can we approach the phenomenon of AI from a global justice perspective?

For Kate Crawford, *Artificial Intelligence* is more than just *Machine Learning* which she describes as "a range of technical approaches" (Crawford, 2021, p. 9) within computer science. She proposes to move beyond the technical notion of AI to understand its serious social implications. To this end, Crawford drafts an "Atlas of AI" by describing and analysing selected microcosms of the AI sector and involved practices and operations. Using an ethnographic approach, she identifies the material and human-made underpinnings of the power structures at work in and around AI. She concludes that AI is "fundamentally political" (Crawford, 2021, p. 9), as it follows the specific interests of its creators, primarily private BigTech companies based in the Global North. In addition, by understanding AI as a "massive industrial formation that includes politics, labour, culture, and capital", Crawford (2021, p. 9) points to the multiple societal dimensions involved in AI—and to the economic, political, and ideological interests that drive its development. Considering the extractive practices of BigTech corporations and the impact of (especially generative) AI on public discourse and knowledge production, AI can be conceptualized as a set of "physical infrastructures that are reshaping the Earth, while simultaneously shifting how the world is seen and understood" (Crawford, 2021, p. 19). With this definition, Crawford acknowledges that AI has a major impact on the structuring of global orders, both at the physical and the epistemic levels: AI can be considered a "registry of power" (Crawford, 2021, p. 8), a system based on infrastructures that both reflects and reinforces unequal global power relations.

Crawford's approach seems promising for further reflection from an infrastructural perspective, that is, from a perspective that focuses both on *the infrastructures on which AI is built* and on *AI as an infrastructure* that profoundly transforms social and epistemic orders on a global scale. Drawing on the definition by Brian Larkin who describes infrastructures as "built networks that facilitate the flow of goods, people, or ideas and allow for their exchange over space" (Larkin, 2013, p. 328), I will elaborate on why a differentiated infrastructural view holds promise for thinking about AI and global justice:

First, the key infrastructures on which AI is built—such as digital communications infrastructure, IT hardware and software, skilled and unskilled labour, private and public research institutions—are deeply transnational. Although AI development is often carried out at the national or even local level (think of the Silicon Valley or the Tübingen Cyber Valley), the big players such as Alphabet (Google), Meta (Facebook) or Amazon think and act transnationally. Likewise, the huge data sets that form the core of AI technologies are usually collected across borders. Moreover, the material basis for high-performance computers, servers, digital hardware, and communication infrastructures (such as metals, plastics, fiber optics), as well as the human workforce involved in the production of AI and its components, are spread across the globe. As noted above, these transnational infrastructures have been criticized for reproducing and reinforcing colonial hierarchies. However, the coloniality of AI infrastructures has often been projected onto AI itself, conflating different spheres without further consideration. An infrastructural perspective provides a more nuanced view, assessing the infrastructures that support AI and AI technologies separately.

Second, AI itself can be regarded a particularly powerful transnational infrastructure with the potential to transform not only information and communication technology (ICT) but almost every sphere of life: (industrial) production; governance, administration, security, and defence; housing, transportation, and health; entertainment and arts; and even knowledge production and creation. However, as contributions from gender studies, *Black* feminism, or decolonial theory show, the AI-driven transformation of life is often accompanied by discriminatory and harmful effects on minorities and vulnerable groups. Here, the infrastructural perspective serves to identify which groups are most advantaged or disadvantaged by AI as infrastructure.

Third, AI is transforming traditional infrastructures, taking over functions that were previously reserved for humans. For example, AI is widely used to conduct, moderate, and filter online communication and information, taking on tasks that touch on fundamental civil rights (namely freedom of speech and non-discrimination) and require moral consideration. In addition, AI is increasingly being used for public surveillance and security purposes, such as smart policing, airport security, or even warfare, exacerbating existing ethical and moral dilemmas. Here, an infrastructural perspective helps to reflect on the shift in human–machine interaction and its implications for social and global orders.

With respect to global justice, the infrastructural perspective on AI raises the following questions: How do AI-supporting transnational infrastructures impact global power relations? For whose benefit and at whose expense do they operate? How does AI as infrastructure, or as part of traditional infrastructures, affect social and epistemic orders, including the human–machine hierarchy? Do these transformations have a global dimension, and to what extent are they just?—The present article outlines a first approach to answer these questions. Drawing on insights from AI-related research in the social sciences and humanities, including decolonial theory and Critical Technology Studies, the article reflects on AI and global justice from an infrastructural perspective. It follows Crawford's approach of focusing on the (infra)structures upon which AI is built, to which I add the consideration of the transformation of life and traditional infrastructures *through* AI.

2 AI Infrastructures and Their Implications for Global Justice

To identify how AI and related infrastructures affect global justice, it is crucial to clarify what is meant by 'global justice' and what criteria are used to assess it.

In decolonial theory, the key to understanding global injustice is what Aníbal Quijano (2014) has called the "coloniality of power". Coloniality has been described by decolonial scholars concerned with AI as "the long-term global asymmetries in economic, cultural and knowledge production" (Couldry & Mejias, 2021, p. 789), or as "what survives colonialism" (Mohamed et al., 2020, p. 663). Consequently, from a decolonial perspective, it is the colonial world order and the resulting power asymmetries that divide the world into those who dominate and those who are being dominated. Global justice from a decolonial perspective thus means decolonization. With respect to AI, decolonization is understood as "an invocation to make intelligible, to critique, and to seek to undo the logics and politics of race and coloniality that continue to operate in technologies and imaginaries associated with AI" (Adams, 2021, p. 190).

Another approach to describing what decolonial scholars have called the "colonial matrix of power" (Mignolo, 2009, p. 163) has been the classification of the world into the "Global North" and the "Global South". The North/South terminology derives from foreign development aid, replacing the former and more discriminatory "first world"/ "third world" terminology. It has been criticized for reproducing colonial and capitalist worldviews (Arun, 2019, p. 4) and for misleadingly suggesting that the categories of "North" and "South" were purely geographical and homogeneous (Milan & Treré, 2019, pp. 325–326). However, as Stefania Milan and Emiliano Treré point out, in most contexts the term refers to structural power inequalities that need to be made terminologically transparent. They propose "the Souths" (in the plural, and as opposed to "the *Global* South") as an alternative term that subsumes all individuals or groups that "suffer discrimination, and/or enact resistance to injustice and oppression" (Milan & Treré, 2019, p. 325). Besides coloniality, the term includes gender, race, class, and intersectional discrimination. Global justice from a Norths/Souths perspective thus means the elimination of structural inequalities, including those (re)produced by AI and related infrastructures.

In this article, I combine the decolonial perspective on global justice with the more comprehensive Norths/Souths concept by Milan and Treré. Given the strong impact of historical colonialism on global orders and related (trade) infrastructures and the historical link between colonialism and capitalism as a main driver of AI development (Couldry & Mejias, 2021, p. 787), the decolonial perspective is essential for any consideration of global justice. The concept of the "Souths" adds to it the consideration of structural inequalities beyond the category of colonial power. Moreover, the concept is helpful in distinguishing between issues of *social* justice (within and beyond societies) and *global* justice (understood as social justice from a global perspective). But what exactly does 'global justice' mean when it comes to AI technology?

Regina Ammicht Quinn et al. (2014, p. 257) point out that shaping technology means, first and foremost, shaping society. Ethical values are inscribed in technologies, affecting their design, accessibility, and potential uses. Therefore, the key question behind any technology development must be: "What kind of society do we want to live in?" (Ammicht Quinn, 2014, p. 28; my translation) Consequently, from an ethical perspective, we must further ask how a technology should be designed to contribute to an ideal society. To assess whether a technology can be considered just, Ammicht Quinn suggests a simple and effective rule: "A [...] technology is just if those who enjoy its benefits are the same ones who bear its (not only monetary) costs [...] and if these costs are distributed approximately equally." (Ammicht Quinn, 2014, p. 37; my translation) In the following, this rule serves as a rough guideline for assessing the level of justice of AI and its infrastructures. Thus, my exploratory reflections will focus on the question of who is benefited and who is harmed by these infrastructures, and whether the negative and positive consequences between these groups are balanced.

2.1 Infrastructures that Sustain AI: Reinforcement of Colonial World Orders

The interactive "Map of Internet Territories" (Coding Rights, 2024) provides an overview of the main infrastructures sustaining the Internet. It shows a dense concentration of servers, connectivity infrastructure such as satellites and cables, and IT-producing companies in the (geographic) Global North. In the Global South, it reveals a high incidence of natural resource extraction, exploitative labour, and the dumping of e-waste and related hazardous substances. Aluminium, potassium, copper, lithium, and gold are among the most needed materials for digital hardware components. In some cases, they are illegally extracted from indigenous lands to supply BigTech companies. China is the world's leading producer of electronics—and the largest importer of e-waste. Meanwhile, the US, globally the second largest producer of digital hardware, exports its toxic e-waste to countries in the Global South, such as Malaysia, India, Nigeria, or Ghana. In terms of connectivity infrastructure, both the US and China are on the winning side: the more than 420 undersea cables that allow data to flow around the world mainly connect the Global North (US-Europe-North Asia-Japan-US). The submarine cables—cynically—follow the former routes of colonial navigation (Coding Rights, 2024). The only example of Global North countries paying a proportionate share of the (non-monetary) infrastructural costs is the high energy and water consumption of their servers, which notably affect local ecosystems: The world's largest data centre, located in Oregon, USA, consumes a quarter of the city's water supply—with a rapid upward trend (Coding Rights, 2024). However, the AI-driven increase in water and energy consumption and CO_2 emissions (Li et al., 2023; Luccioni et al., 2022) also has a *global* dimension, as climate change hits hardest those countries that do not have the resources to effectively adapt. The map draws a picture of global injustice: While the Global North largely benefits from good connectivity and BigTech's production, nature and people in the Global South are being exploited and endangered by hazardous substances. In this sense, people in the Global South bear a high proportion of the harms associated with these infrastructures, while not being their main beneficiaries.

The impact of AI infrastructures on global ordering has been (implicitly) described in contributions focusing on the coloniality of practices of the AI industry. To structure the main findings in light of an infrastructural perspective, it is worth referring to Sareeta Amrute (2019) and her characterization of colonial relationships as "hierarchical, extractive, and exploitative". *Hierarchical* global power relations emerge from the monopoly position of BigTech, giving way to a one-way export of IT from the Global North (including China) to the South, intensifying the digital divide in terms of access and design (Schopp et al., 2019, pp. 13–14). In addition, there are epistemological hierarchies reflected in a pronounced male, *white* mainstream in AI research and even AI ethics (Adams, 2021; Roche et al., 2021). As Walter Mignolo (2009, p. 159) notes, Latin and Native Americans have historically been denied the ability to do science: "As we know: the first world has knowledge, the third world has culture; Native Americans have wisdom, Anglo Americans have science." In AI research, the gap between the Global North and South is particularly pronounced: only 1.3% of the journal publications come from Latin America, only 0.3% from Sub-Saharan Africa (Hakopian, 2024, p. 31). Colonial hierarchies are further reproduced in *extractivism*. In addition to the extractive mining of natural resources in Global South countries, which reinforces colonial dependencies and causes massive environmental damage (Warnecke-Berger et al., 2022, pp. 5–7), Couldry and Mejias (2019, p. 337) point to BigTech's practice of data extractivism in the Global South, which they refer to as "data colonialism". *Beta testing* is a form of data extractivism that particularly affects the Global South: BigTech companies offer free use of their products in Global South countries, circumventing stricter data protection policies in their home countries (Mohamed et al., 2020, pp. 668–669). A well-known example is Facebook's "Free Basics" program that has been implemented mostly in African countries. It provides access to limited and predefined online services while collecting users' data. In India, the program was banned, due to massive protests by activists fighting for freedom of information and data protection (Nothias, 2020, p. 330). People in the Global South are furthermore affected by the *exploitation* of low-wage human labour all along the AI supply chain (Crawford, 2021; Gray & Suri, 2019). The stressful work in hardware manufacturing, data labelling, or content moderation is mostly performed by workers from Africa, Latin America, or South-East-Asia. BigTech companies and their subcontractors have actively recruited workers from countries in crisis, such as Venezuela or Syria, taking advantage of their precariousness (Gruber, 2024; Hao & Hernández, 2022). As revealed by the Time Magazine (Perrigo, 2023), during the training of ChatGPT, underpaid Kenyan workers had to clean the chatbot's beta version of toxic language and images, causing severe psychological harm to the workers. In some cases, the IT industry even relies on forced labour (Verité, 2014), making its labour infrastructure, including that of AI, an arena for new forms of slavery.

In light of these findings, I conclude that the infrastructures on which AI is built are deeply unjust, as they contribute to the maintenance and reinforcement of colonial power relations, and as those who benefit the most are not the same as those who are most harmed.

2.2 AI as Infrastructure: Unjust Transformations of Social Structures

Mohamed et al. (2020, p. 663) have defined coloniality as a result from "territorial appropriation, exploitation of the natural environment and of human labour, and direct control of social structures". In the previous section, I have shown that the first two aspects apply to extractive and exploitative practices in the AI industry. The third aspect, the control of social structures, comes into focus when considering AI *as* infrastructure.

There are (at least) three levels of consideration that indicate that AI is unjustly transforming social and epistemic orders: First, AI is often associated with being objective, neutral, and therefore "just", while being loaded with social biases that lead to discrimination against underrepresented groups, such as women or *People of Color* (Buolamwini & Gebru, 2018). When biased AI systems are applied to public infrastructure, there is a serious risk of intensifying structural violence against those groups that Milan and Treré (2019, p. 325) refer to as "the Souths". Second, AI tends to reproduce dominant patterns of knowledge in written language and images. This is especially true for generative AI tools that rely on deep learning algorithms. Large Language Models (LLMs) such as ChatGPT as well as image and video generation tools like DALL.E, Stable Diffusion, or Runway, are built on massive datasets with notable gender and racial biases which are reproduced in the (re)creative outputs of the tools (Gondwe, 2023; Sun et al., 2023). These outputs often end up back on the web and become part of future datasets, further replicating the biases they contain (Ananya, 2024, p. 723). In this sense, generative AI deepens unjust hierarchies of information and knowledge, intensifying epistemic injustice (Fricker, 2010) and contributing to the "epistemicide" (Santos, 2014) of Southern knowledge. Third, as noted in the introduction, AI is being incorporated in all kinds of technical, social, and public infrastructures, carrying the attribution of being 'just' while being discriminative, and promoting the reinforcement of dominant knowledge, with severe implications for social and global justice.

2.2.1 Discrimination

Whiteness is a dominant norm in datasets. As a result, facial recognition tools built on these data struggle to correctly recognize *People of Color* (Buolamwini & Gebru, 2018). This leads to discriminatory results, as in the case of an early version of the facial recognition feature in Google Photos that misclassified two *Black* persons as "gorillas" (Spiegel Netzwelt, 2015). Similarly, a *Black* woman in the U.S. was arrested for a crime she had not committed after a false facial recognition match (Hill, 2023). While it could be argued that errors in facial recognition systems are less common than racial discrimination by human police officers, it must be countered that the use of AI in smart policing and other sensitive areas is deeply problematic, given our tendency to assume AI's judgments to be fact-based and objective.

Also, women have frequently become victims of algorithmic discrimination, with training datasets showing biases against them. For example, an AI-driven Amazon recruiting tool trained to select top candidates by scanning summaries of job applications actively downgraded women because it looked for patterns in the profiles of successful candidates over the past 10 years that had been predominantly male (Dastin, 2018). Amazon didn't notice the problem until years later, and the developers failed in their efforts to eradicate the bias. In fact, the gender gap among BigTech's employees in technical roles is immense (Huang, 2017), which resonates in a lack of diversity-awareness in tech design (Schelenz, 2023). Another example of AI-driven discrimination against women is the chatbot "Berufsinfomat" that was developed by the Austrian Public Employment Service (AMS) to help high school graduates choose a career (Proschofsky, 2024). Shortly after its launch, it became apparent that the GPT-based chatbot was advising young men to pursue careers in IT, while young women with the same interests were advised to study gender studies or work in the restaurant industry. The chatbot was reproducing the social biases contained in the training data of ChatGPT, which cover large swaths of the Internet.

The examples show that the impact of AI-driven classification is not limited to the technical realm: the use of AI in public services has real-life consequences for the affected groups. Given the multiple harms faced by *People of Color*, women, and other underrepresented groups, algorithmic discrimination can be considered "infrastructural violence". Rodgers and O'Neill (2012, p. 404) have defined infrastructures as both "a material embodiment of violence (structural or otherwise)" and the "instrumental medium" of violence. In this sense, infrastructures not only reflect but also reinforce social orders. In light of the given examples, this is clearly the case with AI as infrastructure, which therefore cannot be considered "just".

Finally, the infrastructural violence of AI has a symbolic dimension that is reflected in visual designs and representations. As Stephen Cave and Kanta Dihal (2020) show, *whiteness* is also a dominant norm in the visual design of robots, smart home assistants, and other AI tools (Cave & Dihal, 2020, pp. 688–693). The authors argue that *whiteness* has historically been associated with intelligence to legitimize *white* supremacy (Cave, 2020, pp. 29–32). They further reason that the white design of intelligent machines implicitly elevates *white* people (as particularly intelligent) and devalues *Black* people (as less intelligent) (Cave, 2020, pp. 698–699). Since smart devices are frequently used in the field of domestic labour—a traditional work domain of the *Black* U.S. population since the colonial era—Cave and Dihal (2020, p. 699) argue that the predominantly *white* design of smart home assistants is an implicit attempt to exclude *People of Color* from *white* utopia, marking the *whiteness* of machines an extreme form of discrimination by design—and *People of Color* its main victims.

2.2.2 Knowledge

"Artificial Intelligence is the development of computer systems that can perform tasks requiring human-like intelligence, such as learning, reasoning, problem-solving, and perception." (ChatGPT, personal communication, 19.01.2024) This definition of AI by ChatGPT is the condensation of countless texts that were scraped from the Internet and used to train the chatbot's underlying program GPT3.5. However, ChatGPT's (self-)definition is not based on comprehensive reasoning, but on the statistical probability that a particular word will be followed by another. As a result, it reproduces and, if widely used, reinforces dominant patterns of knowledge that, in the given example, tend to emphasize AI's technical domain rather than its political or social dimensions. Underrepresented knowledge, such as that found in indigenous languages, worldviews, and wisdom, is rarely integrated into AI datasets and thus has little impact on the outcomes of generative AI—despite evidence that indigenous AI is feasible and that users would benefit from a greater diversity of perspectives (Abdilla et al., 2020; Maitra, 2020; Williams & Shipley, 2021).

In addition to increasing epistemic injustices, generative AI spreads misleading or false information. This has serious implications for democracy if, for example, electorally relevant information is misrepresented. This was the case with Microsoft's Bing Chat, which was asked by a team of researchers working at the German NGO AlgorithmWatch (2023) about the candidates of the Bavarian and Hessian state elections. Since the chatbot provided incorrect information about the representatives, their party affiliations, poll ratings, and political goals, it is certainly not advisable to rely on generative AI models when making voting decisions (algorithmwatch.org 2023). Even scientific work seems to be at risk if ChatGPT is used as a research tool. When being asked about the state of research in a particular field, the chatbot provided a list of scientific papers that did not exist (Amaro et al., 2023, p. 31). A major shortcoming of ChatGPT is its inability to mark its 'invented' answers as such. However, the user is inclined to trust the chatbot due to its consistently competent language style—and our tendency to believe in the 'objectivity' of AI systems.

In addition, generative AI reinforces gender and racial stereotypes. Popular text-to-image generators such as Stable Diffusion or Dall.E are "overwhelmingly resorted to common stereotypes, such as associating the word 'Africa' with poverty, or 'poor' with dark skin tones." (Ananya, 2024, p. 723) Similarly, Dall.E reproduces gendered occupational stereotypes as it "systematically underrepresents women in male-dominated occupations and overrepresents them in female-dominated jobs" (Sun et al., 2023, p. 13). Furthermore, generated images of women in different occupations tend to show them smiling and looking up, making them appear more submissive than men in similar created images (Sun et al., 2023, p. 13). These biases do not disappear even if users try to actively avoid stereotypes by prompting for the desired genders or skin tones (Ananya, 2024, p. 725).

There are several reasons why image generators are particularly susceptible to stereotyping: Images depicting people are hardly neutral since they visually express gender and skin tone. Furthermore, colours are not always taken into account when labelling image data (e.g., a banana is labelled as "banana", not as "yellow banana") (Ananya, 2024, p. 723). When the desired colour is specified by a prompt, the meanings associated with that colour are inevitably incorporated into the image, which leads to stereotyping (Ananya, 2024, pp. 723–724). *Prompt engineering* (that is, learning how to prompt efficiently) is often cited as a solution, shifting the responsibility to the user. AI companies are also making efforts to eliminate the bias in image generators—so far with moderate success (Ananya, 2024, p. 724).

2.2.3 Traditional Infrastructures

A striking example of how AI is transforming traditional infrastructures and thereby affecting social orders is the impact of AI-driven algorithms on online information and communication. As scholars studying the impact of social media on democracy have demonstrated, algorithms create *echo chambers*, in which the content we are shown reveals a limited range of perspectives, reinforcing our attitudes and opinions (Cinelli et al., 2021). *Echo chambers* are suspected of fostering radicalization and extremism, often directed against minorities (Cinelli et al., 2021, p. 1). In addition, the content that receives the most interactions tends to be the content that ranks highest on users' profiles. Yet a key factor in getting high interactions is negativity, which is created in part by using provocative or even offensive language (Fine & Hunt, 2023). Hate speech and other forms of defamation are not exclusively, but disproportionately, directed at minorities and vulnerable groups, such as the LGBTQ+community (Gorenc, 2022, p. 420). Automated content moderation has also been found to discriminate against minorities on social media: According to Oliver Haimson et al. (2021), social media posts containing typical expressions and slang words associated with the transgender or *Black* communities, as well as those using their respective hashtags, are most likely to be censored. In line with this, a report by the Brennan Center for Justice (Díaz & Hecht-Felella, 2021, p. 3) criticizes that "all too often, the viewpoints of communities of colour, women, LGBTQ+communities, and religious minorities are at risk of over-enforcement, while harms targeting them often remain unaddressed."

These examples illustrate how the use of AI in online communication infrastructure contributes to the limitation and radicalization of public discourse and aggravates the situation of minorities. It is evident that the delegation of the traditional gatekeeper function of journalists to automated systems is accompanied by social risks that, once again, affect the most vulnerable groups in society the most.

AI has furthermore fundamentally changed the infrastructures of industrial production and logistics. One example that particularly affects the Global South is the phenomenon of *reshoring*. The term refers to the relocation of production facilities from emerging markets back to the established industrialized countries where the companies are based. *Reshoring* has become profitable thanks to automation and intelligent systems that make automated production in the Global North cheaper than human labour in the Global South. Workers in emerging economies, where thousands of jobs are at stake, are most affected by *reshoring* (Ripani et al., 2020, p. 18). The transformation of the logistics industry through automation and *coboting* as well as AI-driven surveillance has been described by Crawford (2021, pp. 53–57) with reference to Amazon's warehouses. There, unskilled, low-wage workers work alongside robots against which their performance and error rates are measured. Amazon warehouse workers are even automatically fired if they fall below a minimum workload. This example illustrates how AI is not only transforming workflows and related infrastructure, but also challenging the human–machine hierarchy: Instead of using intelligent systems to help human workers solve logistical challenges, machines are being used *against* humans, competing with them, monitoring them, and even punishing them (Burkhardt forthcoming). In the logic of Amazon's semi-automated workflows, intelligent systems paradoxically stand above the low-wage workers in the social order, threatening not only labour rights but human dignity in general.

A final and particularly startling example is the increasing role of AI in warfare. According to an investigation by + 972 Magazine and Local Call (Abraham, 2024), the Israeli army has used an AI system called Lavender to identify potential Hamas operatives in Gaza in the 2024 conflict. The system relies on facial recognition, public space surveillance, and other types of data the nature and origin of which are not made transparent to the public. By analysing this data, Lavender assesses how likely it is that an individual is involved in terrorist activities. These calculations become decisive for targeting and killing individuals—and those who happen to be close to them. As the investigative report reveals, the soldiers carrying out the Israeli army's operations were instructed to accept unusually high numbers (up to 20) of civilian casualties, even for low-ranking potential Hamas members. The AI-driven system proved to have a high error rate of 10%, which officials deemed acceptable (McKernan, 2024). Lavender created a list of tens of thousands of potential terrorists to be monitored and targeted with 'dumb bombs', a particularly cheap and highly destructive type of weapon, while they were in their homes: "We were not interested in killing [Hamas] operatives only when they were in a military building or engaged in a military activity. [...] It's much easier to bomb a family's home. The system is built to look for them in these situations", explains one of the military officials interviewed (Abraham, 2024). The targeting of civilians based on error-prone AI-based assessments marks a new level in the history of warfare. Since it seems more likely that highly developed industrialized nations will be able to develop and deploy such systems, this example raises questions not only about infrastructural violence but also about global justice.

3 Conclusion

This exploratory study has demonstrated that both the infrastructures on which AI is built and AI as infrastructure tend to create or reinforce structural injustices. In this sense, AI has an ordering effect that can be considered global in several respects: first, because unequal (e.g. colonial or patriarchal) world orders are recreated by AI infrastructures; second, because social structures and epistemic orders are influenced to the detriment of vulnerable or marginalized groups (that is, the "Souths")—all over the world, but particularly in the Global South where some of the most disadvantaged groups are strongly represented. By employing an infrastructural perspective, I have shown that corporations and societies in the Global North, and particularly the male, *white* mainstream, tend to benefit the most from AI, while people in the Global South, minorities, marginalized groups, and women are most affected by the risks and harms associated with it. AI in its current form and related practices thus cannot be considered just.

There still seems to be a long way to go to achieve a form of AI that promotes global justice and reduces coloniality and structural inequalities. Decolonial scholars and activists have emphasized the need for a globally inclusive and equal exchange of knowledge and experience between the Norths and the Souths, and for the willingness of corporations and governments in the Global North to respond to the needs of people in the Global South (Cruz, 2021, pp. 1850–1851; Mohamed et al., 2020, p. 659). A fundamental problem is certainly that the big players in the AI industry are private companies that primarily pursue economic interests and whose regulation, especially at the global level, is challenging. According to Couldry and Mejias (2021, pp. 797–798), users and governments should put pressure on companies by boycotting their extractive products and switching to alternatives that pursue resource ecology, fair labour, and non-discrimination. Much could also be done by researchers, programmers and designers, e.g., with regard to a diversity-aware design of AI technologies that addresses the needs of users outside the Western norm. The question of whether the use of AI should be avoided altogether in certain areas should also not be taboo. After all, "the solution to a problem should not create worse problems than originally existed." (Ammicht Quinn, 2014, p. 43; my translation).

References

Abdilla, A., Arista, N., Baker, K., Benesiinaabandan, S., Brown, M., Cheung, M. et al. (2020). *Indigenous protocol and artificial intelligence.* Honolulu: Indigenous Protocol and Artificial Intelligence Working Group (Position Paper). https://doi.org/10.11573/SPECTRUM.LIBRARY.CONCORDIA.CA.00986506

Abraham, Y. (2024, April 3). 'Lavender': The AI machine directing Israel's bombing spree in Gaza. *+972 Magazine; Local Call.* https://www.972mag.com/lavender-ai-israeli-army-gaza/

Adams, R. (2021). Can artificial intelligence be decolonized? *Interdisciplinary Science Reviews, 46*(1–2), 176–197. https://doi.org/10.1080/03080188.2020.1840225

AlgorithmWatch (2023, October 5). *ChatGPT and Co: Are AI-driven search engines a threat to democratic elections?* Algorithmwatch. https://algorithmwatch.org/en/bing-chat-election-2023/

Amaro, I., Della Greca, A., Francese, R., Tortora, G., & Tucci, C. (2023). Ai unreliable answers: A case study on ChatGPT. In H. Degen & S. Ntoa (Eds.), *Artificial Intelligence in HCI. Lecture Notes in Computer Science,* vol 14051 (pp. 23–40). Springer. https://doi.org/10.1007/978-3-031-35894-4_2

Ammicht Quinn, R. (2014). Sicherheitsethik. Eine Einführung. In R. Ammicht Quinn (Ed.), *Sicherheitsethik* (pp. 15–47). Springer.

Ammicht Quinn, R., Nagenborg, M., Rampp, B., & Wolkenstein, A. F. X. (2014). Ethik und Sicherheitstechnik. Eine Handreichung. In R. Ammicht Quinn (Ed.), *Sicherheitsethik* (pp. 277–296). Springer.

Amrute, S. (2019). Tech colonialism today. *EPIC2019* (Keynote Talk). https://medium.com/datasociety-points/tech-colonialism-today-9633a9cb00ad

Ananya. (2024). Ai image generators often give racist and sexist results: Can they be fixed? *Nature, 627*(8005), 722–725. https://doi.org/10.1038/d41586-024-00674-9

Arun, C. (2019). AI and the global south: Designing for other worlds. In M. Dubber, F. Pasquale & S. Das (Eds.), *Oxford Handbook of Ethics of AI.* University Press (Pre-Print). https://papers.ssrn.com/sol3/papers.cfm?abstract_id=3403010

Buolamwini, J., & Gebru, T. (2018). Gender shades: Intersectional accuracy disparities in commercial gender classification. *Proceedings of Machine Learning Research, Conference on Fairness, Accountability, and Transparency, 81*, 1–15. http://proceedings.mlr.press/v81/buolamwini18a/buolamwini18a.pdf

Burkhardt, A. (forthcoming). Von der technischen Erweiterung des Menschen zur menschlichen Erweiterung der Technik: Hierarchie, Extraktion und Ausbeutung in Sleep Dealer (Alex Rivera, 2008). In B. Reiter & A.-K. Reulecke (Eds.), *Imaginationen künstlicher Menschen. Interdisziplinäre Perspektiven auf zeitgenössische Romane, Filme und Serien.* Graz: University Library Publishing.

Burkhardt, A. (2023). 'Centering the south(s)': Dekoloniale Perspektiven auf Künstliche Intelligenz. In A. Burkhardt, S. Marschall & O. Kramer (Eds.) (forthcoming), *Artificial Turn.* Freiburg: Herder (Pre-Print). https://rhet.ai/2023/12/13/centering-the-souths-dekoloniale-perspektiven-auf-kuenstliche-intelligenz/

Cave, S. (2020). The problem with intelligence: Its value-laden history and the future of AI. In A. Markham, J. Powles, T. Walsh, & A. L. Washington (Eds.), *Proceedings of the AAAI/ACM Conference on AI, Ethics, and Society (AIES '20, ACM),* 29–35. https://doi.org/10.1145/3375627.3375813

Cave, S., & Dihal, K. (2020). The whiteness of AI. *Philosophy & Technology, 33*(4), 685–703. https://doi.org/10.1007/s13347-020-00415-6

Cinelli, M., de Francisci Morales, G., Galeazzi, A., Quattrociocchi, W., & Starnini, M. (2021). The echo chamber effect on social media. *Proceedings of the National Academy of Sciences of the United States of America, 118*(9), 1–8. https://doi.org/10.1073/pnas.2023301118

Coding Rights (2024). *Map of Internet Territories.* https://www.cartografiasdainternet.org/en

Couldry, N., & Mejias, U. A. (2019). Data colonialism: Rethinking big data's relation to the contemporary subject. *Television & New Media, 20*(4), 336–349. https://doi.org/10.1177/1527476418796632

Couldry, N., & Mejias, U. A. (2021). The decolonial turn in data and technology research: What is at stake and where is it heading? *Information, Communication & Society, 26*(4), 786–802. https://doi.org/10.1080/1369118X.2021.1986102

Crawford, K. (2021). *Atlas of AI: Power, politics, and the planetary costs of artificial intelligence.* University Press.

Cruz, C. C. (2021). Decolonizing philosophy of technology: Learning from bottom-up and top-down approaches to decolonial technical design. *Philosophy & Technology, 34*(4), 1847–1881. https://doi.org/10.1007/s13347-021-00489-w

Dastin, J. (2018, October 11). Insight - Amazon scraps secret AI recruiting tool that showed bias against women. *Reuters.* https://www.reuters.com/article/idUSKCN1MK0AG/

Díaz, Á., & Hecht-Felella, L. (2021). Double standards in social media content moderation. *Brennan Center for Justice.* https://www.brennancenter.org/our-work/research-reports/double-standards-social-media-content-moderation

Fine, J. A., & Hunt, M. F. (2023). Negativity and elite message diffusion on social media. *Political Behavior, 45*(3), 955–973. https://doi.org/10.1007/s11109-021-09740-8

Fricker, M. (2010). *Epistemic injustice: Power and the ethics of knowing*. University Press. https://doi.org/10.1093/acprof:oso/9780198237907.001.0001

Gondwe, G. (2023). CHATGPT and the global south: How are journalists in sub-Saharan Africa engaging with generative AI? *Online Media and Global Communication, 2*(2), 228–249. https://doi.org/10.1515/omgc-2023-0023

Gorenc, N. (2022). Hate speech or free speech: An ethical dilemma? *International Review of Sociology, 32*(3), 413–425. https://doi.org/10.1080/03906701.2022.2133406

Gray, M., & Suri, S. (2019). *Ghost work: How to stop Silicon Valley from building a new global underclass*. Houghton Mifflin Harcourt. https://learning.oreilly.com/library/view/-/9781684419869/?ar

Gruber, K. (2024, May 3). Training für KI als Schlüsselfrage. *ORF.* https://topos.orf.at/inside-ai-machine-learning-data100

Haimson, O. L., Delmonaco, D., Nie, P., & Wegner, A. (2021). Disproportionate removals and differing content moderation experiences for conservative, transgender, and black social media users: Marginalization and moderation gray areas. *Proceedings of the ACM on Human-Computer Interaction, 5*(CSCW2), 1–35. https://doi.org/10.1145/3479610

Hakopian, M. F. (2024). Art histories from nowhere: On the coloniality of experiments in art and artificial intelligence. *AI & SOCIETY, 39*(1), 29–41. https://doi.org/10.1007/s00146-023-01768-0

Hao, K., & Hernández, A. P. (2022). How the AI industry profits from catastrophe. *MIT Technology Review.* https://www.technologyreview.com/2022/04/20/1050392/ai-industry-appen-scale-data-labels/

Hill, K. (2023, August 6). Eight months pregnant and arrested after false facial recognition match. *New York Times*. https://www.nytimes.com/2023/08/06/business/facial-recognition-false-arrest.html

Huang, H. (2017). Dominated by men. *Reuters*. https://fingfx.thomsonreuters.com/gfx/rngs/AMAZON.COM-JOBS-AUTOMATION/010080Q91F6/index.html

Larkin, B. (2013). The politics and poetics of infrastructure. *Annual Review of Anthropology, 42*(1), 327–343. https://doi.org/10.1146/annurev-anthro-092412-155522

Li, P., Yang, J., Islam, M. A., & Ren, S. (2023, April 6). Making AI less "thirsty": Uncovering and addressing the secret water footprint of AI models. arXiv. https://doi.org/10.48550/arXiv.2304.03271

Luccioni, A. S., Viguier, S., & Ligozat, A.-L. (2022, November 3). Estimating the carbon footprint of BLOOM, a 176B parameter language model. arXiv. https://doi.org/10.48550/arXiv.2211.02001

Maitra, S. (2020). Artificial intelligence and indigenous perspectives. *Proceedings of the AAAI/ACM Conference on AI, Ethics, and Society (AIES '20, ACM)*, 320–326. https://doi.org/10.1145/3375627.3375845

McKernan, B. (2024, April 3). 'The machine did it coldly': Israel used AI to identify 37,000 Hamas targets. *The Guardian*. https://www.theguardian.com/world/2024/apr/03/israel-gaza-ai-database-hamas-airstrikes

Mignolo, W. D. (2009). Epistemic disobedience, independent thought and decolonial freedom. *Theory, Culture & Society, 26*(7–8), 159–181. https://doi.org/10.1177/0263276409349275

Milan, S., & Treré, E. (2019). Big data from the south(s): Beyond data universalism. *Television & New Media, 20*(4), 319–335. https://doi.org/10.1177/1527476419837739

Mohamed, S., Png, M.-T., & Isaac, W. (2020). Decolonial AI: Decolonial theory as sociotechnical foresight in artificial intelligence. *Philosophy & Technology, 33*(4), 659–684. https://doi.org/10.1007/s13347-020-00405-8

Nothias, T. (2020). Access granted: Facebook's free basics in Africa. *Media, Culture & Society, 42*(3), 329–348. https://doi.org/10.1177/0163443719890530

Perrigo, B. (2023, January 18). Exclusive: OpenAI used Kenyan workers on less than $2 per hour to make ChatGPT less toxic. *Time*. https://time.com/6247678/openai-chatgpt-kenya-workers/

Proschofsky, A. (2024, January 4). Vorurteile und zweifelhafte Umsetzung: AMS-KI-Chatbot trifft auf Spott und Hohn. *Der Standard*. https://www.derstandard.de/story/3000000201774/vorurteile-und-zweifelhafte-umsetzung-der-ams-ki-chatbot-trifft-auf-spott-und-hohn

Quijano, A. (2014). Colonialidad del poder, eurocentrismo y América Latina. In A. Quijano (Ed.), *Cuestiones y horizontes: De la dependencia histórico-estructural a la colonialidad/descolonialidad del poder* (pp. 777–832). CLACSO. http://biblioteca.clacso.edu.ar/clacso/se/20140507042402/eje3-8.pdf

Ripani, L., Kugler, A., Kugler, M., Soler, N., & Rodrigo, R. (2020). The future of work in Latin America and the Caribbean: What is the impact of automation on employment and wages? *Inter-American Development Bank*. https://publications.iadb.org/publications/english/document/The-Future-of-Work-in-Latin-America-and-the-Caribbean-What-is-the-Impact-of-Automation-on-Employment-and-Wages.pdf

Roche, C., Lewis, D., & Wall, P. J. (2021). Artificial intelligence ethics: An inclusive global discourse? *Proceedings of the 1st Virtual Conference on Implications of Information and Digital Technologies for Development*, 643–658. https://doi.org/10.48550/arXiv.2108.09959

Rodgers, D., & O'Neill, B. (2012). Infrastructural violence: Introduction to the special issue. *Ethnography, 13*(4), 401–412. https://doi.org/10.1177/1466138111435738

Santos, B. (2014). *Epistemologies of the south: Justice against epistemicide*. Routledge. https://doi.org/10.4324/9781315634876

Schelenz, L. (2023). Diversity and social justice in technology design. *International Journal of Critical Diversity Studies, 5*(2), 33–53. https://doi.org/10.13169/intecritdivestud.5.2.0033

Schopp, K., Schelenz, L., Heesen, J., & Pawelec, M. (2019). Ethical questions of digitalization in the Global South. *TATuP - Zeitschrift Für Technikfolgenabschätzung in Theorie Und Praxis, 28*(2), 11–16. https://doi.org/10.14512/tatup.28.2.s11

Spiegel Netzwelt. (2015, July 2). Google entschuldigt sich für fehlerhafte Gesichtserkennung. *Spiegel Netzwelt*. https://www.spiegel.de/netzwelt/web/google-fotos-bezeichnet-schwarze-als-gorillas-a-1041693.html

Sun, L., Wei, M., Sun, Y., Suh, Y. J., Shen, L., & Yang, S. (2023). Smiling women pitching down: Auditing representational and presentational gender biases in image-generative AI. *Journal of Computer-Mediated Communication, 29*(1), Article zmad045, 1–15. https://doi.org/10.1093/jcmc/zmad045

Verité (2014). Forced labor in the production of electronic goods in Malaysia: A comprehensive study of scope and characteristics. *Verité*. https://verite.org/wp-content/uploads/2016/11/Verite-ForcedLaborMalaysianElectronics2014.pdf

Warnecke-Berger, H., Burchardt, H.-J., & Ouaissa, R. (2022). Natural resources, raw materials, and extractivism: The dark side of sustainability. *EXTRACTIVISM-Project* (Policy Brief No. 1). https://extractivism.de/wp-content/uploads/2022/01/extractivism_policy_brief-1-2022.pdf

Williams, D. H., & Shipley, G. P. (2021). Enhancing artificial intelligence with indigenous wisdom. *Open Journal of Philosophy, 11*(01), 43–58. https://doi.org/10.4236/ojpp.2021.111005

Anne Burkhardt is a postdoctoral researcher at the *Center for Rhetorical Science Communication Research on Artificial Intelligence* (RHET AI Center) at the University of Tübingen. Her current work focuses on AI and global justice, with an emphasis on decolonial theory and (audio) visual culture. Previous projects have focused on media ethics, migration and populism, and discourses of violence.

Anne Burkhardt received her Ph.D. from the Institute for Media Studies at the University of Tübingen. For her work on the cinematic treatment of the Colombian armed conflict, she was awarded the dissertation prize of the German Latin American Studies Association (ADLAF). During her Ph.D., she lived in Colombia on a doctoral scholarship from the German Academic Exchange Service (DAAD) and the State Postgraduate Fellowship Program of Baden-Württemberg. Before joining the RHET AI Center, she worked as a research assistant at the *International Center for Ethics in the Sciences and Humanities* (IZEW).

Part III

Socioeconomic and Ecological Development

The Ambivalence of Infrastructures: The Complex Interplay of Development and Conservation in the Garhwal Himalayas

Karin Polit and Lokesh Ohri

Abstract

This chapter looks at the conflicts and ambivalences of infrastructure projects such as dams and roads in the Himalayan region and highlights the different views on safety, environmental integrity and spirituality as key points of friction in these ambivalences. Garhwal, a region in the Indian Himalayas is known as Dev Bhumi or the land of the gods. The conflicts over infrastructure projects reflect the differing views of locals, environmentalists, non-human actors, authorities and tourists. The landscape serves as a social space where sacred and practical uses intermingle, e.g. as grazing and pilgrimage sites, biodiversity hotspots and water sources for millions of people. Local populations and rural communities, connected to divine beings through daily rituals, are disrupted by infrastructure-related disasters. People strive for modern conveniences such as roads and healthcare while maintaining their spiritual and ecological ties. The chapter explores the tensions between conservationists arguing for non-interference, proponents of economic progress, pilgrims, and various local needs. The need for sustainable development that respects social and ecological complexity and incorporates local knowledge and perspectives is emphasized for balanced progress in Garhwal.

K. Polit (✉)
Abteilung für Ethnologie, Universität Tübingen, Tübingen, Germany
e-mail: karin.polit@uni-tuebingen.de
L. Ohri Jaswant Modern Sr. Sec. School, Dehradun, India

H.-J. Bieling et al. (eds.), *Transnational Infrastructures and the Transformation of Global Orders*, RaumFragen: Stadt – Region – Landschaft,
https://doi.org/10.1007/978-3-031-74846-2_7

Keywords

Himalaya · Ambivalence · Non-human agents · Environmentalist movements · Divine landscapes · Road construction

1 Introduction

On 12 November 2023 a road tunnel still under construction near Uttarkashi—a small town in the state of Uttarakhand in northern India—collapsed. The construction of the 4.5 km long tunnel between the villages Barkot and Silkyara at the Dharashu bend near the National Highway 134 in the Uttarkashi district of Uttarakhand began in March 2018. On behalf of the Ministry of Road Transport and Highways (MoRTH), at a total estimated cost of Indian Rupees 1383 crore (about € 155 million), the National Highways & Infrastructure Development Corporation Limited (NHIDCL) and the Austrian company Bernard Gruppe, began building a two-lane, bidirectional tunnel as part of the all-weather road project in the region. The main purpose of the tunnel is to connect the Yamnotri Valley with the Gangotri Valley to facilitate travel during the pilgrimage season. After the construction of the tunnel, which passes under the Radi Pass, the 25.6 km long journey would be shortened to 4.5 km and provide a considerably time benefit. Especially, because travelling on mountain roads rolls usually at 30 km per hour. The construction of the all-weather road in Uttarakhand provides a prime example on the ambivalence of infrastructure projects and shows that the benefits promised are often outweighed by a multitude of disadvantages, especially considering local populations in the Global South.

Like some other Himalayan regions, Garhwal is known as the land of the gods—Dev Bhumi. However, various actors living, working, or travelling there have different interpretations of what constitutes the land of the gods. This tension is crucial for understanding the ambivalences of infrastructure projects in the region. Our central argument is that various conflicts come to light through the illumination of different infrastructure projects. All of these very different endeavors—dam construction, road construction, tunnelling and railway line construction—are interrelated and the conflicts can only be explained by the different positioning and perspectives on the region.

Discussions about disasters such as the tunnel collapse reveal such contrasting views. Safety measures are questioned, environmentalists argue that the ecological balance of the Himalayas has been destroyed, while many locals believe that the spiritual order is threatened by the government's modernist ambitions. Contrasting protests and socio-economic movements in the region demand slow tourism, mindful pilgrimage, and respectful treatment of the people, gods, and landscapes, while others demand the expansion of infrastructures as part of their rights as citizens of India. The Dev Bhumi of pilgrims and tourists is merging with the politically utilized land of the gods, serving as a starting point for expanding roads and train routes. Also, this increase in infrastructure projects leaves the impacts and the benefits for the local population unclear.

For many people in Garhwal, the land of the gods is more than stories from ancient scriptures or grand temples. The gods live alongside other non-human actors, and the relationship with humans is maintained through ritual practices, processions, stories, music, and drums. These continuous relationships deepen daily through interactions, movement, and agricultural labour. Regular divine processions imprint the landscape with memories and personal engagement. This fabric of existences, involving many non-human actors, is an embodied, existential experience, an experience that is being disrupted by disasters related to infrastructure projects. Modernity and development are not rejected; people want better connections to the rest of India, associating roads and infrastructure with improved access to, for example, education and healthcare. However, when their needs, closely linked to the gods and the landscape, are overlooked in modern development efforts, the experience is one of disrespect, exclusion and invisibility.

2 The Collapse of the Tunnel and It's Connection to Local Deities

At around 05:30 on 12 November 2023, while the 40 workers were engaged in tasks in a section between 260 and 265 m inside the tunnel, a part of the tunnel suddenly crumpled. The drilling from the other side of this collapsed section was still incomplete. As a result, 40 workers were trapped for several days. After seventeen days all workers were saved and fortunately no deaths were reported. While the rescue mission was still ongoing, the press and the wider public heatedly discussed the missing safety measures for workers in projects like this in general. It became clear that India would need to implement stricter regulations in that respect as the workers' lives were constantly endangered. In this chapter, we want to focus on another problem that was uncovered by the accident, albeit much less debated. It also became clear that the infrastructure project and the construction work on the tunnel had once again been negotiated without taking into consideration the needs of local people and local deities. Immediately after the disaster, dwellers in the villages of Uttarkashi district began discussing the causes for the collapse amongst each other. One of the reasons stated by many was the destruction of a small local temple, home to the local Hindu deity Baukh Nag. His temple had been destroyed to create space for the construction of the road and the tunnel. A promise had been made by the private companies involved in the construction work to rebuilt it, alas this never happened. Instead, as was shown in a news film from India Today (2023), shot during the seventeen days of the rescue mission, several local men are seen building a temporary temple right next to the tunnel where the workers were trapped for 17 days. The local population immediately insisted on appeasing Baukh Nag and made the people in charge pay their respects to him, the film proclaimed.

2.1 Deities and Disasters

Similar narratives previously took place when disasters happened in the region. For example, when a devastating flood in 2013 destroyed the homes of thousands of villagers and killed hundreds in the Kedar Valley, it was said that Dhari Devi, whose temple had just been moved in favour of a dam project, was showing her displeasure. The disaster itself affected an important pilgrimage temple for Hindus in India. Kedarnath, where Shiva once resided in isolation, attracts close to 50,000 pilgrims per day during the summer months. The word Kedar itself refers to the marshes in this bleak, snowy landscape where Shiva came to live to avoid, amongst other humans, the Pandava siblings. These five protagonists of the great epic Mahabharata, are said to have come to the Himalayas after the long and bloody battle of Kurukshetra where the great warriors of their time, including their 100 cousins died as a result of a feud for the throne of the kingdom. The Pandava brothers survived but were now looking for emancipation after committing this sin of fratricide in the Mahabharata battle. They were in search of Shiva, hoping that he, the great god would help them find salvation. Shiva hid from them and left behind pieces of his own body at the places that have now become great pilgrimage centres around Shiva temples. After the flood, the marshes were covered in concrete, and the all-weather road, of which the collapsed tunnel is a tiny part, was built to allow for a rush of visitors. Local people proclaim that Shiva does not live in the shrine anymore and has stopped protecting the region. In the pilgrim town of Joshimath, since January 2023, people's homes have begun to sink due to the tunnels being dug for various infrastructure projects. Inhabitants were temporarily settled in hotels and guest houses which were promptly vacated at the start of the pilgrimage season, forcing them to either return to their nearly collapsing homes or migrate to other places. Local people, who spoke to us, bring the sliding of Joshimath is brought into connection with cracks discovered in the town's Narsingh Temple due to the construction works. This temple holds sacred texts clearly mentioning that as long as the local deity Narsingh resides in his temple, Lord Badrinath, the incarnation of Vishnu, would stay in his shrine at nearby Badrinath, a site most sacred to those devoted to the Hindu faith.

2.2 Deities—Guardians and Lords of Land and People

Often, the local deities referred to in these instances, such as Baukh Nag, Narsingh or Dhari Devi serve the communities as so-called *kshetrapals* or guardians of the landscape, its people, wildlife and resources as well as *bhumiyals*, lords of the land. The relationship with the gods is to be understood less as religious believes but more as a relationship between human, divine and non-human actors in the region. The divine beings need the humans just as much as the humans need them. The divine beings belong to the region, like the trees, the mountain goats and Pahari people. They make it possible for people to live there. This understanding is based on other categories than those that consider nature and culture as separate spheres. The gods of the Himalayan mountains live here together with other non-human agents and the relationship with people is maintained through recurring performative ritual practices, processions, stories, music and the sound of drums. Many people in Garhwal generally understand themselves to be in a continuous, substantial relationship with the places they live in and the divine beings who dwell here (Polit, 2012). This relationship continues to deepen through daily interaction, moving in the landscape and agricultural work. Through the practice of regular divine processions, the Garhwal landscape is imprinted with memories and an ongoing personal engagement with the landscape. The movements of various local divine beings, which are commonplace here, not only connect villages, temples and other visible places, but also harbour the mythical past, epic tales, stories and meanings embedded in many ritual practices. The landscape is infused with ritual actions, and these inscriptions shape the way people understand their surroundings and position themselves within them. If mountain lives are rudely and violently disrupted and endangered in favour of large infrastructure projects, the damage is not merely ecological. In the eyes of many mountain dwellers, the destruction of the sensitive mountain landscape has devastating consequences for them and for humanity, because it is about the world in which they exist and of which they are a part, and not merely about an environment to be preserved.

Therefore, we argue, the construction work on the all-weather road is a prime example for the ambivalence of infrastructure projects. On the one hand, it is a sign of the marginalization of the needs of the local population, it shows grave disregard for divine rights, and constitutes practices of humiliation and disrespect for the needs of the above mentioned Himalayan eco-system. On the other hand, the construction work is necessary to fulfil other people's needs—quick access to pilgrimage sites and access to resources that make modern life in India's urban centres possible. As such, the discussions we observed during the Barkot tunnel rescue mission can be interpreted as part of global ordering processes, or rather global processes of hierarchizing needs, knowledge and ways of life. Locally, the large infrastructure projects are perceived as a continuation of a long history of colonial or neo-colonial domination, in which both the mountains and all their human and non-human actors must submit to the needs of the rulers. However, it is not the road, the dam or the railway line itself that is called into question, but the actions of these outside rulers and their handling of infrastructure-related deeds and decisions.

3 Logics of Infrastructures

The idea of roads as a highly visible network, as described by Edward Simpson (2022) in his book *Highways to the End of the World*, tends to be positive. Roads are often portrayed as making people's lives easier, connect people, and foster development. This perspective aligns with widespread modernist depictions of infrastructure as inert, almost invisible, and highly functional—operating in the background to keep our societies running. However, this modernist understanding isolates infrastructure as a domain of technical solutions, seemingly independent of politics and lived experiences (Graham & Thrift, 2007). To account for the ambivalences associated with infrastructure development, a more nuanced understanding is needed. Larkin's (2013, p. 328) definition of infrastructures as material structures and networks that "facilitate the flow of goods, people, or ideas and enable their exchange across space" is useful here. It allows us to view infrastructures as "matter that enables the movement of other matter," recognizing that their ontology lies in being both, things and the relationships between things. This perspective shifts our attention from assuming automatic positive effects to viewing built landscapes and the processes involved in their construction as contested realms.

In a positivist interpretation infrastructure only becomes visible through its inadequacies. Simultaneously, infrastructures, streets, buildings and other structures are part of people's experience of home and self (Jensen & Morita, 2017; Larkin, 2015; von Schnitzler, 2015), signifying an embodied sense of modernity as "material experience on which individuals, nations, and societies ground identities, aspirations, and expectations" (Di Nunzio, 2018, p. 1).

However, the local people of the Garhwal Himalayas do not share this experience, highlighting the fragile foundation infrastructure provides for self-image in the modern world. Here, infrastructure projects serve as the basis for highly segmented and fragmented societies, excluding certain citizens from benefits, even destroying their worlds in favour of modern developments and endangering other non-human mountain dwellers lives. It is therefore necessary to understand the processes through which infrastructures render marginalized groups and agents invisible. We argue that the positivist notions of infrastructure are part of these processes as the muting of agents takes place by the very process that presents infrastructure projects as serving the "public good" (Batt, 1984; Beeferman & Wain, 2016). Instead of accepting these narratives, we want to pay attention to the particular interests served by the development of certain transport infrastructures (Lefebvre, 2003; Anand, 2012; Graham, 2004, 2010; Graham & Marvin, 2001; Smith, 1996; Harvey & Knox, 2015; Mbembe, 2004; Caldeira, 2001; Rodgers & O'Neill, 2012), in our case mainly the all-weather road through Garhwal. These narratives are powerful because aspirations for functioning infrastructure relate to and at the same time shape understandings of participation and civil rights (Anand, 2012; Appel et al., 2015; Humphrey, 2003). In other words, while infrastructures can serve powerful interests and produce landscapes of segregation, they also generate claims and demands from marginalized groups (Barry, 2013; Das, 2011; Holston, 2008). At the same time, when infrastructures are treated "as material conditions of possibility for human or even non-human life", what is at stake is "less about the question of how a system is created, but about the life worlds that sustain and/or destroy such systems" (Venkatesan et al., 2018, p. 1).

4 Marginalization Through Infrastructure Development? Past and Present

The authors have been working in the Himalayan region of Uttarakhand for 23 years and a lifetime respectively, witnessing many rapid changes. Recently, we both observed a new kind of marginalization emerging. A marginalization that leads to the destruction of people, trees, animals, and deities as an effect of large infrastructure projects. Our acquaintances, friends, and colleagues in Uttarakhand and beyond are embroiled in discussions about the lack of respect and recognition for the local population and other mountain dwellers, closely tied to these infrastructure projects, such as road construction, dam building, and railway lines. These projects highlight issues not only in the Himalayas or India but globally—the need for communication, electricity, and mobility linked to a modern lifestyle, which is, we argue, part of colonial and post-colonial ordering processes connected to power structures and an economy that builds on exploitation rather than solidarity and mutual respect.

These infrastructure projects are not built for the benefit of the region but at the expense of a sensitive mountain environment. Understandably, local actors express substantial ambivalence about the ongoing developments, with each actor's response being nuanced by their unique standpoint. While some support the progress, most are deeply suspicious and aware of the environmental repercussions of relentless construction. Some who initially supported the projects, now realize that the roads and railways are depleting the landscape rather than ushering in prosperity.

Previous discourses on this Himalayan landscape have been polarized, viewing it as either inviolable or exploitable—pristine sacred nature or significant resource. The region remained largely unexplored by outsiders until colonial times. For example, the first accounts of the Gangotri region, from where the Ganga emanates, were published as late as 1808. The British research expedition to the source of the Ganges did not reach beyond Batheri (now Bhatwari), about 70 km short of Gangotri. Only in 1815 did sketch artist Fraser reach Gangotri, and even then, local people persuaded him not to venture beyond the shrine at Gangotri towards the glacier at Gaumukh, indicating the value locals placed on the landscape's inviolability. However, soon after, individuals like Fredrick Wilson, a deserter from the British army also known as Pahadi (of the mountains), began discovering and plundering the region's timber wealth (Hutchison, 2010). With the spread of colonialism that coincided with the high tides of the industrial age, the Himalayas' rivers and forests began to be seen as economic resources for hydropower, irrigation, and timber. A view of the region that did not change even after India's independence and only shifted the colonized impression from the British colonial power to the Indian elite.

Post-independence in 1949, the extractive policies were expected to change, but the new India led by Jawarhalal Nehru pursued radically modernist goals. Communities in Uttarakhand resisted the ongoing exploitation. The state sometimes relented, earmarking conservation spaces but often shut out locals in the process. At other times it argued for mountain communities' sacrifice for the "greater common good." The struggle for control over nature continued throughout the remaining half of the twentieth century and culminated in the separation of Uttarakhand from Uttar Pradesh in 2000. However, the new state, desperate for economic growth, disappointed communities again by adopting similar exploitative policies, transforming sustainable pilgrimage practices into pleasure-seeking tourism and thereby continuing colonial structures.

Between the poles of conservationists advocating complete non-interference and those pushing for economic progress without environmental impact assessments, are local populations with their needs, hopes and aspirations, other mountain dwellers and divine agents. This chapter explores the invisible relationships between these people, the mountains and divine beings by understanding the Himalayan landscapes as social spaces rather than sacrosanct places or economic resources. The landscape is understood as home to diverse social groups, with varied life practices. For example, alpine grasslands are grazing commons, and Nanda Devi, the second-highest peak in India, is both a biodiversity hotspot and a goddess central to local culture. At the same time, the region accounts for the water security of nearly one billion people and acts as a significant carbon sink. Most economic progress of Uttarakhand has been achieved in the plains since the formation of the new state, but it continues to pose a challenge for politicians to satisfy mountain dwellers' needs and demands. Pilgrimage, aggressively promoted by the state, is seasonal, agricultural incomes are minimal and the non-human mountain dwellers have needs that are in direct opposition to the plans on what is understood as progress by urban politicians.

Government data indicates that tinkering with the Himalayas can have widespread negative impacts on the region's fragile ecology. Significant parts of Ganga's tributaries have already been fragmented by hydro projects, causing irreversible damage (IMG Report 2013). For example, the Tehri Dam has affected the Ganga's self-purifying quality (NEERI, 2011, 2018). Further, between 2013–2015, Uttarakhand lost 268 sq. km of forests, with only 45.3% forest cover remaining (Forest Survey of India, 2015). Water bodies are drying up, and soil loss is critical, while landslides and destabilization from road and railway construction exacerbate the situation (NITI AAYOG, 2017, Chopra Committee report 2013). Given these realities, both extremes of resource exploitation and complete non-interference seem untenable, the need to find a more balanced approach that recognizes the region's social and environmental complexities and pays attention to the less visible agents and mountain dwellers is urgent.

5 The Different Meanings of the Land of the Gods and Their Impact on the Ambivalence of Infrastructures

Like some other Himalayan regions, Garhwal is also often referred to as the land of the gods—Dev Bhumi. On closer inspection, however, it quickly becomes clear that the various actors living, working, or traveling in the region have very different ideas of what actually constitutes the land of the gods. It is this tension that is worth exploring, if we want to understand the ambivalences of infrastructure projects in the region.

In 2020, a deadly ice-rock mass avalanche occurred in the cradle of Chipko (lit. hug the trees movement), the village of Reni in the district of Chamoli. Claiming over two hundred lives, the flood also wiped out two under-construction hydropower plants. Soon after, Narendra Singh Negi, a popular folk singer, released a song named *Devbhoomi ki nau badli*..., (The name of the land of the gods has changed...) with opening lines stating that Uttarakhand's name had now been changed to *bijli-bhoomi*, the land of electricity generation, with the next line specifying that the land of gods has been shaken up by dams.

In October 2022, while driving on National Highway 7 to Chamoli District in the Garhwal Himalayas, we saw what Negi meant. We had not driven on this road for four years and we noticed that the landscape we were crossing was much quicker to traverse than it had been. We zoomed from Dehra Dun to Srinagar in three hours and took another four hours to reach Gopeshwar, almost twice as fast as before the roads had been expanded. This expansion was highly contested until 2021, known as the Char Dham road debate, but ultimately it was implemented. Almost at the same time, Indian Railways began the ambitious project of building a railway line through the mountains to Karanprayag, and some dam projects had already been commissioned. The landscape we now drove through gave the impression of a war raging between humans and the mountains. Everywhere, parts of the slopes had been blown away or slid down, and the protruding rocks looked like wounds inflicted on the mountainside. Construction sites, landslides, earthmovers at work, broken road sections, and debris completed the picture.

This scenario encapsulates for us the ambivalence produced by the human desire for infrastructure that often clashes with concerns for preserving the fragile mountain ecosystem, as articulated by the mountain inhabitants and the needs of various non-human mountain dwellers. Just 15 years ago, people like Anil Bandhari, Udai Singh Rawat, and Mohan Singh Rawat, three men Karin Polit met for the first time in their village Maikot Kujaum during her research on the Jakh pilgrimage in 2006/2007, recounted feeling cut off from the country's major infrastructural developments because their village was not connected to basic services by a paved road or stable electricity and telecommunication lines at the time. Some locals had formed an association demanding an end to the treatment of hill people as second-class citizens. Stories of pregnant women dying in hill villages because they couldn't be taken to health centres in time due to the lack of paved roads were common. There were also numerous cases of frustrated villagers who, after decades of waiting, decided to build roads to their villages themselves rather than rely on government aid.

In 2022, many roads had already been built, the temporary job creation measures in road construction were over, and many villages were connected to basic infrastructures such as paved roads, electricity networks and basic telecommunication. Cars were parked everywhere, but the sense of marginalization had increased rather than improved. There were still few jobs. Thanks to the more or less well-developed roads, pilgrimage tourists could reach the region's temples better, faster, and more comfortably, making them even less dependent on the villagers as hosts than before. The road and dam construction projects mainly employed workers and specialists from other parts of the country.

5.1 The Gods as Protectors of Land and People

At the same time, after the nightmare that COVID-19 had caused, especially for people in urban areas, the people in the villages of Chamoli agreed that they were lucky to live in the land of the gods—the relative remoteness led to low death rates and the fact that many, even the poorest families, had at least one cow, the fields were still being cultivated and gardens with fruit and vegetables were the reasons why there was little food shortage. However, the local population remain used to having limited access to the health system of the country. In a conversation with Semwal-ji, a Brahmin in the village of Urgam in October 2022, he said: "The others have doctors, hospitals and medical care, we here have our gods. We live in Dev Bhumi, that protects us". He said this in the context of a conversation about people's relationship with Jakh, a god who in his various manifestations is the patron god (*Bhumiyal*) of this region. One of the manifestations had just visited the village Urgam. In this understanding the land of the gods refers to the experience of co-dwelling and care. Gods and people are understood as living together in the mountains, taking care of each other. This differs significantly from the understanding contemporary pilgrims usually have who enter the region from other parts of India every year.

5.2 The Land of Gods as a Pilgrim Tourist Destination or a Spiritual Experience

The region's designation as Dev Bhumi is partly based on its mention in ancient scriptures and the fact that it is home to some of the major and important pilgrimage temples for Hindus from all over India. Garhwal is home to the small Char Dham temples: Badrinath, Kedarnath, Gangotri, and Yamnotri. Except for Kedarnath, these temples are now accessible on relatively well-maintained roads. Until the road was expanded, the journey to Badrinath used to be much longer than to Gangotri and Yamnotri, as the pilgrims first had to cross the whole of Garhwal to reach Badrinath, the largest and most important of the local temples in India. Kedarnath is a 15 km trail that can only be covered on foot, by mule, or by helicopter. Every year between April and October, thousands of pilgrims from all parts of India set off on a journey to one of these pilgrimage sites.

Even the flash flood that claimed the lives of 5,000 people in the Kedarnath Valley on 16 and 17 June 2013 did not stop the influx of pilgrims, although it disrupted the pilgrimage in 2013 and 2014. The trail and temple area were redesigned and optimized for the massive amounts of pilgrims in the following years, the roads and helicopter services were expanded. This suits the many tourist pilgrims who visit Kedarnath to have been there and share their selfies in front of the temple on social media. This new form of pilgrim outnumbers those who make the pilgrimage for spiritual reasons. These people usually try to move at a slower pace, some walk the whole way and take months to do so. Pilgrims Lokesh Ohri and his team interviewed shared that to them, the hardships of the pilgrimage purified and transformed them as they wandered through the land of the gods. To them, every step on the grounds and every river they crossed had a cleansing and purifying effect on their bodies and souls. For these pilgrims, Dev Bhumi meant a total, holistic transformation of their body and soul in the context of the journey through the land of the gods.

5.3 Environmental Movements in the Land of the Gods

In addition to the perspectives connected to religious associations with the land of the gods, the Garhwal Himalayas are also home to some of the most pristine and biodiverse ecosystems in the world. However, the pressure to develop the region for economic gain has led to significant environmental degradation. Deforestation, dam construction, and road building have all taken a toll on the region's fragile ecology. The loss of forest cover has led to soil erosion, landslides, and a decline in water quality. The construction of dams has fragmented rivers, disrupted ecosystems, and displaced local communities. This destruction has led to several environmental movements in the region.

For example, the famous Chipko movement, began as a local initiative in 1974 to prevent the government from selling their trees to a tennis racket manufacturer. A local woman, Gaura Devi, urged the loggers to shoot her instead of harming the forests. At the same time, Sudesha Devi led an initiative of women to protect the forests of Rampur from the loggers by hugging trees and spending nights among the trees to protect them from abuse and destruction (Linkenbach, 2007). The movement successfully raised awareness about the need for conservation and led to a ban on commercial logging in the region. However, the pressure to develop the region for economic gain has continued, leading to ongoing conflicts between local communities, the government, and conservationists.

The above examples show that there are different perceptions of Dev Bhumi. The first perception is that of the villagers, who see their home as Dev Bhumi. The trust in their gods gives them security and confidence and is a refuge for them in emergencies. The second view is that of tourists from outside, who see the land of the gods as a destination that primarily confirms their affiliation with the upwardly mobile Hindu nationalist middle class. This is in stark contrast to the pilgrims, who undertake arduous journeys to the sacred temples in order to achieve transformation, purification, and salvation. The fourth perception is that of the government, which seeks to control the land to build roads, dams, and railways to develop the infrastructure to attract more tourists and pilgrims to the region. They see Dev Bhumi as an opportunity to generate electricity and income. This view meets with resistance from environmentalists who are trying to prevent the infrastructure projects or modify them in such a way that they are compatible with the goals of preserving the ecosystem. Additionally, as we mentioned throughout the text, there are perspectives of non-human actors which further complicate the picture.

These different perceptions of Dev Bhumi create tension and conflict, which make the finding of a balanced approach to development and conservation in the region challenging. The future of the Garhwal Himalayas lies in finding a balanced approach that recognizes the region's social and environmental complexities. This requires acknowledging the different perceptions of Dev Bhumi and the various actors' needs and aspirations. It also requires a commitment to sustainable development that respects the region's ecological integrity and cultural heritage. This could involve enhancing the role of local communities in decision-making processes, improving the enforcement of environmental regulations, and promoting greater transparency and accountability in resource management. Ultimately, this requires a commitment to sustainable development that respects the needs and aspirations of the various agents involved.

6 Conclusion

After the creation of the state of Uttaranchal (later Uttarakhand) in the early twenty-first century, people's expectations of participation, recognition and improvement of their living conditions increased. However, like the previous regimes, the new state was no longer able to fulfil people's expectations or even give them control over natural resources. Instead, the region was heading for ever greater disasters. The question of sustainable modernisation of the region, which can be in the interests of both the local population and the ecosystem, is as topical as ever. Research with the people of the Himalayan region is about whether and how we are able to understand and pass on knowledge about local movements and local ways of being-in-the-world without ignoring the historical and political constraints that colonial and post-colonial structures and global political and economic developments exert on the local and the particular. Perhaps a closer look at the way people in the Himalayas view their position in the mountains in relation to other actors could be a step towards bridging this gap. Paying attention to local knowledge could help to develop alternative ideas for the future, which would also involve restructuring and rethinking global processes of ordering, i.e. global processes of hierarchisation of needs, knowledge and ways of life. If infrastructures are "built networks that facilitate the flow of goods, people or ideas and enable their exchange across space" (Larkin, 2013), we must begin to consider reordering processes under the current deepening of the subsumption of nature.

References

Anand, N. (2012). Municipal disconnect: On abject water and its urban infrastructures. *Ethnography, 13*, 487–509.

Appel, H., Anand, N.,& Gupta, A. (2015, September 24). Introduction: The infrastructure toolbox. Society for Cultural Anthropology. https://culanth.org/fieldsights/714-introduction-the-infrastructure-toolbox (Accessed 31 May 2024)

Barry, A. (2013). *Material politics. Disputes along the pipeline*. Wiley Blackwell.

Batt, H. (1984). Infrastructure: Etymology and import. *Journal of Professional Issues in Engineering, 110*, 1–6.

Beeferman, L., & Wain, A. (2016). Infrastructure: defining matters. SSRN. https://papers.ssrn.com/sol3/papers.cfm?abstract_id=2714308 (Accessed May 31, 2014)

Caldeira, T. (2001). *City of walls: Crime, segregation, and citizenship in São Paulo*. University of California Press.

Chopra Committee (2013). *Report of the expert body of supreme court constituted after june-2013 Kedarnath disaster.* New Delhi.

Das, V. (2011). State, citizenship, and the urban poor. *Citizenship Studies, 15*, 319–333.

Di Nunzio, Marco. (2018). Anthropology of infrastructure. London: LSE. (*Governing Infrastructure Interfaces—Research Note 01* (June 2018)).

Forest Survey of India. (2015). *Annual Report*. New Delhi.

Graham, S. (2004). Constructing urbicide by bulldozer in the occupied territories. In S. Graham (Ed.), *Cities, War, and Terrorism: Towards an Urban Geopolitics* (pp. 192–213). Blackwell.

Graham, S. (2010). *Disrupted cities: When infrastructure fails*. Routledge.

Graham, S., & Marvin, S. (2001). *Splintering urbanism: Networked infrastructures, technological mobilities and the urban condition*. Routledge.

Graham, S., & Thrift, N. (2007). Out of order: Understanding repair and maintenance. *Theory, Culture & Society, 24*, 1–25.

Harvey, P., & Knox, H. (2015). *Roads: An anthropology of infrastructure and expertise*. Cornell University Press.

Holston, J. (2008). *Insurgent citizenship: Disjunctions of democracy and modernity in Brazil*. Princeton University Press.

Humphrey, C. (2003). Rethinking infrastructure: Siberian cities and the great freeze of January 2001. In J. Schneider & I. Susser (Eds.), *Wounded cities: Destruction and reconstruction in a globalized world* (Chapter 5). Berg.

Hutchison, R.A. (2010). *The Raja of Harsil: The legend of Frederick "Pahari" Wilson*. Lotus Collection. Roli Books.

IMG. (2013). Report of Inter-Ministerial Group (IMG), Govt. of India. (March-2013).

India Today. (2023). Uttarkashi rescue op: Expert offers prayers at temple built at tunnel entrance. India Today. https://www.indiatoday.in/india/story/uttarkashi-rescue-op-expert-arnold-dix-offers-prayers-temple-built-tunnel-entrance-2465478-2023-11-20 (Accessed 15 July 2024)

Jensen, C. B., & Morita, A. (2017). Introduction: Infrastructures as ontological experiments. *Ethnos, 82*(4), 615–626.

Linkenbach, A. (2007). *Forest futures: global representations and ground realities in the Himalayas*. Orient Longman.

Larkin, B. (2013). The politics and poetics of infrastructure. *Annual Review of Anthropology, 42*(1), 327–343.

Larkin, B. (2015, September 24). Form. Society for Cultural Anthropology. https://culanth.org/fieldsights/form (Accessed 31 May 2024)

Lefebvre, H. (2003). *The urban revolution.* University of Minnesota Press.
Mbembe, A. (2004). Aesthetics of superfluity. *Public Culture, 16*, 373–405.
NEERI. (2011). National Environment Engineering Research Institute (NEERI) *Report on the river quality of Bhagirathi/ Ganga River in Himalayan region.*
NEERI. (2018). National Environment Engineering Research Institute (NEERI) *Report on the river quality of Bhagirathi/ Ganga River in Himalayan region.*
NITI AAYOG. (2017). *Report on water security of Indian Himalayan region.* (Dec-2017).
Polit, K. (2012). *Women of honour: Gender and agency among Dalit women in the Central Himalayas.* Orient BlackSwan.
Rodgers, D., & O'Neill, B. (2012). Infrastructural violence: Introduction to the special issue. *Ethnography, 13*, 401–412.
Simpson, E. (2022). *Highways to the end of the world: Roads, roadmen and power in South Asia.* Hurst.
Smith, N. (1996). *The new urban frontier: Gentrification and the revanchist city.* Routledge.
Venkatesan, S., Bear, L., Harvey, P., Lazar, S., Rival, L., & Simone, A. (2018). Attention to infrastructure offers a welcome reconfiguration of anthropological approaches to the political. *Critique of Anthropology, 38*(1), 3–52. https://doi.org/10.1177/0308275X16683023 (Accessed 31 May 2024)
Von Schnitzler, A. (2015). Ends. Society for Cultural Anthropology. https://culanth.org/fieldsights/ends (Accessed 31 May 31 2024)

Karin Polit is professor for social and cultural anthropology at the University of Tübingen. She is an expert on the ethnography of Uttarakhand in North India, a specialist on gender in South Asia and has published on global hierarchies of value within the realm of heritage and ritual studies. She is author of the monographs *Women of Honour*, and *When Gods Set Out to Wander.* Her current research projects evolve around the various ways hierarchies of knowledge are entangled with economic and political dominance and ultimately become embodied forms of power and marginalization in its local variants.

Lokesh Ohri is an Anthropologist, Author and Activist. Born and raised in the Himalayas in Uttarakhand, he has worked in the region for more than three decades. He has successfully developed strategies for countering migration from the Himalayan villages by implementing sustainable livelihoods generation programs with nine village communities in Uttarakhand and Himachal Pradesh. Besides several other projects, he co-founded the Virasat Arts and Heritage Festival in Dehradun city. As an Anthropologist, he has focused on the Himalayas, developing insights into the social dynamic here. He was awarded a PhD by the University of Heidelberg, Germany. His research focused on traditions in the Western Himalayas describing how ritual impacts social and political life. He was also awarded the Marsilus Van Inghen Fellowship at the Radboud University, Netherlands, for ritual studies. He has authored the monograph, Till Kingdom Come: Medieval Hinduism in the Modern Himalaya.

The Political Economy of Transport Infrastructure and Energy Crisis: A Regional Study in 19th Century Germany

Bernd-Stefan Grewe

Abstract

Energy crises are a fundamental threat to any society and economy, this also applies to the feared wood shortage in the late 18th and early 19th century. This chapter studies the relevance of the transnational, regional and local transport infrastructures for the supply of energy and examines the political economy of the local transport systems in interaction with the transnational systems of the Rhine rafting and later the railway from the 1840s onwards. The creation and maintaining of the forest infrastructure in the Palatinate is region is examined in order to investigate the extent to which the much-lamented shortage of wood could possibly be due to a lack of transportation options. The chapter describes the existing and new-built infrastructures and what interests were decisive for this. It can be shown that the transport systems led to lower transportation costs, but at the same time significantly increased the commercialization of wood.

Keywords

Energy crisis · Transport revolution · Wood shortage · Forest history · Environmental history · Political economy · Netherlands · Palatinate · Bavaria

B.-S. Grewe (✉)
Institut für Geschichtsdidaktik und Public History, Universität Tübingen, Tübingen, Germany
e-mail: bernd.grewe@uni-tuebingen.de

H.-J. Bieling et al. (eds.), *Transnational Infrastructures and the Transformation of Global Orders*, RaumFragen: Stadt – Region – Landschaft,
https://doi.org/10.1007/978-3-031-74846-2_8

1 Shortage of Energy and the Relevance of Infrastructure

The oil price crises of 1973 and 1979/80 gave politicians and people a new awareness of how dependent society and the economy are on central energy sources. After half a century of relative energy security, the cutback in Russian natural gas in 2022 and the open future of gas pipelines sparked renewed fears in Europe of a new energy crisis. During these crises, economic dependence on energy sources came back into public awareness, as did the relevance of infrastructure.

About two centuries earlier, there had been similar concerns about a shortage of wood in Central Europe, a shortage which, according to the sociologist and economic historian Werner Sombart, almost meant the end of the early capitalist economy. In his famous book *The Modern Capitalism* (1917) he described the era before industrialization as the "Wooden Ages." He emphasized that wood and timber were the material basis of preindustrial production and everyday life. He interpreted the countless complaints about wood shortages as an indicator of a profound crisis (Sombart, 1917, p. 1138). Indeed, wood was needed for many reasons: as fuel, as raw material for the crafts, as timber for ship and house construction, to burn charcoal for iron founders, to cook potash, and to produce glass and soap; tanbark was needed in leather production; pitch and tar for different purposes (Radkau & Schäfer, 2007). The Wooden Ages reached their climax with the historic debate about the shortage of wood in the 1770s and 1780s. In German historiography, the rediscovery of this debate initiated a new controversy between traditional schools of forestry (Hasel, 1985; Mantel, 1990; Schmidt, 2002) and some economic historians who expressed doubts about the thesis of a general shortage of wood (Sieferle, 1982; Radkau, 1986; Allmann, 1989; Ernst, 2000; Grewe, 2004). They were able to show that many of the contemporary complaints about shortages were actually self-interested and often just meant to keep competitors away from the local timber and wood markets. These complaints only made sense in the mercantilist economy of the eighteenth century. In a market with free access for all consumers, these complaints would have been pointless, and in fact they disappeared in the early nineteenth century, often called the "Age of Liberalism". The revisionist historians also distinguished between the absence of timber and its inaccessibility, but few concrete studies of the infrastructure of timber transport followed.

The fact that there was apparently not enough wood available for consumers is therefore attributed by historical research to different explanations: (1) The wood resources in the forests were exhausted due to over-exploitation and could no longer produce enough wood (forestry narrative). (2) A mercantilist distribution of timber instead of a free market prevented effective satisfaction of demand (capitalist or market-liberal narrative). (3) The timber and wood resources in the forests were insufficiently developed, so that only part of it reached the market (narrative of inadequate infrastructure). Another explanation is also conceivable, which has been little discussed in the debate between forestry scientists and revisionist historians: (4) The wood was so expensive that it was no longer affordable for large parts of the population, and they therefore suffered from a lack of wood (political-economic narrative).

The issue of a well-developed infrastructure is central to this debate: if there were no well-developed infrastructure to transport the wood from the forests to the consumers, then the overexploitation of forests would only be limited to the easily accessible areas and could be better controlled. By expanding the transportation routes logging could then be spread over a larger area. Even a free timber market was inevitably dependent on effective transportation options. The infrastructure also had a decisive influence on timber prices (political-economic thesis).

This chapter examines the relevance of the transnational, regional and local transport infrastructures for the supply of energy (and that of indispensable raw materials). Using the example of a southwest German region, the Bavarian Rhine Palatinate, it examines the political economy of the local transport systems in interaction with the transnational systems of the Rhine rafting and later the railway from the 1840s onwards. In the following, the infrastructure in this region is examined in order to investigate the extent to which the much-lamented shortage of wood could possibly be due to a lack of transportation options.

2 The Bavarian Palatinate as a Study Region

First of all, the Palatinate as the region under investigation will be briefly introduced as well as some basic geographical and political conditions that could be relevant for the development of infrastructure. In 1815, after two decades of French rule, several territories on the left bank of the Rhine—north of Alsace—were given to the Kingdom of Bavaria at the Congress of Vienna and were renamed Rhenish Palatinate (*Rheinkreis* or *Rheinpfalz*). The French had not only introduced the Napoleonic Code, but also a highly centralized administrative structure, which left historians with an unusually rich source material. The state's ability to intervene in municipal affairs was much more far-reaching than in the rest of Bavaria (Haan, 1977).

The Palatinate is a particularly suitable region for the study, not only because of the excellent source material—more than two kilometres of forestry files are stored in the Speyer State Archives—but also because several conditions make the Palatinate a first-rate candidate for a general shortage of wood at the beginning of the nineteenth century. During the eighteenth century rich and powerful regions like the Netherlands tended to import the wood and timber that they needed from economically less wealthy and less developed regions further up the Rhine. It is therefore reasonable to examine one of these regions, for example in the South and South-West of Germany. Among the territories upstream from the Netherlands, the forests in Bavaria had the lowest documented wood production in relation to their surface. Among Bavarian forests, the lowest output is to be found in the Palatinate on the left bank of the Rhine. There was no lack of forests, as 39 percent of the region was covered with trees. The population pressure was also high, between 1817 and 1855 the population rose from 73 to 99 inhabitants per square kilometre (for comparison: the current population density in an industrialized country like France is 107 inhabitants/km^2). From an economic perspective, intensive agriculture with specialty crops (wine, tobacco, dye plants etc.) was strongly geared towards exports, and there were also some early industrial textile factories, chemical plants, iron industry and glassworks. Compared to other German regions, the Palatinate was well developed and by no means a semi-periphery that would have primarily supplied raw materials and semi-finished products for further processing in other regions. Where, if not in this region, should a general shortage of wood be found? (Grewe, 2004).

While there was a very dynamic private economy, the forests and thus the key resource wood were almost entirely under state control. The Bavarian administration in the Palatinate had inherited an extremely strong position and controlled about 88 percent of the regional wood and timber supply. The state foresters also managed the communal forests, only about 12 percent of the forests were in private hands. (Königlich Bayerisches Ministerial Forstbureau, 1861). At the beginning of the nineteenth century, many of the communal woodlands had been coppices, in the 1850s more than 70 percent of them had been transformed into high forests. This change in forestry usually happened against the will of the owners. The newly planted high forests had to be spared for many years before they could be cut down. But the income from the sale of wood ultimately benefited the communities, which in turn invested it in local infrastructure. The vast majority of municipal school buildings, town halls, washhouses and wells, as well as the fire stations in the nineteenth century, were actually paid for from forestry revenues and did not have to be raised through additional municipal levies (Franz, 2006). Therefore, the local councils and the Bavarian state ultimately shared an interest in high revenues from the sale of wood. For the Bavarian government, too, the revenue from forestry was also very relevant politically, although unlike taxes, the approval of the Bavarian parliament was not required for this state revenue. In early constitutionalism, the Liberals in the Landtag used their right to approve taxes to demand additional political rights from the crown. This was the political relevance of forest revenues, which accounted for an average of between 8 and 16 percent of total revenues (Grewe, 2004, pp. 91–99). The government, and thus the crown, could dispose of such revenues from state enterprises, which included the forestry administration, without involving parliament. This convergence of interests was responsible for the very high prices for wood and timber in this region (Grewe, 2004, pp. 388–403).

In fact, the prices for wood and timber that had to be paid at auctions in the Palatinate were often the highest of Bavaria. In the northern and western part of the region, around Kaiserslautern and close to the Saar River, where coal or peat were found, these were used to substitute firewood despite all practical disadvantages. But the most notable indicator of an unsatisfied demand for wood and other forest products was the very high rate of theft of wood and other offences against the forest regulations: In 1843, when the Palatinate had about 595.000 inhabitants, more than 180.000 cases of forest offences were reported and sanctioned. Between 1830 and 1850, on average, more than 20 percent of the total population were fined or arrested every year for forest law offences. This amounts to one person in each family per year. In addition, there was also a very high number of undetected cases. Obviously, a large part of the population in the Palatinate could not satisfy their daily need for forest resources (Grewe, 2004, pp. 195–219). This raises the question of the extent to which this undersupply was due to transportation problems and the resulting increase in wood prices.

3 Transportation Infrastructures

The most important basic prerequisite for being able to use wood at all was the accessibility of the forests. Logging was only worthwhile where cheap means of transportation and roads were available. The high transportation costs by land could drive up timber prices to such an extent that the timber could hardly be sold, or only at a low profit. In this respect, the lack of a well-developed road network and inexpensive means of transportation could be one of the main reasons why there was not enough wood available despite the fact that there were actually sufficient supplies. In some cases, wood shortages were due to the inaccessibility of the forests rather than the non-availability of wood.

The transportation of timber supplies took place on three levels:

- Firstly, transport routes had to be available within the forests on which the timber could be transported easily and cheaply to the main transport axes.
- These axes formed the second level of wood transportation within the region. They were used to transport the timber from the forests to the places of consumption and market. The condition of the roads was decisive for land transportation, while the development of the drift streams and the existence of rivers were crucial for water transportation. From the middle of the century, the railroad became increasingly important for timber transport.
- The third level comprised the supra-regional transport routes and was thus a central prerequisite for the import (Netherlands, Great Britain) or export of timber (Baltic, German states). For centuries, the timber trade between different regions had been dependent on the river systems, but the construction of the railroad changed everything.

3.1 Transporting Wood and Timber Within the Forests

An important task of the forest workers was to bring the felled timber to the forest roads and drift streams, from where it was transported onwards. Horses and oxen were used to pull logs attached to chains or ropes out of the forest. Small sawn or hewn timber, on the other hand, was often transported down to the drift streams or forest roads on sledges. In contrast to toboggans in the high mountains, “sledging” took place at all times of the year and not just when there was snow. The local author August Becker (1858) provided a literary, but all the more vivid idea of what this form of transportation looked like in practice:

> At the mountain dumps, you lay out a wooden track by placing the logs crosswise on top of each other. On this sloping log embankment, the loaded sleds descend the mountain, one behind the other, at the speed of an arrow on the rough track. One wrong step and the poor wooden sledger is lost; either he is crushed by the following sledges or he is thrown against a tree and crushed. Great care is needed, especially when arriving in the valley. (Becker, 1858)

The danger of "sledging" was not a dramatizing exaggeration by Becker. Folklore literature and interviews with forest workers in the early twentieth century confirm the veracity of the literary source.

Not only forest maps with marked sledge paths, but also the deep gullies on many mountain slopes are lasting traces of how important and widespread this transportation technique had been. The fact that the Palatinate state forests had the densest network of paths in relation to all the administrative districts is evident from overviews of the forest administration. The good development of this network concerned not only the logging and hauling roads, but above all the forest roads. As many as 29 percent of all forest roads built by the administration in Bavaria's state forests were in the Palatinate administrative district: 3,030 km out of a total of 10,434 km. Although slightly more than 292 km of these were only used as forest protection paths, the development of roads in this region was nevertheless much more advanced than in the rest of Bavaria. An overview of the existing road network in Bavaria (Königlich Bayerisches Ministerial Forstbureau, 1861) shows that in the Palatinate it was not the more primitive sledge and draw paths that dominated, but above all the better developed, leveled forest roads. The state administration had invested considerable sums of money in the forestry infrastructure here. From an economic point of view, these investments made sense because they reduced transportation costs and increased profit margins on timber sales.

A similar picture can be seen in the municipal forests. For the period 1843 to 1858, reliable information is available on how many forest roads had to be built at the expense of the municipalities. The state management of the Palatinate's municipal forests meant that a particularly large number of forest roads were developed and built here compared to the other regions. Almost 60 percent of all paths built in municipal forests in Bavaria between 1843 and 1858 were built in the Palatinate! If one relates these path constructions to the planted area in municipal and foundation forests, the construction of paths was even five times more intensive than in the rest of Bavaria (Königlich Bayerisches Ministerial Forstbureau, 1861).

The forest roads were ordered and planned by the forest administration but financed by the municipalities. Resistance to these financial burdens therefore arose time and again. In no other administrative district were the state and municipal forests covered with such a dense network of mostly very well-developed forest paths as in the Palatinate. The state forest road network was about three times as dense as that of the municipalities.

To better understand the significance of this change, it is worth taking a look at the transportation conditions at the beginning of Bavarian rule. The authors of a forest report on forestry in the Palatinate (*Forstlich-charakteristische Skizze,* 1845) described the progress of timber transportation in very positive terms: The "inhibitions and determinants, which 25 years ago still flowed from the inaccessibility of the forests," had now been "largely eliminated". The expansion of the forest roads and the drift system had made it possible to distribute the "claims over a larger forest area". Apparently, the road network no longer played the decisive role in the question of how intensively timber could be used in the individual forest districts.

Although this official description of forestry wanted to show the efforts of the forestry administration in the very best light, their report probably corresponded to reality in essential respects. Historic research has shown the poor condition of the transportation infrastructure in the early years of Bavarian rule, not only regarding the forest roads (Hehr, 1977). According to the description of 1844, the "roads, even in the main valleys, were almost impassable" at this time. In the side valleys, even poor roads were missing, so that the timber trucks had to use the stream beds as a transport route. In many cases, "the wood had to be carried out on pack animals". In the eighteenth century, the so-called "high roads" leading out of the forest on the mountain ridges were used in particular. Because it was very difficult to get the wood up the mountains to the high roads, the felling was often limited to the mountain ridges, while "the stands in the inner forest became obsolete and considerable amounts of wood remained unused". The construction of roads by the state forestry administration had thus laid the foundation for distributing forest utilization over the entire area of the forests and thus incorporating the previously unused stands into sustainable yield planning.

> The accessibility of the forest has developed immensely in this way, and it is not only possible to reach all parts of the forest with carts, but with the use of the existing paths, there will be no place left in the whole forest where one could not lead with little effort, and from where one could not transport the wood in often very different directions (*Forstlich-charakteristische Skizze,* 1845, p. 47).

This description of the forest road network was no exaggeration. The sources of the nineteenth century suggest that some timber shortages in the previous centuries were probably due more to the lack of development of the forests roads than to a lack of timber reserves. Forest history research has therefore the greatest need to catch up in order to systematically investigate the internal development of the forests through forest roads and sledge paths. On such a basis, different forest conditions in stands near and far from settlements can be assessed more reliably.

3.2 Road Transportation from the Forests to the Consumers

From the 1840s at the latest, there were no longer any transportation problems in the Palatinate, as the investigation of the second level of timber transport will show.

Within the Palatinate, the wood had to be transported from the forests to the places of consumption or market. Compared to the water route, land transportation was the more expensive option. It is no longer possible to determine exactly how high the costs were, but they were certainly even higher for wood than for charcoal. These charcoal transports did not take place all year round. The more expensive the product was in relation to its weight, the more profitable it was to transport it over longer distances. In this case, the transportation of charcoal was still economical in relation to wood, even over longer distances. This meant that charcoal burning and potash boiling were profitable ways of using woodlands that were difficult to reach by road. These forest products made transportation worthwhile, which the heavier wood would have made unaffordable. Thus, one could effectively utilize forest areas that could not otherwise be used by the pre-industrial economy due to their location.

The construction of forest paths and roads thus changed the options to use the more remote forests in a decisive way. It was an indispensable prerequisite for a planned forestry that covered the entire forest area. If glassworks, potash boilers and charcoal burning disappeared from the forests, this was not necessarily due to a lack of wood—as was often claimed by traditional forest history. In the vast majority of cases, new transportation options merely led to a change in use and thus a change in the forestry.

Transportation costs had a decisive impact on the supply of wood. One historian assumes that it was no longer worthwhile to transport timber from a journey time of 6 to 7 h and firewood from 3 to 4 h. This would correspond to a distance of 15 to 30 km, but only in very good weather conditions (Sieferle, 1982).

But if overland transportation of timber was so expensive, did the expansion of the road network have any effect on prices? And how important was the quality of these roads? The contemporary handbook by Jägerschmid answers this question:

> The more comfortable and better the roads are managed and maintained, the more favorable the wages are calculated, because the wagoner can load and carry more draught and pack animals on a certain number than on uncomfortable and bad roads... (Jägerschmid, 1827/28, p. 264)

With a good network of paths and roads with a stable surface, the same amount of timber could be transported with fewer carts. It can be assumed that the performance of horse-drawn carts, which were the most important means of transportation in the region, doubled or tripled as a result of the expansion of the roads. So fewer carters were needed to transport timber and could eliminate an additional source of income for farmers and winegrowers in the winter months. But this effect was more than offset by increased freight volumes. The main beneficiaries of this expansion of transport routes were therefore timber merchants and forest owners who marketed their timber themselves. If they passed on the cost savings to consumers in the form of lower timber prices, they also benefited. If these cost savings were not passed on, only the suppliers' profit margin increased. For forest owners, this was certainly an incentive to build paths and roads.

Road construction was intensively pursued by the government from 1835: "For the flourishing of agriculture, industry and trade" after the founding of the Customs Union, "no task was more important and urgent than the material and numerical completion of those means of communication" (Hehr, 1977, p. 1160). There is no doubt that the Palatinate road network was already very dense around 1845. However, it is almost impossible to quantify the volume of traffic and transportation on the Palatinate roads.

3.3 The Drifting of Wood

In contrast, the sources for water transport are exceptionally favourable because there existed an own department of the forestry administration in the Palatinate for this purpose: the Royal Drift Office in Neustadt (*Königliches Trift-Amt*). If it may be true for other regions that historical–geographical research does not address the importance of the *Trift* for regional economic and cultural landscape development, this does not apply to the Palatinate.

In Bavaria, "*Trift*" refers to the transportation of firewood and shorter timber in unbound form by water. The timbers floated individually and were repeatedly brought into the correct position from the bank with poles by raftsmen running along. The actual rafting mainly took place on larger streams and rivers. Long timbers were joined together and often transported over long distances, in the Rhine region mostly to the Netherlands ("*Holländer*", lit. "Dutch timber"). Rafting was therefore often a supra-regional and transnational form of timber transportation that began in the forest itself, while drifting was primarily an intra-regional function. Even small streams were suitable for drifting if they were developed accordingly.

The drifting of timber from the Palatinate forests to the Rhine plain had a long regional tradition dating back to the late Middle Ages. The most important drifting stream, the Speyerbach flowing through Neustadt, had been free to flow since 1403, although this was restricted in the eighteenth century. The Palatine electors even had a raft ditch built to connect the Speyerbach with the saltworks in Dürkheim and the manufacturing town of Frankenthal.

From 1816, the Bavarian state set about taking over the rafting business itself. "The raft streams are considered to belong to the state property". This was the central legal basis (Code Civil, Art. 538) with which the state forestry administration established the nationalization of rafting. Due to a lack of experience, the forestry administration hired private contractors to transport the timber to the Neustadt timber yard. Interference from timber merchants initially prevented this. However, the Neustadt forestry office managed to poach three master raftsmen from the traders and let them raft successfully. Profits of more than 40,000 guilders were made from the sale of the timber in the very first year

(*Die Holzvertriftungs-Anstalten der Pfalz,* 1858). This was certainly a stronger incentive for further investment and for the expansion of the drift streams than the concern about the supply of wood for the population. The nationalization of the drift ultimately meant nothing other than the detour of profits from timber exploitation, which had previously flowed into private pockets, into the state coffers.

In 1823, a total of 33 streams were fully or partially designated as drift streams and declared "flowable". Undoubtedly, not all of these streams were actually suitable for drifting; extensive technical measures had to be taken first. On the one hand, this involved careful management of the water volume. Because there was usually little snowfall in the Palatinate mountains in winter, it was not possible to rely on meltwater as in the Alps or the Black Forest, and the annual rainfall was also relatively low. For this reason, numerous reservoirs, called "*Wooge*" (*Klausen*), were created in the upper reaches, the outlets of which were opened for drifting. On the other hand, gradients had to be overcome, usually by means of masonry waterfalls. In the Erlenbach valley, for example, it was possible to reduce the original gradient of 2.7 percent to 1.64 percent by installing around 40 waterfalls. Until the 1830s, a large number of wooden structures were built for this purpose, later these construction works were mostly carried out in stone.

Furthermore, the existing mills along the streams, especially the mill wheels, had to be protected from damage caused by wood wedged in them. For this purpose, special raft channels ran around the mill wheels at numerous mills, while at others the timbers were caught in the water by so-called rakes. Stream straightening and canalization not only accelerated the flow speed, but also shortened the transport route. Because the raft personnel had to repeatedly loosen the timbers with long poles and make them float, the banks had to be fortified. Reinforcing the banks of the stream with masonry and, in some cases, wattle and daub, also prevented undercutting and bank erosion and accelerated the flow of water. In addition, timber yards and timber storage areas were built along the drifting streams (the so-called "*Bollerplätze*").

In 1859, when some streams were no longer used for drifting, the drift streams still had a length of more than 240 km. More than one third of these streams were corrugated and bordered with stone walls on both banks. 55 "water-swelters", brick-built enclosures, weirs, falls and outlets from the waves show how heavily the Bavarian administration had invested in the drift streams. What was new about the water transportation of timber in the nineteenth century was that not only the main streams, but also tributary streams and springs were included in the drift system. Basically, the expansion of the drift meant a more efficient use of the available waterpower. Although the direction of transportation was still dependent on the natural conditions, namely the direction of flow of the streams, the waterpower was used optimally and to its limits, right up to the headwaters and springs. It is therefore justified to see the development of a region for drifting and rafting as a "transportation revolution" for the timber industry (Radkau & Schäfer, 2007, p. 111). Like inland navigation on many smaller rivers, rafting was also seasonal work, usually lasting from September 20 to April 23 of the following year.

The fact that drifting was extremely inexpensive compared to land transportation is shown by the different prices for firewood at timber yards that were located on the same drift stream and were therefore often supplied with wood from the same forests. According to other sources, transporting wood by water was said to be profitable over a maximum of 50 h, but only over a distance of around 10 h by land (Hauck, 1866). By opening up the forests with sledge paths right into the valleys and with developed drift streams, the transportation costs were reduced to a fraction of the cost of the original route.

4 Transnational Infrastructures of Timber and Wood Transportation

The infrastructure for long-distance trade in particular proved to be a driver of transnational and even economic interdependencies. As forestry history and economic history studies show, it was the Dutch trade in timber and the huge Rhine rafts, which were often several hundred meters long, that gave the forestry industry a decisive boost. The financial profits from the long-distance timber trade led to an increasing profit orientation and systematization of forestry, which applied to sovereign forest owners as well as to many municipalities (Ebeling, 1997). Over the following decades, they gradually began to restrict the population's rights of use to free logging or common forest grazing or—wherever possible—to exclude them altogether (Allmann, 1989). In this respect, the long-distance timber trade became the initiator, but not the sole cause, of a far-reaching commercialization of forest products. This commercialization of wood reached its peak from the 1830s onwards. Its social consequences were felt particularly strongly in the Prussian Rhine Province and the Bavarian Rhine Palatinate, which led to a sharp rise in timber theft and forestry crimes in particular. One of the first newspaper articles by the young Karl Marx therefore also dealt with the issue of timber theft and denounced the economic ruthlessness of the forestry industry. In most forests, firewood became a good that was sold to the highest bidder.

Although the long distance timber trade in the eighteenth century created a valuable resource of income for the forest owners, the larger part of wood and timber was still needed in the region itself. Only the long trunks from Rhenish forests, especially firs for the masts and oak trunks for the ship's hull, were used by the Dutch shipyards for the East Indiaman that linked Europe with India and China. The Rhenish forests provided indispensable building materials for the Dutch shipyards and thus contributed to global economic integration, but the local impact of this network remained rather limited, acting more indirectly as an impetus for the commercialization of the forests.

The rivers in northern and northwestern Europe were essentially a connecting axis for the transnational timber trade, but touched those forest regions where the required timber for construction could be found, which were close to floatable rivers that ran toward the Netherlands. This timber export via rivers continued during the nineteenth century, but its economic importance declined (Lotz, 2018).

From the 1840s onwards, the construction of railways set two fundamental changes in motion: Firstly, the timber and wood trade became more independent from the current of the streams and rivers. Even the remotest mountain forests became increasingly integrated in a wood market that no longer depended on the river systems. The steam engine was less important for production processes than for a revolution in the transport system. The railroads and regular steamship lines connected the different industrialising centres in Europe and the Atlantic region. The railways brought a major change in the directions of the wood trade, import became possible for regions without direct access to the sea or navigable rivers (which for about two centuries had been a decisive advantage for the British and Dutch economy). The railroad soon crossed mountains and valleys by tunnels and bridges, and the steamship brought people and materials upstream rivers. All this changed the vector of transport and made it independent from waterways, they helped to overcome natural barriers that had limited wood transport for centuries. The costs and the range of transport were no longer determined by the physical strength of humans and draught animals (Sieferle, 2008).

Mass import of timber and wood from the Baltic also affected wood prices in Central Europe. From the 1860s on, even Germany, which compared to other industrialized countries had many forests, depended on wood and timber import. The imperialism at the end of nineteenth century and the falling costs of transport by ship and by train favoured the formation of an increasingly international and global wood market. Formerly peripheral forests were gradually integrated into global economic development (Grewe, 2003).

The second turning point was that the railways made it possible to substitute firewood by coal. The coal mines in the Saar region were connected to the urban centres on the Rhine by the Palatinate *Ludwigsbahn*, and the coal was also exported to Switzerland and Alsace in this way. On a macro level, this could have had the effect of substituting conventional fuel, but on a regional level it relieved the wood market, as the additional fossil fuel was able to satisfy the growing demand, particularly in the commercial sector. In the private sector, coal did not displace firewood, but rather provided price relief. This enabled households to continue using firewood for many decades until the 1950s, when inexpensive heating oil and natural gas became the most important means of heating. The regional wood supply with sledge paths and forest roads and the drift streams therefore remained profitable and continued to operate into the twentieth century.

5 Conclusion

At three levels—transnational, regional and local—it was possible to show how the state forestry administration and the municipalities ensured that all the forests in the region were accessible by road. It can therefore be excluded that the well-documented scarcity of wood for large sections of the population was due to the inaccessibility of the wood reserves inside the forests. Rather, the forests in the Palatinate were more easily accessible than average and ensured comparatively cheap timber transportation. It was this infrastructure that made it possible to manage the forests evenly and sustainably over the entire area. The bitter shortage of wood for the poorer sections of the population must therefore have been caused by other factors and was due in particular to the commercialization of the forests (Grewe, 2004).

References

Allmann, J. (1989). Der Wald in der frühen Neuzeit. Eine mentalitäts- und sozialgeschichtliche Untersuchung am Beispiel des Pfälzer Raumes 1500–1800. Duncker & Humblot.

Becker, A. (1858). *Die Pfalz und die Pfälzer.* J.J. Weber.

[N.N.] (1858). Die Holzvertriftungs-Anstalten der Pfalz, betrachtet nach ihrem Ursprung, Wesen, sowie nach dem Nutzen und den Schäden, welche dieselben für den Staat, die Industrie, die Landwirtschaft und die Holzkonsumenten im Gefolge haben. Zweibrücken.

Ebeling, D. (1997). Der Holländerholzhandel in den Rheinlanden. Zu den Handelsbeziehungen zwischen den Niederlanden und dem westlichen Deutschland im 17. und 18. Jahrhundert. Franz Steiner.

Ernst, C. (2000). *Den Wald entwickeln: Ein Politik- und Konfliktfeld in Hunsrück und Eifel im 18. Jahrhundert.* Oldenbourg.

[N.N.] (1845). *Forstlich-charakteristische Skizze der Waldungen auf dem bunten Sandsteingebirge der Pfalz, welche hier unter dem Namen "Pfälzerwald" bezeichnet werden, und Hauptwirtschafts-Regeln für dieselben.* Daniel Kranzbühler.

Franz, N. (2006). Durchstaatlichung und Ausweitung der Kommunalaufgaben im 19. Jahrhundert. Tätigkeitsfelder und Handlungsspielräume ausgewählter französischer und luxemburgischer Landgemeinden im mikrohistorischen Vergleich (1805–1890). Kliomedia.

Grewe, B.-S. (2003). Das Ende der Nachhaltigkeit? Wald und Industrialisierung im 19. Jahrhundert. *Archiv Für Sozialgeschichte, 43*, 61–79.

Grewe, B.-S. (2004). *Der versperrte Wald. Waldressourcenmangel in der bayerischen Pfalz (1814–1870).* Böhlau.

Haan, H. (Ed.) (1977). Hauptstaat—Nebenstaat. Briefe und Akten zum Anschluß der Pfalz an Bayern 1815/17. Landesarchivverwaltung Rheinland-Pfalz.

Hasel, K. (1985). *Forstgeschichte. Ein Grundriss für Studium und Praxis.* Parey.

Hauck, H. (1866). Das Steigen der Holzpreise seit dem Anfange des vorigen Jahrhunderts, dessen Ursachen und Wirkungen und die Mittel dagegen. *Supplement Zur Allgemeinen Forst- und Jagdzeitung, 2*, 47–66.

Hehr, E. (1977). Verkehrsverhältnisse im 19.Jahrhundert (Die Straßen als Verkehrsträger). In Alter, W. (Ed.), Pfalzatlas (Vol. 2, pp. 1108–1167). Pfälzische Gesellschaft zur Förderung der Wissenschaften.

Jägerschmid, K. F. V. (1827/1828). *Handbuch für Holztransport- und Floßwesen zum Gebrauche für Forstmänner und Holzhändler und für solche, die es werden wollen.* (Vol. 2). Müller.

Königlich Bayerisches Ministerial Forstbureau. (1861). *Die Forstverwaltung Bayerns, beschrieben nach ihrem dermaligen Stande.* Wolf.

Lotz, C. (2018). *Nachhaltigkeit neu skalieren. Internationale forstwissenschaftliche Kongresse und Debatten um die Ressourcenversorgung der Zukunft im Nord- und Ostseeraum (1870–1914).* Böhlau.

Mantel, K. (1990). *Wald und Forst in der Geschichte. Ein Lehr- und Handbuch.* Schaper.

Radkau, J. (1986). Zur angeblichen Energiekrise des 18.Jahrhunderts: Revisionistische Betrachtungen über die "Holznot." *Vierteljahrsschrift Für Sozial- und Wirtschaftsgeschichte, 73,* 1–37.

Radkau, J., & Schäfer, I. (2007). *Holz—wie ein Naturstoff Geschichte schreibt.* Oekom.

Schmidt, U.E. (2002). Der Wald in Deutschland im 18. und 19. Jahrhundert. Das Problem der Ressourcenknappheit am Beispiel der Waldressourcenknappheit in Deutschland im 18. Und 19. Jahrhundert—eine historisch-politische Analyse. Conte.

Sieferle, R. P. (1982). *Der unterirdische Wald. Energiekrise und Industrielle Revolution.* Beck.

Sieferle, R. P. (2008). *Transportgeschichte.* LIT.

Sombart, W. (1917). *Der moderne Kapitalismus. Historisch-systematische Darstellung des gesamteuropäischen Wirtschaftslebens von seinen Anfängen bis zur Gegenwart. Das europäische Wirtschaftsleben im Zeitalter des Frühkapitalismus* (Vol. 2). Duncker & Humblot.

Bernd-Stefan Grewe (Dr. phil., University of Trier) is history professor and director of the Institute of History Didactics and Public History at the University of Tübingen. Research interests include environmental and rural history, the history of colonialism and of global commodities with a special focus on Southern Africa, India, and Great Britain. His books include *Der versperrte Wald. Vorindustrieller Waldressourcenmangel am Beispiel der bayerischen Rheinpfalz 1815–1870* (Böhlau, 2004), *Luxury in Global Perspective: Objects and Practices* (with Karin Hofmeester, Cambridge University Press, 2016), *Gold: Eine Weltgeschichte* (Beck, 2019), *Modern Germany: A Global History* (with Eric Kurlander Douglas McGetchin, Oxford University Press, 2023). In the field of public history he has published several articles and books on Germany's handling of its colonial heritage such as Koloniales Erbe(n), in: Geschichte in Wissenschaft und Unterricht 2021, pp.493–500; *Freiburg und der Kolonialismus: Vom Kaiserreich zum Nationalsozialismus* (with Heiko Wegmann et al., Stadtarchiv Freiburg, 2018).

Open Veins or Lifelines of Society? Infrastructures and the Order of Global Resource Extractivism in Latin America

Riccarda Flemmer

Abstract

Resource extraction projects heavily rely on infrastructures for the exploration, exploitation, and export of raw materials. In the order of "global extractivism", which represents an unsustainable development model reliant on the excessive exploitation of our planet's natural resources, colonial patterns between Global North and Global South persist. This manifests in an unequal distribution of the benefits and impacts of projects between and within states. Reviewing interdisciplinary academic literature and case material from Latin America, infrastructures play a three-fold role in resource extractivism: First, infrastructure is promising development and modernisation including labour opportunities, market access as well as compensation payments. Second, streets, railways, pipelines, and ports are part of the destructive force of resource extractive projects causing harm to humans and nature. Third—and less reflected in the existing literature—infrastructural installations not only incite opposition, but the latter may turn them into leverage for change. Disrupting resource extraction infrastructures may therefore exert pressure against states and companies to transform extractivism as the dominant development model.

I thank Micha Bröckling, Lillian Eichorst, and Zahid Zamudio for the valuable research assistance provided during the elaboration of this chapter.

R. Flemmer (✉)
Institut für Politikwissenschaft, Universität Tübingen, Tübingen, Germany
e-mail: riccarda.flemmer@uni-tuebingen.de

H.-J. Bieling et al. (eds.), *Transnational Infrastructures and the Transformation of Global Orders*, RaumFragen: Stadt – Region – Landschaft,
https://doi.org/10.1007/978-3-031-74846-2_9

Keywords

Latin America · Resistance · Resource extraction · Infrastructural harm · Development promises

1 Introduction

> Latin America is the region of open veins. Everything, from the discovery until our times, has always been transmuted into European—or later United States—capital, and as such has accumulated in distant centers of power. Everything: the soil, its fruits and its mineral-rich depths, the people and their capacity to work and to consume, natural resources and human resources. (Galeano [Spanish original 1971] 2006, p. 2)

In his 1971 work "*The Open Veins of Latin America*", the Uruguayan economist Eduardo Galeano examined the continuous drain of raw materials (and workforce) out of Latin America. The extraction of these natural resources heavily relies on infrastructures that enable their exploration, exploitation, and export. The "open veins" stand for the Latin American flip side of the positive connotation of infrastructures as societal 'lifelines' (van Laak, 2018; English 2023) — installations that sustain progress, development, and wealth. Both, Galeano's and Van Laak's bodily metaphors point to the essential role of infrastructures in directing flows of goods. However, these flows are not "natural" but designed and used for certain purposes and interests. Yet by the same token, this also means that infrastructures can be disrupted, changed and replaced by alternatives.

Originally conceptualised in critical Latin American thought, extractivism is widely seen as an unsustainable development model reliant on the excessive exploitation of our planet's natural resources (Chagnon et al., 2022). Infrastructures play a central role in the expansion as well as the transformation of the physical, legal and symbolic order of global resource extraction. In the global order of our "extractivist age" (McNeish & Shapiro, 2021), colonial patterns between Global North and South persist in the unequal distribution of resource extraction's economic, social, and environmental costs and benefits. These patterns have expanded so that Latin America today does not only sustain industries at the hearts of European and Global North's centres but also in Asia, especially China (Burchardt & Dietz, 2014, pp. 471–72; Farthing & Fabricant, 2018, p. 5).

Thus, infrastructures are part of the destructive force of expanding resource extractivism (Peluso & Lund, 2011). At the same time, railways, pipelines, and ports are transport ways which promise labour, compensation payments, market access and modernisation. However, the visibility of these installations as critical infrastructures makes them vulnerable and turn them into opportunities for resistance against extractive industries. They also provide leverage for this opposition and create spaces for alternative ideas of how to realise economies and energy projects. Further, anti-extractivist alliances may form between communities and movements in the Global South and North promising transformation towards a post-fossil age combining indigenous cosmologies, de-growth and sustainability (Fladvad, 2023; Temper et al., 2018).

This chapter examines the role of infrastructures in ordering global extractivism in Latin America. The first section provides a definition and an historical embedding of *extractivismo* and global extractivism rooted in critical Latin American thinking. The second section analyses how infrastructures have been part of the promises of modernisation and development that sustain and facilitate extractive industry projects in Latin America. The third section demonstrates how infrastructures play a central role in the violence against people and nature involved in resource extraction. The fourth section looks at how the disruption of infrastructures may be used to stop specific projects or even turned into a leverage for exerting pressure from below to challenge the order of global extractivism. The concluding section gives an outlook on future research on the role of infrastructures in expanding or stopping, and potentially transforming global extractivism.

2 Latin America's "Open Veins" and the Order of Global Extractivism

> As the [World] Bank explains it, most of the loans are for building roads and other communications links, and for developing sources of electrical energy, an essential condition for the growth of private enterprise. In effect, these infrastructure projects facilitate the movement of raw materials to ports and world markets and the progress of already denationalized industry in the poor countries. (Galeano [Spanish original 1971] 2006, p. 234)

The concept of extractivism, rooted in late twentieth-century conceptualisations of "*extractivismo*" in Latin America (Acosta 2013; Gudynas, 2009, 2013), denotes the large-scale and high intensity exploitation of resources for export. This orientation towards export relies on transport infrastructure, such as harbours, railways, streets, and airports. Facilitated by these transport routes, major shares of Europe's supply of primary resources were and continue to be imported from the region. In 2022, 79% of lithium (European Commission et al., 2023, p. 26), 70.32% of sugar (own calculation based on World Bank, 2022c), 50.8% of Soy beans (own calculation based on World Bank, 2022b), 46.7% of copper (World Bank, 2022a), and 12.5% of gold (European Commission et al., 2023, p. 85) were delivered to Europe by Latin American countries.

Extractivism as a relatively new academic concept describes colonially rooted dynamics and structures of violent exploitation of sugar, rubber, timber, minerals, metals, oil, and gas in the Global South. Analyses have then expanded to other contexts, such as the Arctic and Global North settings (Dietz & Engels, 2017; Durante, Kröger, & LaFleur, 2021; Gago & Mezzadra, 2017). Historically, this exploitation can be traced back to colonial dispossession and has been chronicled for Latin America by writers like Galeano. From the mythical allure of El Dorado during the Spanish conquest (1532–1560) to the rubber boom of the late 19th and early twentieth centuries (1880–1920), the exploitation of raw materials, wildlife, and oil has left profound marks on Latin America (Mayor Aparicio & Bodmer, 2009, p. 57). More recently, mining for minerals such as lithium has risen due to demands for electric vehicle batteries and renewable energy technologies (European Parliament and Grieger, 2023, p. 3).

In the 2000s and 2010s, Latin America's experienced a "re-primaritization" (Burchardt and Dietz, pp. 471–472; Farthing & Fabricant, 2018, p. 5) with an increase of raw materials exported from Latin America from 27% in 2000 to 60.7% in 2011 (Burchardt & Dietz, 2014, 471). According to the UN Economic Commission for Latin America and the Caribbean (ECLAC) this rate stands at 54.4% (ECLAC, 2022, p. 31) in 2022. This trajectory of escalating resource demands shows no sign of abating, according to projections from the European Commission's Raw Materials Scoreboard (European Commission, 2021). Infrastructures have historically enabled these markets and are still sustaining the connections within and between places of origin, production, and consumption. The close link between Latin American and European primary resources extractivism is also illustrated by the coal trade, which increased from 26.9% of Germany's coal being imported from Colombia in 2021 to 44% in 2022 (OEC, 2024, May 15) after the war between Russia and Ukraine had begun. Adding to the raw materials, which Europe directly imports from Latin America, large containers of technology products built from these materials, such as mobile phones, arrive every day at European ports (Infante-Amate et al., 2022). These trade relations have reaffirmed the position of Latin America as the supplier of raw materials.

3 Infrastructures as Promise: Ambivalences of Modernisation and Development

> Latin America and the Caribbean [... do] not have the infrastructure it needs or deserves given its income level. Infrastructure also falls short of what is needed to advance social integration and achieve higher growth and prosperity. (World Bank, 2017a, p. 7)

> "Infrastructure investment can be a powerful engine for growth in Latin America and the Caribbean [...]," said Jorge Familiar, World Bank Vice President for Latin America and the Caribbean. (World Bank, 2017b)

Infrastructures have been crucial to connect Latin America as an extraction site for raw materials to the world market. In this context, projects of roads, harbours, rails, and airports directly or indirectly sustaining extractivism have a long historical trajectory of being framed as promises leading to the modernisation and development of the region by the World Bank (2017a, 2022d), the Inter-American Development Bank (Garcia & Schor, 2023), and national governments (Alderman & Goodwin, 2022; Appel et al., 2018). Large-scale infrastructure, energy and resource extraction projects often go hand-in-hand (Silva et al., 2018, p. 33). Inside the countries, discourses around resource extraction projects repeat theses promises.

Extractive projects themselves are framed as promises of modernisation and employment. Infrastructures as part of these extractive projects enable resource access, exploitation and transport. The "extractive imperative" (Arsel et al., 2016) of Latin American development policies is rooted in colonial times and further manifested in foreign private companies directly investing and managing projects in the context of trade liberalisation, deregulation, and privatisation under the Washington Consensus. In the late 1990s and 2000s, new governments in Latin America emerged, symbolizing hope for alternative development approaches, as seen in leaders like Hugo Chavez (Venezuela, 1998: Oil for all!), Evo Morales (Bolivia, 2005: Water and gas for all!) and Rafael Correa (Ecuador 2006: *sumak kawsay* or *buen vivir,* good life). However, the "commodities consensus" (Svampa, 2015) across the region contained a reaffirmation of extractivism. Discussed as the rise of "(neo-)extractivism" (Acosta, 2013; Burchardt & Dietz, 2014), characteristics of resource governance were marked by a shift towards state regulation and redistributive policies using the surplus revenues to finance social programmes. This turned extractivism into "a politically legitimised new development project" (Burchardt & Dietz, 2014, pp. 469–470). Further, scholars have critically examined how promises of local employment and social programmes have fallen short of creating long-term jobs. A common characteristic of large-scale mining and hydrocarbon projects, based on concessions that usually run for several decades, is that companies bring their own skilled employees, leaving only short-term labour opportunities, such as the construction of roads, to the local workforce. This has been criticised as part of the "false developmental promise" (Frynas, 2005) of Corporate Social Responsibility.

Further, social, health or other basic infrastructures are often promised by states and companies to facilitate social approval of resource extraction projects. For state practices, the use of these "development promises" (Schilling-Vacaflor et al., 2018, p. 76) has been documented in the expansion of oil and gas projects into the Amazon. In a study for Peru from 2007 to 2015, based on internal reports from the Peruvian Oil Agency and the Human Rights Ombudsperson (Defensoría del Pueblo), the authors demonstrate how "state institutions joined forces with private companies" (Schilling-Vacaflor et al., 2018, p. 82) committing to provide direct monetary compensation, finance social projects, and build healthcare or transport infrastructures for local communities or leaders. Similarly, a study about indigenous participation in the same context shows that a large share of claims regarding new hydrocarbon projects are—besides labour and environmental demands—requests for basic infrastructure (Flemmer & Schilling-Vacaflor, 2016). In similar contexts, the concept of "infrastructural colonization" (Dunlap & Riquito, 2023) has been coined to critically examine how companies assume infrastructure development concerning basic responsibilities of the state to acquire the "social license to operate" a resource extraction or energy project.

Promises of development are powerful in a symbolic as well as a material way with ambivalent effects for countries as well as for populations affected by extractivism. On the one hand, development causes hope for countries and communities to belong to the modern, progressive, and powerful. Critical Development Studies and decolonial scholarship have well documented the exclusionary practices of labelling parts of the world as "under-developed" (e.g. Escobar, 1995). Inside Latin America, state governments often use the same developmental discourse with repercussions for parts of populations, especially labelling rural and indigenous communities as "backward" (e.g. Schilling-Vacaflor,

2017). On the other hand, economic dependency compels states to engage in extractive activities, albeit at the cost of environmental risks and burdens. Economic dependency or hardship combined with political marginalisation have also been identified as the central factors for communities' acceptance of mining projects (Conde & Le Billon, 2017) or their engagement with them (Orihuela et al., 2022). Framing extractivism through the lens of poverty, this perspective underscores the urgent imperative to address the structural inequalities embedded within extractive industries and to prioritise the well-being and rights of marginalised communities affected by resource extraction. The negative ecological and "human rights trade-off" (Valencia, 2014) is particularly visible in heavily contaminated places, such as the smelter town La Oroya, Peru, which exemplifies the complex dynamics of communities facing difficult choices between economic opportunities offered by extractive projects and the protection of fundamental rights such as health and a clean environment.

4 Infrastructures as Harm: Violence Against People and Nature

The concept of "infrastructural harm" (Kallianos et al., 2023) delves into the complex interplay between coloniality, violence, and the impacts—both material and immaterial—of extractive infrastructures on communities and environments. In the context of extractivism, this can be exemplified by what Truscello (2020) terms "infrastructural brutalism", capturing the decisive role of infrastructures in determining the harsh and often destructive impact of extractive projects on human and non-human lives and deaths. Scholars have emphasised that extractivism is intrinsically linked with violence, representing not a byproduct but a fundamental logic (McNeish & Shapiro, 2021, p. 2). This violence encompasses structural and symbolic forms as well as direct and indirect harm.

The structural dimension of harm caused by extractivism has been criticised as the "ecological debt" from North to South (*Deuda ecológica*, Robleto & Marcelo, 1992). Environmental justice scholars in this regard the interconnected dynamics of global market dependency, growth-oriented development models, centred on raw material exports, and the concentration of negative impacts within project countries and in concrete sites of extraction. This literature focuses on "ecological distribution conflicts" as "social conflicts born from the unfair access to natural resources and the unjust burdens of pollution" (Martinez-Alier, 2018, p. 187) between and within countries. Focusing on elites, the concept of hyper-extractivism (Wapner, 2021), underscores that this unequal distribution of environmental burdens also means that rich privileged individuals can delay or avoid direct exposure to negative impacts in the Global North and South.

Epistemic violence underpins the physical harm caused to people and nature affected by extractive industry projects (Davies, 2022). Scholars stress that inherent to extractivism is an own "onto-logics" (McNeish & Shapiro, 2021, p. 3; Chagnon et al., 2022, p. 773) of converting beings and land into resources to be exploited. This logic subverts other types of knowledge and ways of being with nature, such as indigenous cosmologies, peasant relations with land and communal everyday lives (Flemmer et al., 2024).

Direct violence is particularly acute on the "resource frontiers" (see: Watts 2021) when projects move into new areas and often collide with preexisting human and ecological systems. Infrastructures are part of the destructive force of expanding resource extractivism (Peluso & Lund, 2011). With large-scale hydrocarbon and mining projects entering into indigenous territories, communities are amongst the most affected populations by extractive industries (Martinez-Alier, 2002; Martínez-Alier et al., 2016). Violence at these expanding frontiers of resource extraction has been documented by scholars and activists, highlighting the dangers faced by communities defending their lands (Temper & Shmelev, 2015, p. 260). Attacks against individuals who peacefully oppose the exploitation of natural resources have resulted in several deaths, especially in Colombia and Brazil (Global Witness, 2021, p. 11). The Environmental Justice Atlas documents environmental conflicts categorised by resource type, including those related to infrastructure and built environment. Research by Temper and Shmelev (2015, p. 272) indicates that the most intense conflicts are associated with water management, followed by mineral ore and building material extraction such as gold, copper, lithium, and sand. Mining-related conflicts account for a significant share, with 573 documented cases, while infrastructure-related conflicts have resulted in 248 assassinations of activists (Scheidel et al., 2020, p. 6). These figures underscore the grave risks faced by activists and community members defending their lands and environments against the impacts of resource extraction and infrastructure development.

Indirect forms of violence in the context of extractive industries are deeply entangled with physical violence but operate in more subtle ways. Scholars have explored the concept of "slow violence", referring to the gradual but profound harm inflicted by infrastructures and extractive projects on ecosystems over time (Nixon, 2011). Further, extractive projects can lead to the displacement and resettlement of communities resulting in loss of land or territory, the appropriation of resources, destruction of ecosystems, the disruption of ways of life or livelihoods, and the erosion of values due to compensation payments and royalty incentives (Sempértegui & Báez, 2024, p. 674; Wolff, 2017, p. 245). This can be illustrated by the legacy of the Chevron (formerly Texaco) oil project in the Ecuadorian Amazon. The company's practices have been linked to widespread pollution of water sources and the destruction of indigenous communities' lands and livelihoods. This environmental degradation has had lasting effects on local ecosystems and public health, showing the long-term slow consequences of extractive industries. Communities have sued the company and the Ecuadorian state for compensation payments and environmental remediation. However, responsibilities are passed between corporate lawyers and state courts leading to continuous legal battles (see e.g. Pellegrini et al., 2020).

5 Infrastructures and Resistance "From Below"

> Blockades [...] not only bring visibility to the grievances and demands of protesters but also to the social and political life of Latin American infrastructures (Alderman & Goodwin, 2022, p. 3).

Large-scale infrastructure projects face a significant amount of social dissent in Latin America (Velho & Ureta, 2019). However, state and company responses to protests involving the blocking of infrastructure can substantially vary, ranging from negotiations to repression (Orihuela et al., 2022). Reviewing empirical studies about social movements, contentious politics, and resource conflicts in Latin America indicates that the disruption of infrastructures within the context of resource extraction have served affected communities and social movements to oppose concrete projects or the entire model of extractivism, to issue broader political claims, and to open space for alternative development. These three strategic aims are often raised simultaneously—or even contradictorily—by protesters but are conceptually different in their ambition to change the order of global extractivism.

Primarily, blockades and sabotage are employed to effectively block or oppose extractive projects, preventing their implementation or operation. Research on opposition to infrastructure projects in the developing world has been notably scarce within the field of social movements, as highlighted by McAdam et al., (2010, p. 403) for the "site fight" literature. Single case studies have explored how communities in Latin America use blockades of infrastructure, including access roads, ports, and facilities to avoid projects being imposed on their lands. In a comparative study about the expansion of hydrocarbon projects in Peru, Schilling-Vacaflor et al., (2018, pp. 80–82) illustrate how communities block road or water way access to planned extraction sites in order to oppose these projects on their lands. The concept of extrACTIVISM, as elucidated by McNeish and Shapiro (2021), embodies a multifaceted approach to activism that specifically targets the adverse impacts of resource extraction activities on communities and ecosystems. This form of activism, documented by Jalbert et al. (2017), extends beyond traditional protest tactics to encompass political militancy and strategic engagement with legal institutions. Moreover, extrACTIVISM is characterised by alliances forged among communities, non-governmental organisations (NGOs), legal professionals, and other stakeholders to amplify collective voices and pursue shared objectives.

Secondly, blockades of transport ways are utilised as a means of resistance by exerting pressure on governments or corporate entities, compelling them to acknowledge and address the broader concerns of affected communities (Silva et al., 2018). This can be observed in both urban settings (e.g. Leal, 2020) and rural areas. In 2009, a particularly violent government response to blockades happened in Peru. Indigenous communities and their organisations blocked roads, waterways and access to oil plants to prevent legal changes they feared would lead to further deforestation and open the rainforest for direct investment, particularly in the context of the Free Trade Agreement (FTA) between Peru and the United States. These blockades were met with a violent response from police forces, resulting in the tragic loss of over 30 lives. The Bagua incident drew international attention and led to calls for legal reforms and greater accountability regarding resource extraction and indigenous land rights in Peru. Ultimately, this resulted in Peru adopting Latin America's first national law on indigenous peoples' rights to free, prior, and informed consultation and become a legal forerunner to implement these standards for extractive projects in the region (Schilling-Vacaflor & Flemmer, 2015). Protest and resistance to extractivism entail communities leveraging the absence of state presence and the peripheral nature of their land, strategically slowing down project activities and imposing substantial economic costs on developers. Scholars such as Arturo Escobar (2018) shed light on how protests involving infrastructure blocking are often rooted in demands for land rights, environmental protection, and recognition of indigenous territories. These demands are integral to broader struggles for social and environmental justice.

Thirdly, blockades are instrumental in creating a conducive environment for exploring and advocating alternative development pathways and counterproposals to extractivist development. An example of a strategic blockade to maintain and create an alternative path for development is the Sarayaku Kichwa community in the Ecuadorian Amazon. In the 1990s, the indigenous community of Sarayaku in Ecuador mounted a steadfast resistance against oil exploration and exploitation within their ancestral territories, employing blockades to impede access and thwart development activities. This resistance culminated in a landmark lawsuit filed against the Ecuadorian state in 2002, which eventually led to a favourable ruling by the Inter-American Court of Justice in 2012, affirming the community's rights to prior consultation and consent over projects affecting their lands (see e.g. Verdonck & Desmet, 2017). Embodying the principles of Sumak Kawsay, or "good life," the Sarayaku community has articulated a life plan and implemented zonification strategies. These planification includes for example the installation of a runway and the buying of two small airplanes to ensure transport without opening the territory to road access. The infrastructural planning is oriented towards the holistic relational concept of the "*Kawsak Sacha*" (The Living Forest), which formulates the principles of human and nonhuman coexistence in their territory and was adopted by a broader alliance of indigenous Amazonian networks(Pueblo Originario Kichwa de Sarayaku 2018). On an international level, the Territories of Life initiative (ICCA Consortium, 2021) collects these and other examples of communities creating alternative infrastructures to support their own visions of development. This also speaks to initiatives of indigenous peoples to create more-sustainable, community-run energy and water infrastructure in Global South and North context (Fladvad, 2023).

6 Outlook: Infrastructures and the Order of Extractivism in Latin America

> Infrastructure [...] not only has the capacity to bring life (biopolitics—Foucault, 2008) or accelerate death (necropolitics—Mbembe, 2019) but to disrupt relations between the living and the dead and alter the practices and subjectivities embedded in these relations. (Alderman & Goodwin, 2022, p. 14)

Infrastructures are part of the destructive force for expanding resource extractivism. At the same time, railways, pipelines, and ports, are transport ways and promise labour, compensation payments, market access and modernisation for communities affected. Finally, the visibility of these installations as critical infrastructures makes them vulnerable and turns them into opportunities for resistance against extractive industries. They also provide leverage for opposing extractivism and creating spaces for alternative economies and energy projects.

The disruption of infrastructure at project sites points to the vulnerability of extractivism: if the supply of raw materials is cut off, the whole system will dry out. Beyond the ambivalence of infrastructures as promise or harm, infrastructures therefore also provide leverage to pressure for change. Academic literature emphasises that the impacts of extractivism are inherently multi-scalar as is anti-extractivist resistance: protests against a concrete project imply opposition to a national development model and challenge the global order of extractivism.

To conclude, infrastructures play a multifaceted role in Latin American and global extractivism, serving as both a destructive force and a source of development promises but their disruption also holds the potential for transformative change. The sites of extraction and the locations of protests are intricately connected, with tactics like blockades creating opportunities for solidarity (Haudenschild et al. 2023). Collectives, such as Ende Gelände (2022) in Germany, link their actions against fossil fuel infrastructure to broader global extractivist concerns, opposing infrastructure that perpetuates the climate crisis and reinforces neo-colonial and capitalist exploitation dynamics. This approach emphasises civil disobedience to prevent the operation and construction of climate-damaging infrastructure, utilising demonstrations and physical blockades as means of direct action. Future research exploring the role of infrastructures in challenging and potentially changing the order of global extractivism will benefit from investigating these transnational alliances and the use of such strategies aimed at disrupting and dismantling the systems that enable extractivism and its associated social and environmental impacts.

References

Acción Ecológica. (1999). No more plunder, they owe us the ecological debt! *Bulletin of Acción Ecológica, 78* (October), 1999. Quito: Acción Ecológia.

Acosta, A. (2013). Extractivism and Neoextractivism: Two Sides of the Same Curse. In M. Lang, & D. Mokarni (Eds.), *Beyond Development: Alternative Visions from Latin America* (pp. 61–86). Amsterdam: Rosa-Luxemburg Foundation, Quito; Transnational Institute.

Alderman, J., & Goodwin, G. (Eds.) (2022). *The social and political life of Latin American infrastructures.* University of London. https://doi.org/10.14296/gljm4371

Appel, H., Anand, N., & Gupta, A. (2018). Introduction: Temporality, politics, and the promise of infrastructure. In N. Anand, A. l. Gupta, & H. Appel (Eds.), *The promise of infrastructure* (pp. 1–20). Duke University Press.

Arsel, M., Hogenboom, B., & Pellegrini, L. (2016). The extractive imperative in Latin America. *The Extractive Industries and Society, 3*(4), 880–887. https://doi.org/10.1016/j.exis.2016.10.014

Atlas of Environmental Justice. (n.d.). http://ejatlas.org.

Bebbington, A., & Bebbington, D. H. (2011). An Andean avatar: Post-neoliberal and neoliberal strategies for securing the unobtainable. *New Political Economy, 16*(1), 131–145. https://doi.org/10.1080/13563461003789803

Bryant, B. I., & Mohai, P. (2019). *Race and the incidence of environmental hazards: A time for discourse.* Routledge.

Burchardt, H.-J., & Dietz, K. (2014). (Neo-)extractivism—a new challenge for development theory from Latin America. *Third World Quarterly, 35*(3), 468–486. https://doi.org/10.1080/01436597.2014.893488

Chagnon, C. W., Durante, F., Gills, B. K., Hagolani-Albov, S. E., Hokkanen, S., Kangasluoma, S. M. J., et al. (2022). From extractivism to global extractivism: The evolution of an organizing concept. *The Journal of Peasant Studies, 49*(4), 760–792. https://doi.org/10.1080/03066150.2022.2069015

Conde, M., & Le Billon, P. (2017). Why do some communities resist mining projects while others do not? *The Extractive Industries and Society, 4*(3), 681–697. https://doi.org/10.1016/j.exis.2017.04.009

Davies, T. (2022). Slow violence and toxic geographies: 'Out of sight' to whom? *Environment and Planning C: Politics and Space, 40*(2), 409–427. https://doi.org/10.1177/2399654419841063

Dietz, K., & Engels, B. (2017). Contested extractivism, society and the state: An introduction. In B. Engels & K. Dietz (Eds.), *Contested extractivism, society and the state: Struggles over mining and land* (pp. 1–19). Palgrave Macmillan.

Dunlap, A., & Riquito, M. (2023). Social warfare for lithium extraction? Open-pit lithium mining, counterinsurgency tactics and enforcing green extractivism in northern Portugal. *Energy Research & Social Science, 95*, 102912. https://doi.org/10.1016/j.erss.2022.102912

Durante, F., Kröger, M., & LaFleur, W. (2021). Extraction and extractivism. Definitions and concepts. In J. Shapiro & J.-A. McNeish (Eds.), *Earthscan from Routledge. Our extractive age: Expressions of violence and resistance* (pp. 19–30). Routledge.

ECLAC. (2022). *Statistical Yearbook for Latin America and the Caribbean, 2022* (LC/PUB.2022/21-P). Santiago de Chile: Economic commission for Latin America and the Caribbean.

ELLA. (2012). *Latin American approaches to extractive industry conflicts.* ELLA Guide. http://ella.practicalaction.org/wp-content/uploads/files/120928_ECO%20ExtIndConMan_%20GUIDE.pdf

Ende Gelände. (2022). *Action consensus.* Ende Gelände. https://www.ende-gelaende.org/aktionskonsens-2022/ (Accessed 22 Sept 2023)

Escobar, A. (1995). *Encountering development: The making and unmaking of the third world.* Princeton University Press.

Escobar, A. (2018). *Designs for the pluriverse: Radical interdependence, autonomy, and the making of worlds. New ecologies for the twenty-first century.* Duke University Press.

European Commission: Directorate-General for Internal Market, Industry, Entrepreneurship and SMEs. (2021). *3rd raw materials scoreboard—European innovation partnership on raw materials.*Publications Office of the European Union: European Union. https://doi.org/10.2873/567799

European Commission: Directorate General for Internal Market, Industry, Entrepreneurship and SMEs, Grohol, M. and Veeh, C. (2023). *Study on the critical raw materials for the EU 2023: Final report.* Publications Office of the European Union. https://doi.org/10.2873/725585

Farthing, L., & Fabricant, N. (2018). Introduction: Open veins revisited: Charting the social, economic, and political contours of the new extractivism in Latin America. *Latin American Perspectives, 45*(5), 4–17. https://www.jstor.org/stable/48595255

Fladvad, B. (2023). Infrastructuring environmental (in)justice: Green hydrogen, indigenous sovereignty and the political geographies of energy technologies. *Geographica Helvetica, 78*(4), 493–505. https://doi.org/10.5194/gh-78-493-2023

Flemmer, R., & Schilling-Vacaflor, A. (2016). Unfulfilled promises of the consultation approach: The limits to effective indigenous participation in Bolivia's and Peru's extractive industries. *Third World Quarterly, 37*(1), 172–188. https://doi.org/10.1080/01436597.2015.1092867

Flemmer, R., Gresz, V., & Hein, J. (2024). What is at stake? The ontological dimension of environmental conflicts. *Society & Natural Resources, 37*(5), 608–622. https://doi.org/10.1080/08941920.2024.2329888

Frynas, J. G. (2005). The false developmental promise of corporate social responsibility: Evidence from multinational oil companies. *International Affairs, 81*(3), 581–598. https://doi.org/10.1111/j.1468-2346.2005.00470.x

Gago, V., & Mezzadra, S. (2017). A critique of the extractive operations of capital: Toward an expanded concept of extractivism. *Rethinking Marxism, 29*(4), 574–591. https://doi.org/10.1080/08935696.2017.1417087

Galeano, E. (2006). *Open veins of Latin America: Five centuries of the pillage of a continent.* Monthly Review Press.

Garcia, P. M., & Schor, T. (2023, August 7). The integration of the Amazon region: 14,000 km of opportunities. IDB Blog. https://blogs.iadb.org/integration-trade/en/the-integration-of-the-amazon-region-14000-km-of-opportunities/. (Accessed 1 April 2024)

Global Witness. (2021). *Last line of defense: The industries causing the climate crisis and attacks against land and environmental defenders.* London: Global Witness. https://www.globalwitness.org/documents/20190/Last_line_of_defence_-_low_res_-_September_2021.pdf

European Parliament: Directorate-General for Parliamentary Research Services and Grieger, G. (2023). EU trade with Latin America and the Caribbean—Overview and figures. European Parliament. https://doi.org/10.2861/026323

Gudynas, E. (2009). Diez tesis urgentes sobre el nuevo extractivismo. Contextos y demandas bajo el progresismo sudamericano actual. In J. Schuld, A. Acosta, A. Barandiarán, A. Bebbington, M. Folchi, C. Bolivia, A. Alayza, & E. Gudynas (Eds.), *Extractivismo, política y sociedad* (pp. 187–225). Lima: CAAP (Centro Andino de Acción Popular); CLAES (Centro Latino Americano de Ecología Social).

Gudynas, E. (2013). Extracciones, extractivismo y extrahecciones. Un marco conceptual sobre la apropiacion de recursos naturales. *Observatorio del Desarrollo, 18.*

Haraway, D. (1988). Situated knowledges: The science question in feminism and the privilege of partial perspective. *Feminist Studies, 14*(3), 575–599. https://doi.org/10.2307/3178066

Haudenschild, D., Stühlen, C., & Anderl, F. (2023). Infrastrukturen der Gewalt Lützerath, Dannenröder Forst und die Klimagerechtigkeitsbewegung. *Wissenschaft & Frieden Klimakrise*, (2023/02).

ICCA Consortium. (Ed.). (2021). *Territories of life: 2021 Report.* worldwide. https://report.territoriesoflife.org/

Infante-Amate, J., Urrego-Mesa, A., Piñero, P., & Tello, E. (2022). The open veins of Latin America: Long-term physical trade flows (1900–2016). *Global Environmental Change, 76*, 102579. https://doi.org/10.1016/j.gloenvcha.2022.102579

Jalbert, K., Willow, A. J., & Casagrande, D. (Eds.). (2017). *ExtrACTION: Impacts, engagements, and alternative futures*. Routledge. https://doi.org/10.4324/9781315225579

Kallianos, Y., Dunlap, A., & Dalakoglou, D. (2023). Introducing infrastructural harm: Rethinking moral entanglements, spatio-temporal dynamics, and resistance(s). *Globalizations, 20*(6), 829–848. https://doi.org/10.1080/14747731.2022.2153493

Leal, D. F. (2020). Mass transit shutdowns as a tactical innovation in Bogota. Colombia. *Social Currents, 7*(4), 310–330. https://doi.org/10.1177/2329496520906826

Martinez-Alier, J. (2002). *The environmentalism of the poor: A study of ecological conflicts and valuation*. Edward Elgar Publishing Ltd.

Martinez-Alier, J. (2018). Ecological distribution conflicts and the vocabulary of environmental justice. In V. Dayal, A. Duraiappah, & N. Nawn (Eds.), *Ecology, economy and society* (pp. 187–204). Springer. https://doi.org/10.1007/978-981-10-5675-8_11

Martínez-Alier, J. (2018). Ecological distribution conflicts and the vocabulary of environmental justice. In V. Dayal, A. Duraiappah, & N. Nawn (Eds.), *Ecology, economy and society* (pp. 187–204). Springer.

Martínez-Alier, J., & Walter, M. (2016). Social metabolism and conflicts over extractivism. In F. de Castro, B. Hogenboom, & M. Baud (Eds.), *Environmental governance in Latin America* (pp. 58–85). Palgrave Macmillan UK.

Martínez-Alier, J., Baud, M., & Sejenovich, H. (2016). Origins and perspectives of Latin American environmentalism. In F. de Castro, B. Hogenboom, & M. Baud (Eds.), *Environmental governance in Latin America* (pp. 29–57). Palgrave Macmillan UK.

Mayor Aparicio, P., & Bodmer, R. E. (2009). *Pueblos indígenas de la Amazonía peruana*. CETA (Centro de Estudios Teológicos de la Amazonía).

McAdam, D., Boudet, H. S., Davis, J., Orr, R. J., Scott, W. R., & Levitt, R. E. (2010). "Site Fights": Explaining opposition to pipeline projects in the developing world. *Sociological Forum, 25*(3), 401–427. https://doi.org/10.1111/j.1573-7861.2010.01189.x

McNeish, J.-A., & Shapiro, J. (2021). Introduction. In J. Shapiro & J.-A. McNeish (Eds.), *Our extractive age: Expressions of violence and resistance* (pp. 1–15). Routledge.

Mignolo, W. D. (2007). DELINKING: The rhetoric of modernity, the logic of coloniality and the grammar of de-coloniality. *Cultural Studies, 21*(2–3), 449–514. https://doi.org/10.1080/09502380601162647

Moore, J. W. (2000). Sugar and the expansion of the early modern world-economy: Commodity frontiers, ecological transformation, and industrialization. *Review (Fernand Braudel Center), 23*(3), 409–433.

Nixon, R. (2011). *Slow violence and the environmentalism of the poor*. Harvard University Press.

OEC. (2024, May 15). *Colombia (COL) exports, imports, and trade partners*. The Observatory of Economic Complexity. https://oec.world/en/profile/country/col.

O'Faircheallaigh, C. (2014). IR theory and domestic adoption of international norms. *International Politics, 51*(2), 155–176.

Orihuela, J. C., Pérez Cavero, C., & Contreras, C. (2022). Extractivism of the poor: Natural resource commodification and its discontents. *The Extractive Industries and Society, 9*, 100986. https://doi.org/10.1016/j.exis.2021.100986

Pellegrini, L., Arsel, M., Orta-Martínez, M., & Mena, C. F. (2020). International investment agreements, human rights, and environmental justice: The Texaco/Chevron case from the Ecuadorian amazon. *Journal of International Economic Law, 23*(2), 455–468. https://doi.org/10.1093/jiel/jgaa016

Peluso, N. L., & Lund, C. (2011). New frontiers of land control: Introduction. *Journal of Peasant Studies, 38*(4), 667–681. https://doi.org/10.1080/03066150.2011.607692

Robleto, M. L., & Marcelo, W. (1992). *La deuda ecológica, una perspectiva sociopolítica.* Santiago de Chile: Instituto de Ecología Política.

Santos, B. de S. (2016). *Epistemologies of the South: Justice against epistemicide.* Routledge.

Scheidel, A., Del Bene, D., Liu, J., Navas, G., Mingorría, S., Demaria, F., Avila, S., et al. (2020). Environmental conflicts and defenders: A global overview. *Global Environmental Change, 63*, 102104. https://doi.org/10.1016/j.gloenvcha.2020.102104

Schilling-Vacaflor, A. (2017). 'If the company belongs to you, how can you be against it?': Limiting participation and taming dissent in neo-extractivist Bolivia. *The Journal of Peasant Studies, 44*(3), 658–676. https://doi.org/10.1080/03066150.2016.1216984

Schilling-Vacaflor, A., & Flemmer, R. (2015). Conflict transformation through prior consultation? Lessons from Peru. *Journal of Latin American Studies, 47*(4), 811–839. https://doi.org/10.1017/S0022216X15000826

Schilling-Vacaflor, A., Flemmer, R., & Hujber, A. (2018). Contesting the hydrocarbon frontiers: State depoliticizing practices and local responses in Peru. *World Development, 108*, 74–85. https://doi.org/10.1016/j.worlddev.2018.03.019

Sempértegui, A., & Báez, M. (2024). Ontological conflicts in the plurinational state: The case of indigenous resistance against the mirador mega-mining project in Ecuador. *Society & Natural Resources, 37*(5), 660–667. https://doi.org/10.1080/08941920.2023.2228241

Silva, E., Akchurin, M., & Bebbington, A. J. (2018). Policy effects of resistance against mega-projects in Latin America: An introduction. *European Review of Latin American and Caribbean Studies | Revista Europea de Estudios Latinoamericanos y del Caribe*, *0*(106), 23. https://doi.org/10.32992/erlacs.10397

Smith, K. (2020). Order, ordering and disorder. In A. B. Tickner & K. Smith (Eds.), *International relations from the global south: Worlds of difference* (pp. 76–96). Routledge Taylor & Francis Group.

Sovacool, B. K., & Dunlap, A. (2022). Anarchy, war, or revolt? Radical perspectives for climate protection, insurgency and civil disobedience in a low-carbon era. *Energy Research & Social Science, 86*, 102416. https://doi.org/10.1016/j.erss.2021.102416

Sultana, F. (2022). The unbearable heaviness of climate coloniality. *Political Geography, 99*, 102638. https://doi.org/10.1016/j.polgeo.2022.102638

Svampa, M. (2015). Commodities consensus: Neoextractivism and enclosure of the commons in Latin America. *South Atlantic Quarterly, 114*(1), 65–82. https://doi.org/10.1215/00382876-2831290

Temper, L., & Shmelev, S. (2015). Mapping the frontiers and front lines of global environmental justice: The EJAtlas. *Journal of Political Ecology, 22*(1), 256–278. https://doi.org/10.2458/v22i1.21108

Temper, L., Demaria, F., Scheidel, A., Del Bene, D., & Martínez-Alier, J. (2018). The global environmental justice atlas (EJAtlas): Ecological distribution conflicts as forces for sustainability. *Sustainability Science, 13*(3), 573–584. https://doi.org/10.1007/s11625-018-0563-4

Truscello, M. (2020). *Infrastructural brutalism: Art and the necropolitics of infrastructure.* The MIT Press.

Tsing, A. L. (2005). *Friction: An ethnography of global connection.* Princeton University Press.

Valencia, A. (2014). Human rights trade-offs in a context of "systemic lack of freedom": The case of the smelter town of La Oroya. Peru. *Journal of Human Rights, 13*(4), 456–479. https://doi.org/10.1080/14754835.2014.960962

Valladares, C., & Boelens, R. (2017). Extractivism and the rights of nature: Governmentality, 'convenient communities' and epistemic pacts in Ecuador. *Environmental Politics, 26*(6), 1015–1034. https://doi.org/10.1080/09644016.2017.1338384

van Laak, D. (2018). *Alles im Fluss: Die Lebensadern unserer Gesellschaft—Geschichte und Zukunft der Infrastruktur.* S. Fischer.

van Laak, D. (2023). *Lifelines of our society: A global history of infrastructure.* The MIT Press.
Velho, R., & Ureta, S. (2019). Frail modernities: Latin American infrastructures between repair and ruination. *Tapuya: Latin American Science, Technology and Society*, *2*(1), 428–441. https://doi.org/10.1080/25729861.2019.1678920.
Verdonck, L., & Desmet, E. (2017). Moving human rights jurisprudence to a higher gear: Rewriting the case of the Kichwa indigenous people of Sarayaku v Ecuador (IACtHR). In E. Brems & E. Desmet (Eds.), *Integrated human rights in practice: Rewriting human rights decisions* (pp. 445–504). Edward Elgar Publishing Limited.
Wapner, P. (2021). Thresholds of injustice: Challenging the politics of environmental postponement. In J. Shapiro & J.-A. McNeish (Eds.), *Earthscan from Routledge. Our extractive age: Expressions of violence and resistance* (pp. 48–67). Routledge.
Wolff, J. (2017). Contesting extractivism: Conceptual, theoretical and normative reflections. In B. Engels & K. Dietz (Eds.), *Contested extractivism, society and the state: Struggles over mining and land* (pp. 243–255). Palgrave Macmillan.
World Bank. (2017a). *Rethinking infrastructure in Latin America and the Caribbean spending better to achieve more.* https://documents.worldbank.org/en/publication/documents-reports/documentdetail/676711491563967405/rethinking-infrastructure-in-latin-america-and-the-caribbean-spending-better-to-achieve-more.
World Bank. (2017b, April 7). *Spending better, not necessarily more, key to improving infrastructure in Latin America and the Caribbean.* World Bank Group (Press release No 2017/205/LAC). https://www.worldbank.org/en/news/press-release/2017/04/07/spending-better-not-necessarily-more-key-to-improving-infrastructure-in-latin-america-and-the-caribbean (Accessed 01 April 2024)
World Bank. (2022a). *European Union copper ores and concentrates imports by country. European Union Copper ores and concentrates imports by country | 2021 | Data.* https://wits.worldbank.org/trade/comtrade/en/country/EUN/year/2021/tradeflow/Imports/partner/ALL/product/260300.
World Bank. (2022b). *European Union soya beans; whether or not broken imports by country. European Union soya beans; whether or not broken imports by country | 2022 | Data.* https://wits.worldbank.org/trade/comtrade/en/country/EUN/year/2022/tradeflow/Imports/partner/ALL/product/120100.
World Bank. (2022c). *European Union sugars; cane sugar, raw, in solid form, not containing added flavouring or colouring matter imports by country. | 2022 | Data.* https://wits.worldbank.org/trade/comtrade/en/country/EUN/year/2022/tradeflow/Imports/partner/ALL/product/170111.
World Bank. (2022d, October 4). *Social and infrastructure investments can drive growth and shared prosperity in Latin America and the Caribbean.* World Bank Group (Press Release No: 2023/LAC). https://www.worldbank.org/en/news/press-release/2022/10/04/perspectivas-inversiones-sociales-infraestructura-pueden-impulsar-crecimiento-america-latina-caribe (Accessed 01 April 2014).

Riccarda Flemmer is Junior-Professor for "Political Struggles in the Global South" at the Institute of Political Science at the University of Tübingen. She previously worked as a researcher at the German Institute for Global and Area Studies (GIGA) and the University of Hamburg. She is council member of the Amazonia Section at the Latin American Studies Association (LASA), member of the focal group on 'Ethnographic Methods' of the Deutsche Vereinigung für Politikwissenschaft (DVPW) as well as part of the Environmental Justice Network (EnJust), the Political Ecology Network (POLLEN) and the Red de Estudios sobre las Resistencias Indígenas (RERI). Her research interests include indigenous peoples' rights, environmental conflicts, Rights of Nature and the ontological politics of human-nature relations.

Blue-Green Infrastructure as an Innovative Approach to Sustainable Development

Heidi Elisabeth Megerle

Abstract

The term 'infrastructure' has been predominantly associated with grey infrastructure, which encompasses technical forms thereof such as transport routes and supply and disposal facilities. 'Blue-green infrastructure', however, represents a relatively new and innovative concept. It posits that ecosystems and their associated services—such as intact floodplains, which serve as a natural form of flood protection—are as crucial for the development of a country, the functionality of its settlements and the well-being of its inhabitants as grey infrastructure is. Blue-green infrastructure encompasses both public and private, near-natural and naturally grown water and green spaces which are planned and maintained as a kind of network. The implementation and maintaining of blue-green infrastructure can contribute significantly to adaptation to the effects of climate change and the realisation of Sustainable Development Goal (SDG) 3 (Good Health and Well-being), SDG 6 (Clean Water and Sanitation), SDG 11 (Sustainable Cities and Communities) and SDG 13 (Climate Action), in particular. While there is growing evidence of positive momentum regarding blue-green infrastructure's implementation in the Global North, this has been less noticeable in the Global South to date.

Keywords

Blue-green infrastructure · Ecosystem services · Climate change · Sponge city · Greenbelt movement

H. Megerle (✉)
Hochschule für Forstwirtschaft Rottenburg, Rottenburg, Germany
e-mail: megerle@hs-rottenburg.de

H.-J. Bieling et al. (eds.), *Transnational Infrastructures and the Transformation of Global Orders*, RaumFragen: Stadt – Region – Landschaft,
https://doi.org/10.1007/978-3-031-74846-2_10

1 Introduction: Blue-Green Infrastructure as an Innovative Concept

The term 'infrastructure' is generally associated with grey infrastructure: that is,

> the basic equipment of an economy with facilities that can be counted as part of the economic capital stock [...]. Classic examples are transport networks (roads, railways, waterways) and supply and disposal facilities (energy, water, communication networks), without whose existence private sector production of goods or services would not be possible, or at least only with less efficiency (business-related infrastructure). (Klodt, 2018)

'Blue-green infrastructure' or 'blue and green infrastructure' (used synonymously from here on) is a relatively new concept. It embodies the idea that ecosystems and their services—such as intact floodplains, which act as a natural form of flood protection—are just as indispensable for a country's development as grey, or technical, infrastructure is. Blue-green infrastructure is hereby defined as.

> a network of natural, semi-natural and restored areas designed and managed at different spatial scales (from local to global), that encompasses all major types of ecosystems (marine, terrestrial and freshwater), and that aims to conserve biodiversity, mitigate emissions of greenhouse gases, enable societal adaptation to climate change, and deliver a wide range of other ecosystem services. (da Silva and Wheeler, 2017, p. 33)

Blue and green infrastructure thus includes both public and private, near-natural and naturally grown water and green spaces which are planned and maintained as a kind of network. Green infrastructure can constitute large-scale landscapes, habitats or ecosystems (e.g. floodplain forests) down to individual elements (e.g. trees), while blue infrastructure can encompass both natural bodies of water and newly created water areas (Winker et al. 2020, p. 16), but also 'invisible water elements' (e.g. flood retention basins) Blue-green infrastructure refers, then, to the entirety of these elements and their areas of interaction; as such, urban green spaces or floodplains are not green infrastructure per se but contribute, rather, to the fulfilling of its functions as core parts of the ecosystem. It follows that not all water and green spaces fall under this definition unless they provide certain services (Heiland et al., 2017, p. 23).

Blue-green infrastructure has various advantages over grey infrastructure. It has proven to be a natural tool for generating ecological, economic and social benefits and can help avoid the construction of expensive infrastructure when nature provides not only more cost-effective but also more resilient solutions. The latter, in turn, often offer local employment opportunities, such as planting/maintaining urban greenery to mitigate the urban heat island effect (European Commission, 2013, pp. 2–3). Blue-green infrastructure can also make a significant contribution to the realisation of many Sustainable Development Goals (SDGs), particularly SDG 3 (Good Health and Well-being), SDG 6 (Clean Water and Sanitation), SDG 11 (Sustainable Cities and Communities) and SDG 13 (Climate Action).

To this day, both as a term and as a concept, blue-green infrastructure is used very differently in the literature and in practice depending on the context to hand and perspective chosen (Heiland et al., 2017, p. 22). The term 'green' infrastructure is often used in isolation, despite the great importance of 'blue' infrastructure—with the latter instead being merely subsumed to the former, for example in the European Union's 'Green Infrastructure Strategy' (European Commission 2013, henceforth GIS). Due to the complexity of the topic and the rapidly growing research field on it, only brief insight can be given on its contours in the following.

2 Origins, State of the Art and Implementation

Since the 1980s, there has been ongoing discussion about considering ecosystems a form of infrastructure (da Silva and Wheeler 2017, p. 32). The first mention of 'ecological infrastructure' occurred in 1984 among scientists participating in a meeting on urban planning organised by UNESCO's Man and the Biosphere Programme (UNESCO, 1984, p. 42). The term 'green infrastructure', meanwhile, was first noted in the United States in 2004 (da Silva and Wheeler 2017, p. 33).

A study by Ying et al. (2022) found that scientific publications on green infrastructure increased significantly between 1995 and 2019, and especially after 2013. While less than ten studies were published per year between 1995 and 2008, from 2014 onwards there were consistently more than one hundred studies annually, reaching almost 600 in number in 2019 alone. Dominant here have been publications from the developed world (Europe, US) and China. Studies in developing countries have so far played only a subordinate role. Research projects focus mainly on agglomerations (da Silva and Wheeler, 2017, p. 32), and thematically on stormwater management, ecosystem services, biodiversity conservation and climate change (Ying et al., 2022). To date, the term 'green infrastructure' has, as noted, often taken precedence. Publications explicitly referring to 'blue infrastructure' have mostly appeared only in the last decade and represent a very small proportion of the scientific publications (da Silva and Wheeler, 2017, p. 33).

The European Commission's 2013 GIS includes the following four priority areas:

- Promoting green infrastructure in key policy areas;
- Improving information, strengthening the knowledge base and advancing innovation;
- Enhancing access to finance;
- Contributing to the development of green-infrastructure projects at the EU level

Various other EU strategies also promote blue-green infrastructure, such as its 'Biodiversity Strategy for 2030' (henceforth, BDS 2030). In 2017, Germany published its 'Federal Green Infrastructure Concept' (Heiland et al., 2017) to support the implementation of the GIS. This makes it the only EU member state to have adopted a national strategy hereon to date (European Commission, 2019a, p. 18).

3 Blue-Green infrastructure and Ecosystem Services

Blue-green infrastructure yields a broad spectrum of ecosystem services, ones often multifunctional in character. Ecosystem services constitute the diverse benefits that nature provides to humans. The Millennium Ecosystem Assessment (MA, 2005, p. VI) identifies four categories to such ecosystem services:

- **Providing ecosystem services** include renewable resources such as wood, water, food and similar for human use
- **Supporting ecosystem services** include functions such as oxygen production, carbon sequestration or primary production, soil formation, nutrient and water cycles
- **Regulating ecosystem services** include functions such as regulation of air, soil and water quality, temperature control and CO_2 storage (climate regulation)
- **Cultural ecosystem services**, in contrast to the other three categories, are intangible and satisfy human needs through ecosystems' various aesthetic, contemplative, spiritual, religious, cognitive, educational and recreational effects

Natural ecosystems can provide many of these services simultaneously. This multifunctionality is one of the key functions of blue-green infrastructure. For example, near-natural flood protection solutions can provide additional aspects of groundwater recharge, water purification, CO_2 storage, biodiversity maintenance and microclimate enhancement. Depending on the design, there are also opportunities for recreation, human health and landscape aesthetics (see Fig. 1).

In the following section, three select aspects are examined in more detail, with a particular focus on sustainable water management.

4 Climate Change and Blue-Green Infrastructure

Climate change has many effects, including an increase in extreme weather events (see Sect. 6) as well as periods of drought and higher temperatures. The latter are more pronounced in urban areas than in rural ones due to denser structural development, higher levels of sealing and less air circulation. This urban heat effect poses significant health risks to vulnerable groups (e.g. the elderly) and can lead, among other things, to higher mortality rates (Leal Filho et al., 2018, p. 1140). Among the at least 30,000 additional extreme weather-related deaths in Germany since 2000, 99 per cent can be attributed to heat events (BMWK 2023, p. 5).

Studies suggest that in the two decades between 2000 and 2021 alone, the consequences of climate change have caused damages totalling some €145 billion. Future costs, meanwhile, will be between €280 billion and €900 billion by 2050. However, the total costs are expected to be much higher, as such a forecast only includes those measurable in monetary terms, and in doing so excludes loss of biodiversity (flora and

Fig. 1 Near-natural multifunctional flood protection on the Neckar River near Börstingen, Germany. (Megerle, 2018)

fauna), declining quality of life, additional deaths as well as impacts on water management, coastal protection and other ecosystem services (BMWK 2023, p. 6). Blue-green infrastructure promises, accordingly, to make a significant contribution to reducing climate change impacts and thus associated costs.

Previous policy responses have been based primarily on mitigation. However, as the impacts of climate change are increasingly being felt despite a wide range of efforts to combat it, municipal areas have a particular responsibility here given that these effects closely intersect with the specific characteristics of the urban climate. As such, adaptation measures need to be implemented in parallel with mitigation ones to safeguard inhabitants' quality of life in the long term. Urban greenery is one medium which can help mitigate the effects of climate change. Trees provide shade in hot weather, green roofs improve the insulation of buildings and green spaces of all kinds help to increase the infiltration rate of rainwater.

In addition to their climatic effects, urban green spaces have been an important urban planning tool since at least the nineteenth century to ensure the healthiest possible living conditions, in particular by filtering air pollutants. Green spaces and gardens, in particular the community gardens proliferating in large cities in recent years, furthermore have an important social function and make a significant contribution to preserving biodiversity (see Fig. 2). Urban forests are of particular importance, as they can provide many ecosystem services simultaneously—including cooling, water storage and local recreation (Jay et al. 2015).

Strategically planned blue-green infrastructure can contribute to mitigating urban heat effects (Gunawardena et al., 2017) given green spaces have a cooling impact on the environment (see Fig. 2). Diverse wooded areas are particularly effective in this respect. Measurements in the Hambacher Forest showed that it was on average 11 °C cooler than neighbouring open areas; in summer, the difference in temperature was up to 22 °C (Ibisch et al., 2019, p. 2). Spruce forests can see up to 45,000 L of water evaporate per hectare per day, deciduous forests up to 70,000 l per ha per day. Forester Pertl estimates the evaporation and cooling capacity of forests to be 100 to 150 times higher than the energy value of wood production (interview in Scheub & Schwarzer, 2023, p. 108).

Trees are an essential element in creating a high quality of life in urban areas (see Fig. 3). They also make an important contribution to climate change mitigation, air quality and adaptation. Larger trees can evaporate more than 100 l of water per day (Pallasch et al., 2022, p. 753). These 100 l correspond to a cooling capacity of 70 kilowatt-hours, equivalent to that of two average household air conditioners per day (Ellison et al., 2017, p. 54). The absorption and reflection of solar radiation by large canopy trees can result in temperature differences of up to 18 °C at the street surface, the immediate environment of pedestrians (Pearlmutter et al., 2017, p. 2). Trees with deep-root systems can maintain this cooling capacity even during periods of prolonged drought. Temperature

Fig. 2 Urban gardens in Bordeaux, France; green infrastructure with social and ecological functions. (Megerle 2022)

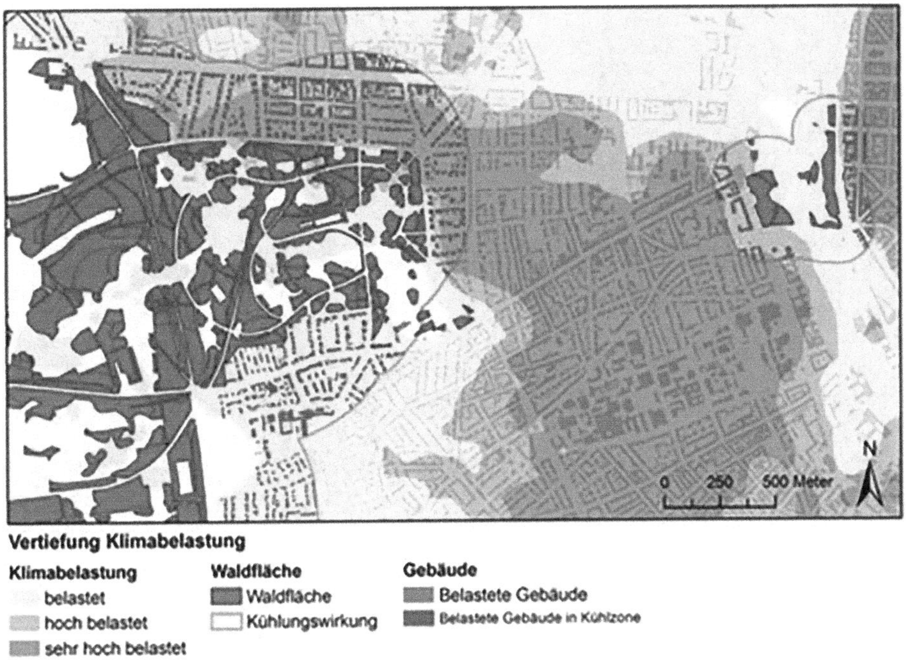

Fig. 3 Cooling capacity of urban forests in Cologne. (Niepmann, 2019, p. 54)

reduction correlates with stand size and can have an effect 200–400 m deep into the surrounding development (Doick et al., 2014). Although larger stands cause greater temperature reductions in their surroundings, small, dispersed stands ultimately impact a more sizeable area due to their larger contact surface with surrounding buildings (Jaganmohan et al., 2016). Green cities have significantly lower temperatures overall (see Mutch et al., 2017). Apart from the fact that urban greenery in general has very positive effects on residents' psyche and well-being, it is estimated that increasing the amount in European cities to 30 per cent could prevent 40 per cent of premature heat-related deaths (Iungmann et al. 2023, p. 577). (Fig. 4)

For historical reasons, the city of Cologne has a relatively high proportion of urban forests. A study of their cooling capacity (from an area of 1 ha) showed that around 40 per cent of Cologne's urban span falls within these forests' cooling areas. Within this geography, there are almost 16 million m^2 taken up by buildings, 62 per cent of which are residential. In total, 35 per cent of the future climate-impacted areas occupied by buildings in Cologne will benefit from the forests' regulation, helping mitigate rising temperatures and make them more bearable (Niepmann, 2019).

In terms of cooling effect, coniferous and deciduous trees are almost equivalent. Although free-standing deciduous trees with open, well-ventilated crowns have a higher transpiration and thus cooling capacity (Lyr et al., 1992; Scholz et al., 2018), coniferous

Fig. 4 Urban greenery in Chambéry, France. (Megerle 2022)

Fig. 5 Biodiversity-rich green spaces on the grounds of the Université Savoie Mont Blanc, France. (Megerle 2022)

stands have greater evapotranspiration values due to the larger leaf mass and the resulting increase in interception evaporation (Zimmermann et al., 2008). In general, loose stands with large-crowned, heat- and drought-tolerant tree species are recommended to avoid the stagnation of air masses. In addition, the soil's water availability and balancing capacity should be ensured by avoiding compaction and guaranteeing a stable stand structure as well as planting and maintaining species of tree supportive of this (Niepmann, 2019). When water bodies are restored or newly created, increased evaporation not only provides greater cooling but also contributes to increased precipitation through heightened water vapour (Scheub & Schwarzer, 2023, p. 61). As outlined above, this applies similarly to green spaces—especially forests.

5 Biodiversity, Species Decline and Blue-Green Infrastructure

Worldwide, there has been a drastic decline in biodiversity. In Germany, almost one-third of all animal and plant species are currently considered to be endangered. The decline in the total number of flying insects by more than 75 per cent is particularly dramatic (Hallmann et al., 2017). Changes in land use (including increasing soil sealing and intensification of agriculture) and the effects of climate change (including increasing periods of drought) are considered to be the main drivers of species decline (Drenckhahn et al. 2020, p. 11).

Blue-green infrastructure can counteract this decline in biodiversity by preserving natural ecosystems, but also by creating green spaces as close to nature as possible and by restoring water bodies to provide diverse habitats. Greenways and green corridors can link habitats and are important elements in biotope networks. Blue-green infrastructure, which helps to mitigate the effects of climate change and contributes to sustainable water management, also has a positive impact on biodiversity and species diversity, especially if it is done with native plants and can therefore provide (new) habitats for numerous species of animal.

6 Sustainable Water Management, the 'Sponge City' Concept and Blue-Green Infrastructure

Climate change is leading, as detailed, to more frequent droughts and a growing number of extreme weather events, often accompanied by floods and heavy rainfall. Low precipitation from 2018 to 2022, however, has caused soils in Germany to dry out and groundwater levels to fall, with significant consequences for vegetation (UFZ, 2023). In the context of climate change, urban areas in particular are facing ever-greater challenges due to periods of drought on the one hand and episodes of flooding and heavy rainfall on the other.

The high degree of sealing combined with a low proportion of green spaces in urban centres results in a reduced infiltration rate and therewith increased surface runoff (Pearlmutter et al., 2017, p. 43) (see Fig. 6). Rainwater either cannot be stored at all or not sufficiently, seeing both the aforementioned increased surface runoff—possibly with flooding—as well as reduced groundwater recharge, which is essential for the drinking water supply as well as for vegetation. Important regulating variables in the soil and groundwater balance, such as evapotranspiration, water storage, groundwater recharge, capillary rise, surface runoff and material shifts, are hereby affected (Haase & Sauerwein, 2016, p. 68). Heavy rainfall often then leads to flooding, as the urban infrastructure is usually not sufficiently dimensioned for these extreme weather events. As up to 90 per cent of rainwater in cities runs off on the surface (Pauleit & Duhme, 2000), pollutants such as particulate matter, fuels, oils, heavy metals and similar are washed into the sewage system and receiving waters (Xiao et al., 1998). The high degree of sealing also results in significantly lower evapotranspiration, which reduces air humidity. All of this, ultimately, has a negative impact on residents, plants and animals.

The 'sponge city' concept was developed to address these challenges. Its overarching goal is a near-natural and climate-adapted rainwater management system. Precipitation

Fig. 6 Completely sealed area in the Europaviertel in Stuttgart, Germany. (Megerle 2013)

is to be retained in the city, stored, used in a targeted manner or allowed to evaporate (Siemer, 2022, p. 55). To this end, extensive new facilities will be built or the blue-green infrastructure redesigned. Wooded areas and ground-covering vegetation provide temporary storage by intercepting water. The capacity of this temporary buffering depends on tree species, tree size and/or crown density (Livesley et al., 2014), stand density (Armson et al., 2013), the greening period of the trees (Inkiläinen et al., 2013; Kermavnar & Vilhar, 2017) and the distribution and intensity of precipitation. In addition, trees stabilise the soil and protect it from leaching and erosion caused by heavy rainfall (Konijnendijk et al. 2005, p. 97). The amount of water stored varies considerably, ranging from 4 to 50 per cent (Kermavnar & Vilhar, 2017; Xiao & McPherson, 2002; Xiao et al., 1998). Trees with large, dense crowns and a high leaf mass store particularly notable amounts of water (Xiao et al., 1998). A high degree of stocking with dense, multilayered stands and ground-covering vegetation is also beneficial. Similar to cooling, the spatial distribution of interconnected small and large green areas is also more efficient (Pearlmutter et al., 2017, p. 45) (see Fig. 7).

A pioneer of the sponge city movement is Denmark's capital, Copenhagen. On 2 July 2011, 20 per cent of the city's annual precipitation fell within the time of just two hours, causing between €1 billion and €1.5 billion in damage (Read & Nielsen, 2013). Following these devastating floods, the municipality developed the 'Cloudburst Management Plan' as part of the 'Copenhagen Climate Adaptation Plan' (City of Copenhagen, 2012, p. 5). Flow analysis showed that wide streets follow old river courses like fingers and meet in the topographically lowest part of the city. These streets have since been

Fig. 7 Greened city of Freiburg im Breisgau, Germany. (Megerle 2023)

redesigned as 'cloudburst boulevards', which drain floodwater to the surface in low-lying areas. Copenhagen's southernmost lake, Sankt Jørgens Sø, was lowered and integrated into a large city park. This has created a backwater volume of 40,000 m^2. The system is complemented by various green spaces which not only provide social (local recreation), health (microclimate) and ecological (biodiversity) benefits but also enable decentralised rainwater management. A total of 30 kms of 'rainwater boulevards' and streets with 500,000 m^2 of green areas are planned as retention basins and 'green streets'. This will relieve pressure on the sewage system to the tune of 1.5 million cubic metres of waste water per year. Although the required financial investment for realising all these outcomes is high (€300–€400 million), it is considerably less than the calculated follow-up costs arising from further heavy rainfall events. The 'blue-green city' concept is, therefore, also 'extremely smart' from an economic perspective (Read & Nielsen, 2013).

7 Blue-Green Infrastructure in the Global North

The key relevance of blue-green infrastructure and its ecosystem services is now increasingly recognised in the Global North, with its implementation—including in spatial, regional and urban planning—becoming more common practice. Within the EU, the GIS and the integration of relevant aspects thereof into the BDS 2030 have played an important role in this regard. Nevertheless, the 'EU Progress Report' (European Commission, 2019b, p. 11) sees both some momentum and positive developments but also further challenges, as a strategic approach to blue-green infrastructure has not yet been taken up at the EU level. Implementation is often small-scale, and the potential economic, health and social benefits of using blue-green rather than grey infrastructure solutions have not been sufficiently considered. Greater effort here should also be made at the member state level.

Overall, blue-green infrastructure will come to be just as 'indispensable' for the functioning of cities and the people inhabiting them as technical and social infrastructure (Breuste et al., 2016, p. 196). Professional planning and implementation as well as sound long-term maintenance are crucial (Stiftung Die grüne Stadt 2020, p. 28). The extensive positive economic gains in play should be better communicated. For example, the European Commission (2019b, p. 1) estimates the monetary value of the Natura 2000 network's ecosystem services alone to stand at €300 billion. If the entire blue-green infrastructure is taken into account, these figures are even higher. If Target 2 of the BDS 2030 ('to conserve and enhance ecosystems and their services through the creation of green infrastructure and the restoration of at least 15 per cent of degraded ecosystems') is achieved, not only could an even wider range of benefits from ecosystem services be realised but so too over €11 billion in direct output and up to 140,000 new jobs.

8 Blue-Green Infrastructure in the Global South

While progress has been made on implementing blue-green infrastructure in the Global North, this is not yet the case in the Global South for a variety of reasons.

African cities in particular are facing rapid urbanisation, which is usually accompanied by the deterioration of existing, often less extensive, blue-green infrastructure. This, in turn, increases vulnerability to climate risks and reduces the already comparatively low quality of life (Breed et al. 2023). Ying et al., (2022, p. 360) therefore see a strong need to accelerate respective studies in/with the Global South. To date, 'green infrastructure' has been under-researched in sub-Saharan Africa, with its benefits often viewed predominantly from the perspective of 'Western' urban considerations alone (Titz and Chiota 2019). As a result, specific planning principles for green infrastructure in the Global South per se are lacking, and its concrete implementation does not yet appear to be gaining the same traction as in developed countries (Breed et al. 2023). Accordingly, the socio-economic, environmental and health benefits of green infrastructure tend to be neglected locally, as related strategies focus mainly on energy, climate adaptation and green growth (Pauleit et al., 2021). In its 'New Urban Agenda', the United Nations explicitly calls for 'safe, inclusive, accessible, green and quality public spaces [in all cities]' (UN Habitat, 2017, p. 5); most major cities in the Global South are far from achieving this, however (see Fig. 8).

Fig. 8 Megacity Tehran, Iran, without green spaces. (Megerle 2018)

The few research projects which do exist concentrate heavily on urban centres. Rural regions, in which a high percentage of the extreme poor live in many countries of the Global South (especially in sub-Saharan Africa), are largely neglected by research on blue-green infrastructure. However, aspects such as 'green grabbing' (see below) and water shortages, which must also be seen within the context of blue-green infrastructure, manifest themselves primarily in these peripheral rural areas. There are, therefore, increasing calls for tangible implementation plans here, as the following quote from Pakistan shows:

> Nature-based solutions have the potential to solve many of our water challenges. We need to do so much more with 'green' infrastructure and harmonise it with 'grey' infrastructure wherever possible by planting new forests, reconnecting rivers to floodplains, restoring wetlands for balancing water cycle for the improvement of human health and livelihoods. (Mirza, 2018)

As a comprehensive examination of blue-green infrastructure in the Global South is not possible within the scope of this chapter, focus will, first, be on the so-called Green Belt Movement and then, second, on the ongoing discussion around green grabbing.

9 The 'Green Belt Movement' and the 'Great Green Wall'

Changes in forest cover are a major driver of climate change. Deforestation caused significant warming of up to 0.28 K/decade relative to average temperature trends in tropical regions (Li et al., 2016, p. 14.372). Further studies have shown that current anthropogenic land-use changes will reduce annual terrestrial evapotranspiration by 5 per cent and increase surface water runoff by 7.6 per cent (Sterling et al., 2013, p. 385).

Extreme rates of deforestation in a country like Burundi (originally 98 per cent Afromontane mountain rainforest, now about 6 per cent forest cover) come with multiple negative impacts. Of particular note here are erosion, a decline both in soil fertility and in farmable land in general, increasing problems with water supply and food security, but also a significant decline in biodiversity. Associated difficulties are with energy supply as well as a noticeable decline in key non-timber products (Megerle et al. 2018) (see Fig. 9).

To address these problems in the African context, Kenyan Nobel Peace Prize winner Wangari Maathai founded the Green Belt Movement in 1977. She had become aware of the link between forest cover and water availability: 'If you destroy the forest then the river will stop flowing, the rains will become irregular, the crops will fail and you will die of hunger and starvation' (The Green Belt Movement, n.d.). After initial difficulties, more than 51 million trees were planted thanks to the increased involvement of women. In 1986, the Pan African Green Belt Network was founded, now spanning 13 African countries. In 2007, the African Union launched its 'Great Green Wall' project, which—with 22 African countries on-board—is working to restore 100 million ha of degraded land, sequester 250 million tonnes of CO_2 and to create 10 million green jobs

Fig. 9 Deforestation in Burundi. (Megerle 2015)

by 2030 (UNCCD 2024). Further relevant initiatives are: UNEP's 'Billion Tree Campaign' launched in 2008; the 'One Trillion Tree Initiative', in support of the 'UN Decade of Ecosystem Restoration' (2020–2030), emerging from the World Economic Forum, Davos, in 2020.

'Green belts' and 'green dams' are seen as infrastructure which 'provides a public ecosystem service' (OSS, 2008, p. 9). They fulfil most of the functions of green infrastructure, to date being found mainly in rural areas of sub-Saharan Africa. There is still great need for further research on them, as well as on blue-green infrastructure in the Global South's urban centres.

10 Green Grabbing and 'Green Colonialism'

The commercialisation of nature—meaning the appropriation of land and resources for environmental purposes (forest reserves, national parks, reforestation for climate compensation)—is frequently called 'green grabbing', in analogy to land grabbing (Fairhead et al., 2012, p. 237). Such practices can play a key role in the instrumentalisation of green infrastructure in the Global South by actors heralding from the Global North. In addition to the general spheres of conflict arising with the appropriation of land and resources (following expropriation, displacement and similar), climate change-related schemes such as carbon credits are of vital importance here, too. The latter are integrated into global power structures and can turn actors in developing countries into winners or losers in these new green markets (Leach et al. 2012). Today's green grabbing has its roots in the colonial appropriation of resources. Lyons and Westoby (2014, p. 14) speak of 'carbon colonialism' in relation to the privatisation and commercialisation of forest resources. According to Fairhead et al. (2012), there is an extraordinarily broad alliance of different actors—environmental and climate activists, (eco)tourism providers but also commodity traders, venture capitalists and pension-fund managers—who are now developing new forms of valuation, commodification and commercialisation vis-à-vis nature and its constitutive elements. Overall, however, individual case assessments should be made, as large protected areas can also represent a vital source of income—especially for the local population, namely via tourism, reforestation measures and CO_2 certificates.

Green grabbing by local actors is also on the rise in the Global South. However, the expansion and development of green infrastructure to mitigate climate risks in the latter's (mega)cities can come at the expense of poorer sections of society and exacerbate inequalities, for example by displacing those concerned from marginal, sometimes illegal, neighbourhoods in order to create green spaces. These sites then become 'green elite ghettos', accessible almost exclusively by the middle and upper classes and tourists (Anguelovski et al., 2019, p. 134).

11 Conclusion and Outlook

Blue-green infrastructure is becoming an increasingly important planning tool in the context of climate change. Torgny Holmgren (2022), Executive Director of the Stockholm International Water Institute, points out that it has long been assumed that grey infrastructure is superior to what nature can provide in the form of mangroves, swamps, meadows and forests. While this is true for technically oriented subsectors, grey infrastructure is often inflexible and thus less adaptable to circumstance, making it less suitable in a changing environment than green infrastructure is. The latter, contrariwise, is more flexible, resilient and self-restoring.

According to Holmgren, combining grey and blue-green infrastructure is the most appropriate way to ensure future-proof and sustainable development. While in the Global North the importance of blue-green infrastructure is increasingly recognised by policy practitioners and thus investigated by researchers, in the Global South there is still considerable need to catch up here. Specifically, both in terms of practical implementation and practice-oriented scholarship.

Acknowledgements The author would like to thank James Powell for his diligent proofreading.

The author would like to thank the state of Baden-Württemberg for funding the research projects in Burundi.

References

Anguelovski, I., Irazábal-Zurita, C., & Connolly, J. T. (2019). Grabbed urban landscapes: Socio-spatial tensions in green infrastructure planning in Medellín. *International Journal of Urban and Regional Research, 43*(1), 133–156.

Armson, D., Stringer, P., & Ennos, A. R. (2013). The effect of street trees and amenity grass on urban surface water runoff in Manchester UK. *Urban Forestry & Urban Greening, 12*(3), 282–286.

Breuste, J., Pauleit, S., Haase, D., & Sauerwein, M. (2016). *Stadtökosysteme. Funktion Management und Entwicklung*. Springer Spektrum.

Breed, C. A., Engemann, K., & Pasgaard, M. (2024). A transdisciplinary multiscaled approach to engage with green infrastructure planning, restoration and use in sub-Saharan Africa. *Urban Ecosystems, 27*(3), 895–907.

Bundesministerium für Wirtschaft und Klimaschutz (2023). Was uns die Folgen des Klimawandels kosten—Zusammenfassung. https://www.ioew.de/fileadmin/user_upload/BILDER_und_Downloaddateien/Publikationen/2023/BMWK-Merkblatt-Klimawandelfolgen_Zusammenfassung.pdf

Christina, A., Du Plessis, T., Engemann, K., Pauleit, S., & Pasgaard, M. (2023). Moving green infrastructure planning from theory to practice in sub-Saharan African cities requires collaborative operationalization. *Urban Forestry & Urban Greening, 89*, Article 128085.

City of Copenhagen (2012). The cloudburst management plan 2012. cph_-_cloudburst_management_plan.pdf (klimatilpasning.dk)

Da Silva, J., Cardoso, M., & Wheeler, E. (2017). Ecosystems as infrastructure. *Perspectives in Ecology and Conservation, 15*(1), 32–35.

Doick, K. J., Peace, A., & Hutchings, T. R. (2014). The role of one large greenspace in mitigating London's nocturnal urban heat island. *Science of the Total Environment, 493*, 662–671.

Drenckhahn, D., Arneth, A., Filser, J., Haberl, H., Hansjürgens, B., Herrmann, B., et al. (2020). Globale Biodiversität in der Krise: Was können Deutschland und die EU dagegen tun? *Deutsche Akademie der Naturforscher Leopoldina. eV-Nationale Akademie der Wissenschaften*. https://www.leopoldina.org/uploads/tx_leopublication/2020_Diskussionspapier_Biodiversitaetskrise_web.pdf

Ellison, D., Morris, C. E., Locatelli, B., Sheil, D., Cohen, J., Murdiyarso, D., et al. (2017). Trees, forests and water: Cool insights for a hot world. *Global Environmental Change, 43*, 51–61.

European Commission (2013). Mitteilung der Kommission an das Europäische Parlament, den Rat, den Europäischen Wirtschafts- und Sozialausschuss und den Ausschuss der Regionen "Grüne Infrastruktur (GI). Aufwertung des europäischen Naturkapitals". COM(2013) 249 final.

European Commission (2019a). Commission staff working document "Additional information on the review of implementation of the green infrastructure strategy". SWD(2019) 184 final.

European Commission (2019b). Report from the Commission to the European Parliament, the council, the European Economic and social committee and the committee of the Regions "Review of progress on implementation of the EU green infrastructure strategy". COM(2019) 236 final.

Fairhead, J., Leach, M., & Scoones, I. (2012). Green grabbing: A new appropriation of nature? *Journal of Peasant Studies, 39*(2), 237–284.

Gunawardena, K. R., Wells, M. J., & Kershaw, T. (2017). Utilising green and bluespace to mitigate urban heat island intensity. *Science of the Total Environment, 584*, 1040–1055.

Haase, D., Sauerwein, M. (2016). Was sind Stadtökosysteme und warum sind sie besonders? In J., Breuste, S.,Pauleit, D. Haase, & M., Sauerwein (Eds.), *Stadtökosysteme. Funktion, Management und Entwicklung* (pp. 61–84). Springer.

Hallmann, C. A., Sorg, M., Jongejans, E., Siepel, H., Hofland, N., Schwan&, H., et al. (2017). More than 75 percent decline over 27 years in total flying insect biomass in protected areas. *PLoS ONE, 12*(10), e0185809.

Heiland, S., Mengel, A., Hänel, K., Geiger, B., Arndt, P., Reppin, N., & et al. (2017). Bundeskonzept Grüne Infrastruktur. Fachgutachten. Bundesamt für Naturschutz-Skripte 457.

Holmgren, T. (2018). Balancing green & grey this world water day. *Global Issues*. https://www.globalissues.org/news/2018/03/20/24037

Ibisch, P., Blumröder, J., & Kriewald, S. (2019). Hambacher Forst in der Krise: Studie zur Beurteilung der mikro und mesoklimatischen Situation sowie Randeffekten. *Greenpeace eV*. https://www.greenpeace.de/publikationen/hambacher_forst.pdf

Inkiläinen, E. N. M., McHale, M. R., Blank, G. B., James, A. L., & Nikinmaa, E. (2013). The role of the residential urban forest in regulating throughfall: A case study in Raleigh, North Carolina, USA. *Landscape and Urban Planning, 119*, 91–103.

Iungman, T, Cirach, M., Marando, F., Barboza, E. P., Khomenko, S., Masselot, P., & et al. (2023). Cooling cities through urban green infrastructure: A health impact assessment of European cities. *The Lancet, 401*(10376), 577–589.

Jaganmohan, M., Knapp, S., Buchmann, C. M., & Schwarz, N. (2016). The bigger, the better? The influence of urban green space design on cooling effects for residential areas. *Journal of Environmental Quality, 45*(1), 134–145.

Jay, M., Selter, A., Wurster, M., & Schraml, U. (2016). Urbaner Wald, urbane Lebensqualität. Die vielfältigen Ökosystemleistungen urbaner Wälder sichtbar machen. Ein Handlungsleitfaden. ifp Arbeitsberichte.

Kermavnar, J., & Vilhar, U. (2017). Canopy precipitation interception in urban forests in relation to stand structure. *Urban Ecosystems, 20*, 1373–1387.

Klodt, H. (2018). Infrastruktur: Definition: Was ist "Infrastruktur"? Springer Gabler. https://wirtschaftslexikon.gabler.de/definition/infrastruktur-39955

Konijnendijk, c., Nilsson, K., Randrup, T., & Schipperijn, J. (Hrsg.) (2005). Urban Forests and Trees. A Reference Book. Berlin, Heidelberg. Springer. http://dx.doi.org/10.1007/3-540-27684-X

Kumar, P. (Ed.) (2010). *The economics of ecosystems and biodiversity: ecological and economic foundations*. Routledge.

Leach, M., Fairhead, J., & Fraser, J. (2014). Green grabs and biochar: Revaluing African soils and farming in the new carbon economy. *Journal of Peasant Studies, 39*(2), 285–308.

Leal Filho, W., Icaza, L. E., Neht, A., Klavins, M., & Morgan, E. A. (2018). Coping with the impacts of urban heat islands. A literature based study on understanding urban heat vulnerability and the need for resilience in cities in a global climate change context. *Journal of Cleaner Production, 171*, 1140–1149.

Li, Yan, Z., Maosheng, M., David J., Motesharrei, S., Mu, Q., Kalnay, E., & et al (2016). Potential and actual impacts of deforestation and afforestation on land surface temperature. *Journal of Geophysical Research: Atmospheres, 121*(24), 14–372.

Livesley, S. J., Baudinette, B., & Glover, D. (2014). Rainfall interception and stem flow by eucalypt street trees–The impacts of canopy density and bark type. *Urban Forestry & Urban Greening, 13*(1), 192–197.

Lyons, K., & Westoby, P. (2014). Carbon colonialism and the new land grab: Plantation forestry in Uganda and its livelihood impacts. *Journal of Rural Studies, 36*, 13–21.

Lyr, H., Fiedler, H.-J., & Tranquillini, W. (1992). *Physiologie und Ökologie der Gehölze*. Fischer.

MA (2005). *Ecosystems and human well-being: Synthesis.* Island Press: Millennium Ecosystem Assessment. https://www.millenniumassessment.org/documents/document.356.aspx.pdf

Mirza, S. (2018). *Water shortage of 31m acre feet expected by 2025.* https://www.dawn.com/news/1398099

Mutch, E., Doick, K., Davies, H., Handley, P., Hudson, M., Kiss, S., & et al. (2017). Understanding the value of Southampton's urban trees. Results of the 2016 i-Tree Eco survey. *University of Southampton, Forest Research, Treeconomics and Southampton City Council.*

Niepmann, J. (2019). *Regulierende Ökosystemleistungen von urbanen Wäldern sichtbar machen. Eine GIS-basierte Analyse am Beispiel der Stadt Köln.* Hochschule für Forstwirtschaft (Abschlussarbeit).

OSS (2008). The Great Green Wall initiative of the Sahara and the Sahel. *Sahara and Sahel Observatory.* https://www.fao.org/3/ax355e/ax355e.pdf

Pallasch, M., Geisler, D., & Kluge, B. (2022). Straßenbäume und dezentrale Versickerung als Beitrag wassersensibler Stadtentwicklung-Teil 2. *Korrespondenz Abwasser, Abfall, 69*(9), 747–758.

Pauleit, S., Vasquéz, A., Maruthaveeran, S., Liu, L., & Cilliers, S. S. (2021). Urban green infrastructure in the Global South. In. C. Shackleton, S., Cilliers, E., Davoren & M. Du Toit. (Eds.), *Urban ecology in the Global South* (pp. 107–143). Springer International.

Pauleit, S., & Duhme, F. (2000). Assessing the environmental performance of land cover types for urban planning. *Landscape and Urban Planning, 52*(1), 1–20.

Pearlmutter, D., Calfapietra, C., Samson, R., O'Brien, L., Ostoić, S. K., Sanesi, G., & del Amo, R. A. (Eds.). (2017). *The urban forest Cultivating green infrastructure for people and the environment.* Springer. https://doi.org/10.1007/978-3-319-50280-9

Read, J., & Nielsen, C. N. (2013). Wolkenbruch in Kopenhagen. *Stadt + Grün, 08.* https://stadtundgruen.de/artikel/wolkenbruch-in-kopenhagen-17724

Scheub, U., & Schwarzer, S. (2023). *Aufbäumen gegen die Dürre.* Oekom-Verlag.

Scholz, T., Hof, A., & Schmitt, T. (2018). Cooling effects and regulating ecosystem services provided by urban trees—novel analysis approaches using urban tree cadastre data. *Sustainability, 10*(3), 712. https://doi.org/10.3390/su10030712

Siemer, A. (2022). *Klimaanpassung und Schwammstadt als Querschnittsaufgabe der Stadtplanung.* Rhombos, *80*, 51–60. https://doi.org/10.26084/14dfns-p006

Sterling, S. M., Ducharne, A., & Polcher, J. (2013). The impact of global land-cover change on the terrestrial water cycle. *Nature Climate Change, 3*(4), 385–390.

Stiftung Die grüne Stadt (2020). Grüne Städte, Städte zum Leben: Daten, Fakten, Argumente für mehr Grün in der Stadt. https://die-gruene-stadt.de/wp-content/uploads/2022/04/dgs-broschuere-gruenestaedte-2021-1.pdf

The Green Belt Movement (n.d.). *Tree Planting and Water Harvesting.* https://www.greenbeltmovement.org/what-we-do/tree-planting-for-watersheds

Titz, A., & Chiotha, S. S. (2019). Pathways for sustainable and inclusive cities in Southern and Eastern Africa through urban green infrastructure? *Sustainability, 11*(10), 2729. https://doi.org/10.3390/su11102729

UFZ (2023). Dürren in Deutschland. *Helmholtz Zentrum für Umweltforschung.* https://www.ufz.de/index.php?de=47252

UN Habitat (2017). New urban agenda. *United Nations Habitat* https://habitat3.org/wp-content/uploads/NUA-English.pdf

UNCCD (2023). Great green wall initiative. *United Nations Convention to Combat Desertification.* https://www.unccd.int/our-work/ggwi

UNEP (2008). Plant for the planet: The billion tree campaign. *United Nations Environment Programme.* https://wedocs.unep.org/bitstream/handle/20.500.11822/7661/- Plant%20 for%20the%20Planet_%20%20The%20Billion%20Tree%20Campaign-2008810.pdf?isAllowed=y&sequence=5

UNESCO. (1984). Final report, programme on man and the biosphere (MAP). International Experts Meeting on Ecological Approaches to Urban Planning. *United Nations Educational, Scientific and Cultural Organization, MAB Report Series, 57*, 1–63.

WE Forum (2020). One trillion trees: World Economic Forum launches plan to help nature and the climate. *World Economic Forum*. https://www.weforum.org/agenda/2020/01/one-trillion-trees-world- economic-forum-launches-plan-to-help-nature-and-the-climate/

Winker, M., Deffner, J., Rohrbach, M., Schramm, E., & Stein, M. (2022). Enhancing blue-green infrastructure in German cities with the involvement of urban society: Insights from Frankfurt/Main and Stuttgart. *Blue-Green Systems, 4*(2), 230–246.

Xiao, Q., & McPherson, E. G. (2002). Rainfall interception by Santa Monica's municipal urban forest. *Urban Ecosystems, 6*, 291–302.

Xiao, Q., McPherson, E. G., Simpson, J. R., & Ustin, S. L. (1998). Rainfall interception by Sacramento's urban forest. *Arboriculture & Urban Forestry (AUF), 24*(4), 235–244.

Ying, J., Zhang, X., Zhang, Y., & Bilan, S. (2022). Green infrastructure: Systematic literature review. *Economic Research-Ekonomska Istraživanja, 35*(1), 343–366.

Zimmermann, L., Raspe, Stephan, S., Christoph, & Grimmeisen, W. (2008). Wasserverbrauch von Wäldern. *LWF aktuell, 66*, 16–20.

Heidi Elisabeth Megerle studied Geography (diploma) at the University of Tübingen with an integrated semester abroad at the University of Aix-en-Provence. After working for several years in applied geography (including international nature conservation, environmental impact assessments, Local Agenda 21), she completed her doctorate and habilitation at the Institute of Geography at the University of Tübingen. Since October 2009, she has been Professor of Applied Geography and Planning at the University of Applied Forest Sciences in Rottenburg am Neckar, Germany, where she is also Director of the programme Water Resource Management. Her research focuses on sustainable regional development and tourism, especially geotourism, with a geographical focus on Southwest Germany, France and Burundi.

Landscape Conflicts within Germany's Energy Transition

Corinna Jenal and Olaf Kühne

Abstract

The transposition from nuclear power and fossil fuels to renewables as part of the energy transition is bringing about a profound change, both technologically and socially, and one which is also reflected in the physical space. However, this evolution is by no means smooth sailing, with it igniting social conflicts of varying intensity. The chapter, accordingly, examines landscape conflicts in the context of Germany's energy transition, particularly in connection with wind turbines and the expansion of the electricity grid. It draws on Karl Popper's three-world theory and Ralf Dahrendorf's theory of social conflicts to shed light on the complexity of the landscape phenomenon and on the resulting tensions. The latter's dimensions and root causes are presented on the basis of empirical studies and theoretical analyses, wherein the diverging demands on the landscape and their interpretations in different social contexts play a central role. The state as key actor in and framework provider for conflict regulation is also considered, as are the associated challenges at various levels. An outlook on the future of landscape conflicts in this context is offered in conclusion, emphasising the importance of a productive and constructive debate on the diverging interests of the different parties involved.

C. Jenal (✉) · O. Kühne
Fachbereich Geowissenschaften, Universität Tübingen, Tübingen, Germany
e-mail: corinna.jenal@uni-tuebingen.de

O. Kühne
e-mail: olaf.kuehne@uni-tuebingen.de

H.-J. Bieling et al. (eds.), *Transnational Infrastructures and the Transformation of Global Orders*, RaumFragen: Stadt – Region – Landschaft,
https://doi.org/10.1007/978-3-031-74846-2_11

Keywords

Landscape · Energy transition · Conflicts · Three-world theory · Social conflict · Dahrendorf · Popper

1 Introduction

The undertaking to convert electricity generation based on nuclear energy and fossil fuels to renewable alternatives necessitates comprehensive technological and social change, with a corresponding impact on the physical space. This shift is not happening without strong pushback, however, with so-called social conflicts of varying degrees of intensity being ignited in the process. These developments—both the (social) change and the experienced conflictuality—do not represent exceptionalisms, but can rather be seen as a normal case of human development (cf. Dahrendorf, 1963, 2017). A key area of conflict in the physical implementation of new (wind turbines, photovoltaics and similar) or upgraded (powerlines) energy infrastructure is that of the landscape. Opponents in particular often speak of a 'destruction' of the latter which must be averted, whereas proponents focus on existing needs (among many others, see: Kühne, 2019b; Kühne & Weber, 2018 [online first 2017]; Weber et al., 2017a, b). It is important, though, to understand 'landscape' as more than just physical space, in being a complex phenomenon which, per Karl Popper (1979), encompasses several worlds or dimensions and can, in consequence, have a conflictual effect both intra- and interdimensionally.

This chapter synthesises, accordingly, the key findings of two studies on landscape conflicts in Germany's energy transition: namely, on how wind turbines and electricity grid expansion are central components here, respectively (Weber et al., 2016). Their findings are supplemented by the surveying of the relevant state of the art as well as by our own studies on changes to material space interpreted as 'landscape', beyond just in the primary context of the energy transition. The results are also classified based on the theory of three landscapes and of social conflicts (Dahrendorf, 1963, 1969b, 1994).

To gain a deeper understanding of this complexity of 'landscape', the phenomenon is first analysed on the basis of Popper's (1979) three-worlds approach. Then we show how social conflicts in Ralf Dahrendorf's (2017) sense can arise. Finally, we look at current developments regarding the energy transition and ignited conflict, before concluding with an outlook on what the future might hold.

2 Theory of Three Worlds and Three Landscapes

Popper divides the world into three worlds: into the one of material objects (World 1); into the one of individual consciousness, which can also include subconscious experience (World 2); and, into the world of cultural content with "all planned or intended products of human mental activity" (Popper, 2019 [1987], p. 17) (World 3). The latter can be understood anthropologically as 'culture' (Popper, 2019 [1987]). With World 3, Popper extends contemporary understandings of the world: according to a materialistic worldview, only World 1 is recognised as 'real'; according to an immaterialist worldview, only World 2 matters. There are also dualistic outlooks which declare Worlds 1 and 2 to both be 'real'—namely, by granting cultural content such as theories and all intellectual, artistic, creative achievements a life of their own.

It should be emphasised that these worlds are not separate from each other, but rather find themselves intertwined in a hybrid manner. For example, when a wind turbine or powerline is a material object it is part of World 1, but as an intellectual and creative achievement it is also constitutive of World 3—as created, indeed, from World 2. This also makes the latter's vital importance clear, as only this World 2 is respectively connected to Worlds 1 and 3 (Popper, 1973). Humans, in turn, have a stake in all three worlds: they have a body (World 1), a consciousness (World 2) and engage in the world of cultural content (World 3). Popper (2011 [1947]) emphasises, furthermore, how Worlds 2 and 3 are constitutively interconnected, in that they not only depend on each other but also owe their existence to one another. Thus, society with its cultural content in World 3 requires human existence; conversely, the development of the individual and their consciousness (World 2) is interwoven into and tied back to the social conditions, dependencies and possibilities informing World 2 (Popper, 2011 [1947]). Popper thus sets himself apart from the classical liberal position, which focuses in particular on the individual's own achievements and merits.

In order to be able to influence Worlds 1 and 3, however, World 2 requires the development of awareness of that potential. Also, the ability to reflect on the moral norms of society—alongside not submitting to them unconditionally (Dahrendorf, 1979, 2002; see also: Kühne et al., 2023; Popper, 2011 [1947]). As part of World 2, humans are, nevertheless, only partially able to exert such influence, "primarily due to the complexity of World 3, which we have created but not controlled" (Alt, 1995, p. 87).

Based on Popper's theory, it is possible to derive—as with other phenomena—approaches to space as well as to landscape, with the latter a special case of space (Kühne, 2020). Taking a social-constructivist perspective, 'landscape' is not understood here as 'objectively' given but instead as a synopsis of physical objects learned via social interaction. In turn, the landscape formed herewith is subject to certain patterns of interpretation tied back to historical, societal, individual and social contexts and is therefore changeable. Accordingly, Landscape 1 denotes the spatial aspects; Landscape 2 represents the individual; Landscape 3 spans the social patterns of interpretation, categorisation and evaluation (see Fig. 1 below). In contrast to the case with space, the constitutive level in relation to landscape is Landscape 3, which contains social patterns of interpretation, categorisation and evaluation, on the basis of which Landscape 2 can only be formed individually. Landscapes 2 and 3 exist in a feedback loop and influence each other, in that the former is conversely also in a position to have an innovative effect on the latter through previously unknown patterns of interpretation, categorisation and evaluation, on the one

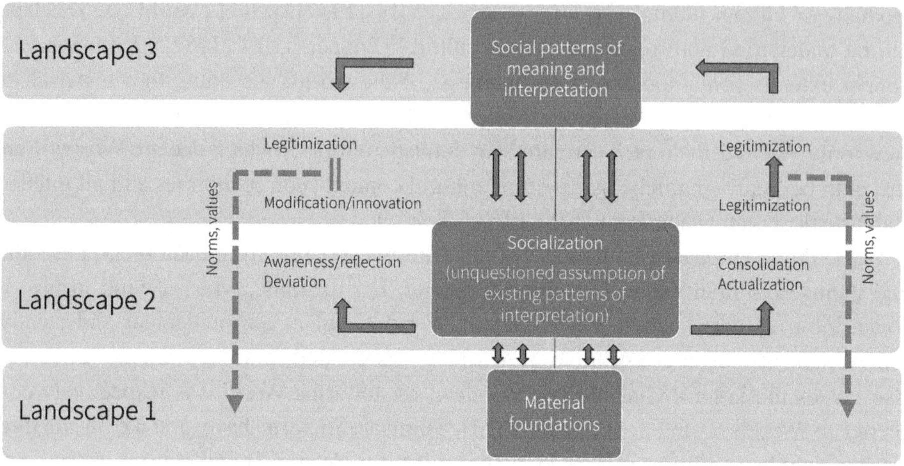

Fig. 1 The theory of three landscapes. (Authors' own representation)

hand, and a perpetuating effect on Landscape 3 through the reproduction of established patterns of interpretation, on the other. A central point, which is particularly important in relation to the implementation of the energy transition, is that norms are directed at Landscape 1 through mediation or revision originating from Landscape 2 (on landscape and morality, see Kühne et al., 2023). This can lead to a material intervention in Space 1 to align the physical foundations of Landscape 1 with the ideas of Landscapes 2 or 3.

The central categories of interpretation for public and non-public, or individual and social, communication about landscape can be divided into three (Ipsen, 2006) or, taken further (Kühne, 2019a), into four dimensions: the aesthetic, the cognitive, the emotional and the functional (see Fig. 2). In Landscapes 2 and 3, for example, the debate about the change in the physical foundations of Landscape 1 in the course of the energy transition deals cognitively with social/technical necessity, aesthetically with its visual consequences and emotionally with the loss of the everyday local landscape (Kühne et al., 2022; on native normal landscape, see Kühne, 2019a). The respective dimensions can

Fig. 2 The dimensions of 'Landscape'. (Authors' own representation, based on Ipsen (2006) and Kühne (2019a))

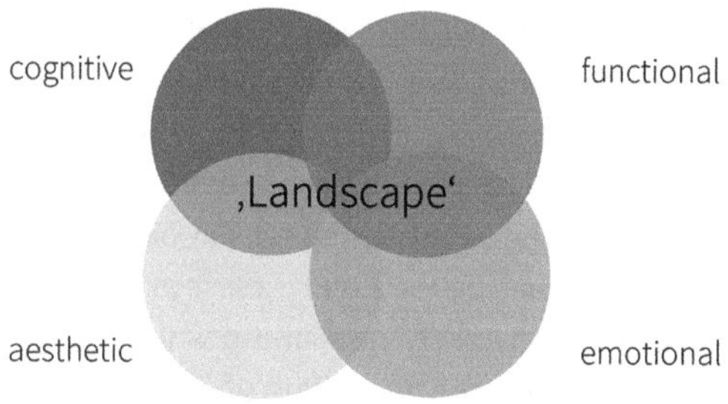

be quite individually different in Landscape 2: in expert mode (grid operators, engineers and similar), for example, the cognitive dimension can outweigh the emotional one (e.g. due to a lack of regional or local referents), while the aesthetics are updated during weekend excursions or when travelling. Local residents, meanwhile, often emotionally fear the loss of 'home' and 'identity', aesthetics-wise the 'destruction of their landscape' while also functionally benefitting from local electricity generation—financially, for instance (Weber et al., 2017a, b).

Following the discussion of the three landscapes, Dahrendorf's conflict theory is now presented. The aim here is to aid better grasp the course of landscape conflicts in the context of the energy transition, and thus to be able to develop constructive options for their regulation.

3 Dahrendorf's Conflict Theory

Dahrendorf adopts a mesosociological perspective in analysing the typical course of social conflicts, providing indications of the conditions under which they can be productive for social development and those under which they are not. This makes his theory stand out among the alternatives vis-à-vis the investigation of spatial and energy conflicts. Namely, by providing a theoretical framework in which specific episodes can be understood against the background of social development (Kühne et al., 2019, 2021).

According to Dahrendorf, social conflicts are a central element in the advancement of society. He emphasises that they occur wherever social life exists. Conflicts are essential for our understanding of social problems, even though they may be unpleasant and disruptive (Dahrendorf, 1968, p. 261). He refers in particular to those tensions resulting from differences in social status (i.e. not individual conflicts). With this view, he distances himself from Talcott Parsons' (1986[1966]) structural-functionalism and also rejects key parts of Karl Marx's (2014[1872]) interpretation of conflict, even if these thinkers share an understanding of such episodes being ultimately productive (for a more detailed introduction to Dahrendorf's sociology, including his conflict theory and biography, see: Kühne, 2017; Kühne & Leonardi, 2020; Leonardi, 2014; Meifort, 2017).

Structural-functionalism understands society as a relatively stable system of parts each possessing defined functions, but ignores the temporal dimensions hereof (Dahrendorf, 1968). Accordingly, Dahrendorf criticises this view as too static due to the tendency towards inertia and laments the interpretation of conflicts as episodes of dysfunctionality. Like Marx, he instead emphasises both the necessity and inevitability of conflict as a driver of social change. However, Dahrendorf rejects Marx's idea of revolutionary (bloody) conflict and of a utopian, tension-free communist society, partly because this teleological conception eschews conflict being a prerequisite for social development.

Dahrendorf (1972, 2017) characterises empirically ascertainable societies by their four common features:

1. Ubiquity of change: every society is subject to constant and omnipresent change;
2. Ubiquity of conflict: social conflicts are omnipresent in every society;
3. Ubiquity of productivity: every member of society makes a contribution to change;
4. Ubiquity of domination: every society is characterised by certain parts of society exercising power over others.

Not only do these specifics illustrate the regularities of human socialisation, but the course of social conflict also follows a certain pattern according to Dahrendorf (1972): The 'structural starting position' is characterised by the formation of 'quasi-groups' which, in specific contexts, have similar interests. The phase of 'becoming aware of latent interests' goes hand in hand with the emergence of the respective parties to a given conflict, as these quasi-groups come to recognise their core interests. The 'phase of developed interests' is associated with an increasing degree of organisation on the part of the conflict parties, with each having a recognisable identity of their own (Dahrendorf, 1972). They confront each other in a dichotomous situation, and any internal differences become conflicts within the individual camps, too (Dahrendorf, 1972).

Dahrendorf (1972) identifies three basic approaches to dealing with conflict: suppression, resolution and regulation. He rejects the first of these out of hand, as neither the conflict itself nor its root causes are eliminated by such suppression. Instead, this approach often leads to increased pressure, which can manifest itself in (potentially violent) outbreaks of conflict. He also rejects conflict resolution, as it does not really do away with the underlying social antagonisms, which is not the case in any empirically ascertainable society. Furthermore, solution robs society of its opportunities for development via tensions being allowed to play out. In consequence, Dahrendorf prefers the third form of dealing with conflicts: regulation. He identifies five key aspects here:

- The specific conflict (as with social ones in general) must be accepted as normal, not as a state of affairs contrary to the norm;
- Regulation relates to a specific object, the forms and manifestations of the conflict but not to its social causes;
- Successful regulation of a conflict is particularly likely if the parties to it each have a certain degree of organisation;
- That success also depends on whether the parties to the conflict adhere to rules. Mutual recognition of the equal value of the parties to the conflict and acceptance in principle of the other party's/parties' worldview(s) are also important prerequisites;
- The ability to regulate the conflict depends on the existence of an institutional framework formed by a third authority. The latter establishes generally binding guidelines for dealing with conflicts and has the ability to end them externally if necessary, which Dahrendorf (1994) describes as 'freedom under the protection of the law'. Another prerequisite is clear accountability regarding responsibility for decision-making, for example through regular assessment of the performance of politicians by the electorate, as is customary in a liberal democracy.

It is, furthermore, possible to differentiate between different types of conflict (Berr et al., 2019; Dahrendorf, 1969a, 1972, 1994, 2007; Kühne, 2018, 2020; Walter et al., 2013):

- The intensity of a conflict reflects the extent of its social relevance, being acute when the stakes are high for those involved and the costs of potential defeat significant (Dahrendorf, 1972, p. 38);
- A conflict can range in degree of violence from subtle non-verbal acts to mass murder and war;
- The complexity of a conflict increases with the number of actors involved, including institutions, administrations, associations, civic organisations and companies. Dahrendorf also points to the latent danger of the 'individualization of conflict' (2007, p. 93). A social conflict can be transformed into a personal one, which then functions individually as an end in itself when participation therein becomes a way of finding meaning in life and social recognition within one's identified group (Dahrendorf, 1971 [1958]).
- The spatial scope of a conflict can range from the local to global level. Complex episodes are often not clearly defined at a specific level, but rather multiscale in nature in terms of intensity. In addition, such multiscale conflicts are often asynchronous in their respective phases. For example, while in region A the conflict over the energy transition's physical effects has already been regulated, in region B we may still be in the phase of group formation (cf. Kühne, 2020).

The controllability of conflicts varies depending on their exact level. In the case of factual conflicts, such as the choice between site A or site B for the construction of a wind turbine, controllability is high. This is because the conflict is at the object level and can be decided by recognised criteria via accepted procedures. In the case of procedural conflicts, on the other hand, there is no consensus on appropriate rules; instead, they have to be negotiated. These protracted discussions often involve different identities and values, which makes regulation much more complicated. Those conflicts involving social self-descriptions are even more difficult to regulate, as own identity is often based on the valorisation of one's group and the devaluation of others, which limits acceptance of the equal value of the other party/parties. Even more challenging to regulate besides are value conflicts, which are not about external objects (factual conflicts), appropriate rules (procedural conflicts) or the divergent social self-descriptions of the respective conflict parties (identity conflicts) but rather the constructs behind different and usually incommensurable worldviews and associated identities (Becker & Naumann, 2018; Berr et al., 2019; Bolz, 2021; Bude, 2014).

Conflicts often have a tendency to spread to other levels: for example, a factual conflict can develop into an identity conflict, which then expands into a conflict over fundamental values and raises the core question of conflict management or its very nature is called into question (Berr et al., 2019; Kühne, 2020). This also occurs due to the tendency whereby each party to the conflict emphasises the danger which the other side poses not only to them but also to an identity formation in need of help (Scheller, 2021). This process can be seen not only as a form of paternalistic care but also as having a moral component to it, because 'to help is power without self-interest, but with self-esteem enhancement' (Paris, 2005, p. 25). The other party to the conflict is often assigned complexity-destroying totalisations such as 'the left', 'the wind-power opponents', 'the city dwellers' and similar (Scheller, 2021, p. 19).

In relation to the energy transition, a factual conflict in origin—one which addressed, for example, the question of suitable locations for wind turbines or powerline routes and upgrades—later expanded into one over identity and values. Initially, as noted, quasi-groups become aware of their common interests (e.g. preventing the construction of a wind turbine) and form parties to the conflict with a more or less developed degree of organisation, which over time develop their own externally recognisable identity (e.g. in the form of citizen initiatives; see also, Jenal 2018; Walter et al., 2013). As the conflict progresses, groups then form which face off in a dichotomous situation (supporters versus opponents). At the same time, the accompanying landscape conflict takes on the dimensions of being one of identity (loss/destruction of 'home') and values (economy/profit vs. nature/natural order)—making it even more difficult to regulate henceforth.

4 Resistance to Germany's Energy Transition

Even if the amount of electricity fed into the German grid—for example, from wind power—has increased overall (Statistisches Bundesamt, 2024), the expansion of wind turbines as the most important renewable energy source in the country still lags behind the legally stipulated milestones needing to be achieved here (Deutsche Windguard, 2024). With the shutdown of nuclear power plants and the curtailment of coal-fired ones, Germany imported more electricity than it exported for the first time since 2002 (Statistisches Bundesamt, 2024). As part of the expansion of the electricity grid in accordance with the Federal Requirements Planning Act (BBPlG) and the Energy Line Expansion Act (EnLAG), only around 2,800 kms out of the total 14,000 km envisaged had been completed by the end of 2023, while a further 1,800 km had been approved and were in the preparation phase or under construction (Bundesnetzagentur, 2024). The remainder of the network is still subject to various planning procedures such as approval/notification, regional planning or federal sectoral planning, or is not yet in the approval process at all (Bundesnetzagentur, 2024).

The rate of implementation lagging behind the targets set can be attributed, on the one hand, to complex approval procedures, extensive supply-chain problems or to cost increases (Deutsche Windguard, 2024). On the other, to local protests in the context of the energy transition. This pushback has repeatedly led to the delay or even prevention of, for example, wind turbines, powerlines, storage plants and similar (Colell et al., 2022;

Hoeft et al., 2017; Kamlage et al., 2020; Kühne, 2020; Schmitt, 2016; Walter et al., 2013; Weber & Jenal, 2016; Weber et al., 2017a, b; Wolf, 2020).

In extensive studies on the expansion of the electricity grid (Weber et al., 2016) and on the landscape and energy transition (Schmidt et al., 2018a, b) as a consequence of the extensive protests faced by political leaders, an analysis of the public discourse on the expansion of the electricity grid and the relationship between the landscape and the energy transition was carried out. In this context, the scholarly literature, Google search results, television programmes, (national, local, regional) daily and weekly newspapers and magazines, guideline-based interviews with experts and representatives of citizen initiatives, the homepages of the latter as well as two case contexts in Bavaria and Lower Saxony all formed key sources of information. Only select key results (from the homepages of citizen initiatives on preventing electricity-grid expansion / of wind turbine opponents; speaker positions; and, patterns of interpretation featuring in national, regional and local newspapers) are discussed in the following.

When analysing the arguments found on the websites of citizen initiatives mobilising against wind turbines (280 homepages examined) or the expansion of the electricity grid (90), concern about the (irretrievable) 'destruction'/ 'disfigurement' of the landscape or homeland is listed as pivotal to their opposition (see Fig. 3). Two basic lines of reasoning are generally used here: first, the 'loss' and 'destruction' of the native normal landscape of the local area (Kühne, 2020; Weber et al., 2017a, b); second, the 'disfigurement' of 'landscape', being 'stereotypically beautiful' according to both individual and collective patterns of interpretation (Kühne, 2019a).

Conservation arguments are particularly relevant when coming out against wind turbines. This applies, in particular, to regulations pertaining to the European Union's Natura 2000 protection system, which are not subject to spatial planning considerations

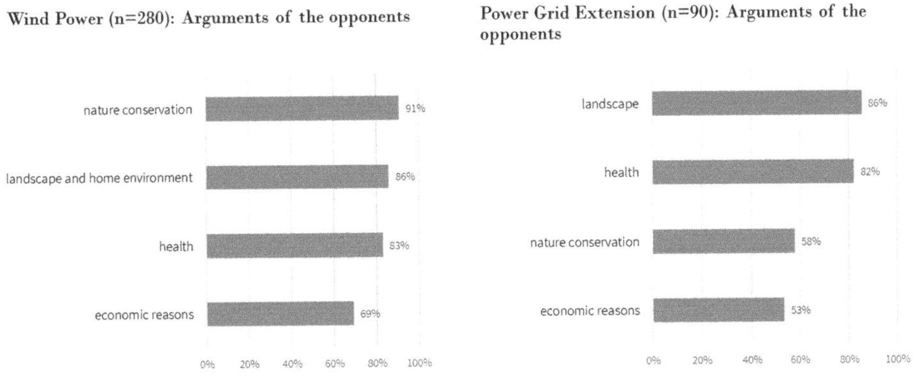

Fig. 3 Citizen initiatives against wind power and electricity-grid expansion. (Authors' own representation, based on Weber et al. (2016); Weber and Roßmeier et al., (2017a, b))

(Dorda, 2018; Moning, 2018). In contrast, 'landscape' is only considered selectively, and even then to a lesser extent due to its high degree of social construction and complexity (which 'landscape' is to be protected exactly, based on what criteria and how? (Bruns et al., 2022). Health risks as well economic impacts (such as a loss of value regarding property and land) are also important factors in the thinking of opponents to wind turbines and powerlines (see Fig. 3).

Turning to newspaper articles to see which speakers stand out in the public discourse on the expansion of Germany's electricity grid, it becomes clear, for example, that in national newspapers it is federal and state politicians who make up the leading voices in this context. Contrariwise, at the sub-state level it is local politicians and especially representatives of citizen initiatives who are primarily represented herein (Fig. 4; see in detail in Weber et al., 2016).

If the respective speaker positions are differentiated out and analysed in relation to the underlying lines of argumentation presented, national newspapers urge the rapid implementation of Germany's grid expansion and its upgrading in order to be able to distribute the electricity generated from renewable sources more effectively (Fig. 5; see also, Weber et al., 2016). In the reporting of newspapers at the sub-state level, on the other hand, the physical manifestations of the German electricity grid's expansion are interpreted as acts of 'destruction' and 'disfigurement', especially of native normal but also 'stereotypically beautiful' landscapes. In these local/regional reports, the (proposed) powerlines are interpreted as 'ugly', 'unsightly' and 'destroying the landscape' (Fig. 5; see also, Weber et al., 2016).

With regards to the consequences ensuing from this, regional differences can be observed. For example when, as in the context of Lower Saxony (*Einbecker Morgenpost*), the 'ugliness' of a conventional powerline is used to call for underground cabling. In our Bavarian case study (*Nürnberger Land*), meanwhile, the planned powerlines were

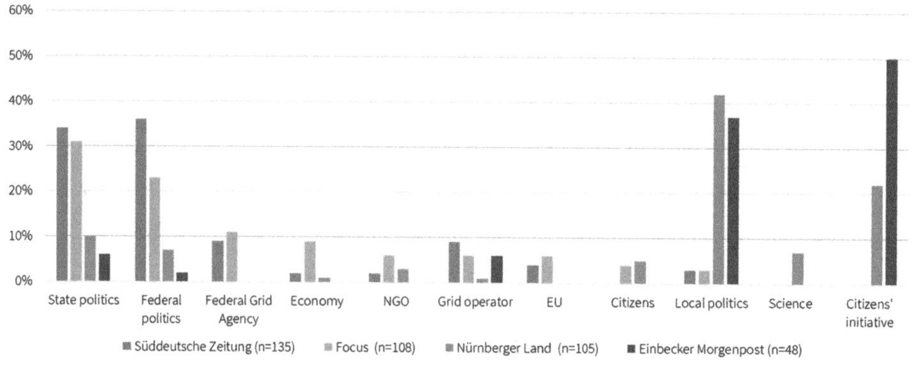

Fig. 4 Newspaper discourse on Germany's grid extension (on a local-regional/national level)—who gets a word in? (Authors' own representation, based on Weber et al. (2016))

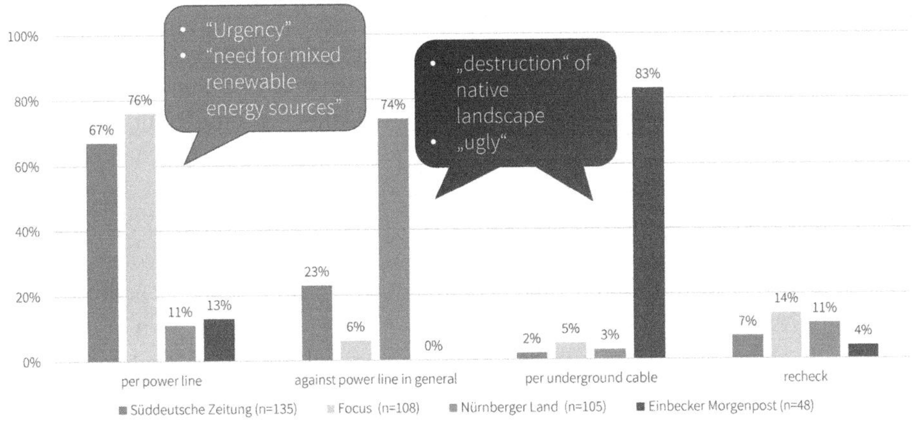

Fig. 5 Newspaper discourses on Germany's grid extension—respective positions (on a local-regional/national level) (Authors' own representation, based on Weber et al. (2016))

not only interpreted as 'ugly' and 'destroying the homeland' but also as merely serving to import nuclear-generated electricity from Eastern Europe (Weber et al., 2016).

Despite the current uncertainty caused by fluctuating energy prices and the new regulations surrounding the Building Energy Act from 2024, approval ratings regarding the expansion of renewables remain high, with around 80 per cent of the German population rating their increased use as either important / very important or extremely important (Agentur für Erneuerbare Energien, 2023). At the same time, however, many ambivalent, dissatisfied people can be identified, who cite the 'discrepancy between the idea ("good") and [actual] implementation ("bad")' (Kerker et al., 2022, p. 4). Overall, the energy transition is a highly complex process which overtaxes the relevant actors in terms of sociopolitical design and technical implementation; it usually completely eludes understanding for the layperson in part, too (Marg, 2023).

Even though recent research has shown that citizens' greater participation can increase their acceptance of related courses of action, all forms of involvement used to date have their weaknesses. This is why a combination of different participation formats appears to be the most promising avenue going forwards (Laborgne & Radtke, 2023). Results thus far show that 'there are numerous gaps in the toolbox for dealing with conflicts and promoting acceptance of the energy transition in the electricity sector' (Püttner et al., 2024, p. 58). In addition, 'energy conflicts reveal phenomena of a democratic crisis that cannot be adequately responded to in the negotiations on specific energy projects' (Krüger, 2021, p. 539). An unintended side effect of this is that conflicts can also be shifted abroad if, for example, the raw materials needed for the production of renewables or electricity generated from renewable sources have to be respectively imported, given the possibility of related tensions in origin countries in both cases (Püttner et al., 2024).

5 Theoretical Interpretation

It becomes clear here that Landscapes 2 and 3 can be regarded as the ones constitutive of existing landscape conflicts in Germany's energy transition, since different demands are placed on Landscape 1. The divergence of which gives rise to landscape conflicts which: a) confirm, question or revise the legitimacy of landscape understandings vis-à-vis Landscapes 1 and 2; and, b), confirm, question or revise the resulting material consequences in Landscape 1 as a consequence of a (see Fig. 6). Such episodes in the context of Germany's energy transition exhibit all the features of a social conflict and its various phases according to Dahrendorf's understanding: from the structural starting point of becoming aware of the divergent construction and interpretation collectively of Landscapes 2 and 3, to the phase of developed interests alongside an increasing degree of organisation in the form of citizen initiatives and interest groups, to the conflict parties then facing off. The conflict intensity here can be classified as high: concerning sociopolitical actors, for example, their mandate, professional future and reputation are all potentially at stake, while opponents of the proposed measures fear the loss of their 'home' and 'identity'.

Accordingly, questions about the regulation of landscape conflicts come to the fore. This represents a major social challenge, particularly due to the conflict in question's expansion to several different levels. For example, the landscape conflicts studied here have gone from originally being a controversial factual issue (routing, siting of wind turbines) to being a conflict in which each upheld value is contrasted with a disvalue (beautiful/ugly, useful/useless, healthy/sick; Berr & Kühne, 2019). Wind turbines and powerlines constituting material objects in Landscape 1 are interpreted as 'ugly' in Landscapes 2 and 3, 'disfiguring' and (irreparably) 'destroying' a Landscape 1 classified as 'beautiful'

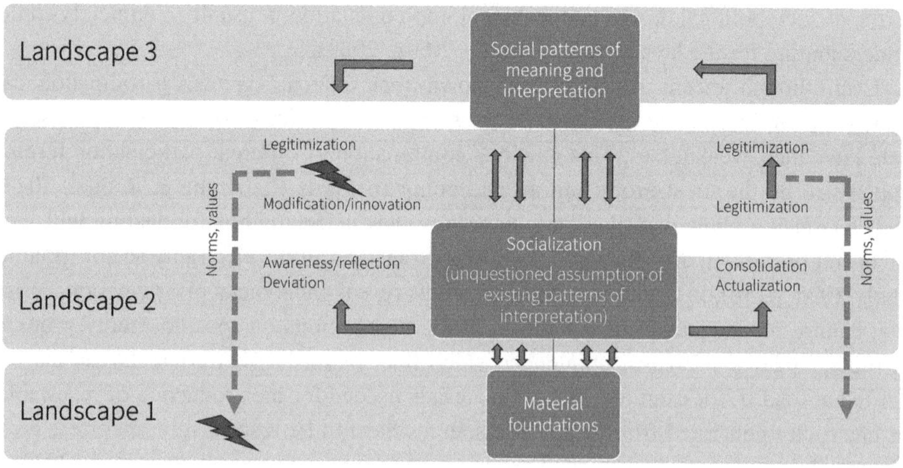

Fig. 6 Conflicts in the context of the three landscapes. (Authors' own representation)

in Landscapes 2 and 3. The changes induced by the energy transition in Landscape 1—previously held as 'health-promoting' by its nature—are seen as (potentially) 'harmful to health' in Landscapes 2 and 3 (Bruns & Münderlein, 2018; Münderlein, 2021).

This also becomes an identity conflict, in the sense that those affected locally see themselves as victims ('we') of the 'financial greed' of others (the owners of wind turbines, grid operators, sociopolitical actors and similar); the latter's activities pose an existential threat to the 'stereotypically beautiful', to the normal native landscape and to one's 'home'. As a result, one's own position is enhanced, which limits the acceptance of the equal value of the other party/parties to the conflict and makes regulation even more difficult. A special feature of these energy transition-related landscape conflicts also worthy of note is the role of the state, which on the one hand is a key actor but on the other is supposed to provide the institutional framework, too. This represents an additional challenge in the context of regulating these forms of conflict.

With regards to changes in Landscapes 2 and 3 in the context of those occurring in Landscape 1, different types of references can be made by the stakeholders involved (see Fig. 7). While cognitive-functional references to Landscape 1 tend to dominate among the actors involved in sociopolitical design and technical implementation, aesthetic-emotional references to landscape are more used in leisure time (e.g. during weekend excursions). Such aesthetic-emotional references and interpretations of Landscape 1 also prevail among opponents of the wind turbines or powerlines to be installed locally. In the expert mode of Landscape 2, the necessary urgency of rapidly generating and distributing electricity from renewable sources is updated with a view to Landscape 1. Questions of technical implementation are hereby placed in the foreground, whereas the local population from the vantage point of Landscape 2—and as also per Landscape 3—criticise the 'destruction' of the 'stereotypically beautiful' but also normal native landscape, consequently rejecting changes in Landscape 1.

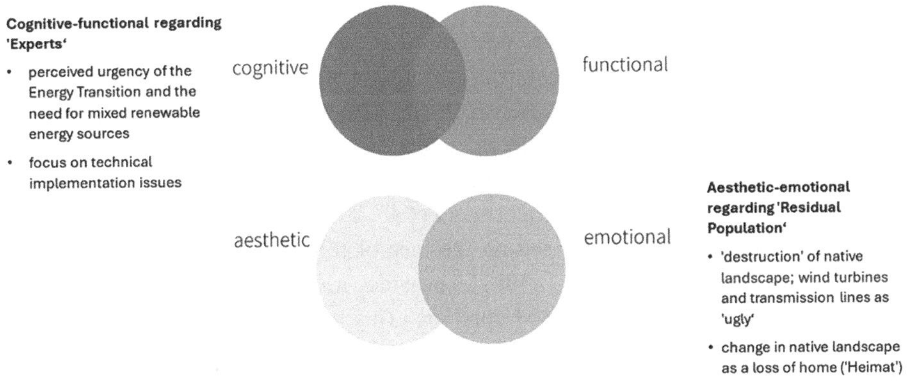

Fig. 7 The dimensions of 'landscape' in energy transition-related conflicts. (Authors' own representation)

Over the course of time it becomes apparent that—also as a result of the expansion of an original factual conflict to the levels of a value and identity conflict—the respective dimensions of the different references increasingly diverge vis-à-vis the involved parties. Accordingly, future regulation must take into account the need to reduce the gap which has arisen between the parties to these landscape conflicts and to bring the respective dimensions closer together again. Doing so will help ensure mutual recognition of the equal value of the other conflict party/parties and the fundamental acceptance of other worldviews, as forming key prerequisites for successful conflict regulation.

6 Conclusion

With a view to what the future holds regarding these landscape conflicts, it is important to take note of intergenerational change in Landscapes 2 and 3 as regards the interpretation of the energy transition's physical manifestations occurring in Landscape 1. There are indications of a key shift here, especially among the younger generations: for example, when they increasingly integrate the wind turbines, powerlines and similar appearing in Landscape 1 into their Landscape 2-related outlooks—while acting as a modifier to their Landscape 3 perspectives as well. Efforts should be made to bring existing and future landscape conflicts back to the factual level while recognising the legitimacy of the interests of the other parties involved, so as to render these tensions more constructive in nature. Energy transition-related conflicts have, however, specific features which make regulation more difficult. As a result of the disjointed expansion of facilities for the generation, transmission but also storage of renewable electricity, the organisation of respective groups is more challenging. The struggle for recognition of one's own position often results in intensified rhetoric. Essentialist understandings of the landscape are often revised, in turn making it more difficult to recognise the legitimacy of the other conflict party's/parties' position. Essentialisation also leads to landscape conflicts being understood not as an everyday negotiation process but as a deviation from an idealised state of harmony. The frequently encountered generalisation of landscape conflicts' nature leads to the situation whereby they are no longer carried out at the level of factual issue but are transformed into questions of identity, which can then become a criticism of the political system itself (here in particular, liberal democracy). The regulation of energy transition-related landscape conflicts is, accordingly, made harder by the reduction of the third independent party to the judiciary (Eichenauer et al., 2018; Kühne, 2020).

It is clear that our approach based on the idea of three landscapes, as derived from Popper's three-world theory (2019 [1987]), provides a useful analytical framework for dealing with energy transition-related conflicts. This outlook helps to address the different levels of 'landscape' and to capture the interconnections between them. It also offers a basis for categorising different theories and methods relevant to this context, which can aid extensive triangulation (Kühne, 2024). Compared to other conflict theories (Thiel, 2015), Dahrendorf's outlined approach is conceptually oriented towards the mesosociological level and offers not only a set of tools for analysing social tensions but also pointers for their productive regulation, making it highly useful for dealing with landscape conflicts.

Acknowledgements The authors would like to thank James Powell for his diligent proofreading.

References

Agentur für Erneuerbare Energien (2023). Erneuerbare Energien in Deutschland: Zwischen Akzeptanz und Unsicherheit. https://www.unendlich-viel-energie.de/erneuerbare-energien-in-deutschland-zwischen-akzeptanz-und-unsicherheit. Accessed: 6. May 2024.

Alt, J. A. (1995). *Karl R. Popper* (2nd ed.). Campus.

Becker, S., & Naumann, M. (2018). Energiekonflikte erkennen und nutzen. In O. Kühne & F. Weber (Eds.), *Bausteine der Energiewende* (pp. 509–522). Springer VS.

Berr, K., & Kühne, O. (2019). Moral und Ethik von Landschaft. In O. Kühne, F. Weber, K. Berr, & C. Jenal (Eds.), *Handbuch Landschaft* (pp. 351–365). Springer VS.

Berr, K., Jenal, C., Kühne, O., & Weber, F. (2019). *Landschaftsgovernance. Ein Überblick zu Theorie und Praxis.* Springer VS.

Bolz, N. (2021). *Keine Macht der Moral! Politik jenseits von Gut und Böse* (Fröhliche Wissenschaft, vol. 196). Matthes & Seitz.

Bruns, D., & Münderlein, D. (2018). "Paysage à votre santé". Gesundheitsfördernde Landschaften—Eine Betrachtung von Naturparken. In F. Weber, F. Weber, & C. Jenal (Eds.), *Wohin des Weges? Regionalentwicklung in Großschutzgebieten* (Arbeitsberichte der ARL, vol. 21, pp. 250–281). Selbstverlag.

Bruns, D., Kühne, O., Leconte, L., & Jenal, C. (2022). *Landschaftshandeln. Grundzüge, Potenziale und Zukunft der Europäischen Landschaftskonvention.* Springer Fachmedien.

Bude, H. (2014). *Gesellschaft der Angst.* Hamburger Edition.

Bundesnetzagentur (2024). Monitoring des Stromnetzausbaus. Viertel Quartal 2023. https://data.netzausbau.de/Vorhaben/Monitoring/Monitoringbericht_Q4-23.pdf. Accessed: 2. May 2024.

Colell, A., Knodt, M., Stoll, P., Kemmerzell, J., Reitz, S., Goshen, L., et al. (Kopernikus-Projekt Ariadne, Ed.). (2022). Konflikte und Akteure—Gesellschaftliche Herausforderungen bei der Umsetzung der Stromwende, Potsdam-Institut für Klimafolgenforschung. https://data.netzausbau.de/Vorhaben/Monitoring/Monitoringbericht_Q4-23.pdf. Accessed: 6. May 2024.

Dahrendorf, R. (1963). Conflict and liberty: Some remarks on the social structure of German politics. *The British Journal of Sociology, 14*(3), 197–211.

Dahrendorf, R. (1968). *Pfade aus Utopia. Arbeiten zur Theorie und Methode der Soziologie.* Piper.

Dahrendorf, R. (1969a). Sozialer Konflikt. In W. Bernsdorf (Ed.), *Wörterbuch der Soziologie* (pp. 1006–1009). Ferdinand Enke.

Dahrendorf, R. (1969b). Zu einer Theorie des sozialen Konflikts [1958 erstveröffentlicht]. In W. Zapf (Ed.), *Theorien des sozialen Wandels* (pp. 108–123). Kiepenheuer & Witsch.

Dahrendorf, R. (1971 [1958]. *Homo Sociologicus. Ein Versuch zur Geschichte, Bedeutung und Kritik der Kategorie der sozialen Rolle* (10th ed.). Westdeutscher Verlag.

Dahrendorf, R. (1972). *Konflikt und Freiheit. Auf dem Weg zur Dienstklassengesellschaft.* Piper.

Dahrendorf, R. (1979). *Lebenschancen. Anläufe zur sozialen und politischen Theorie* (Suhrkamp-Taschenbuch, vol. 559). Suhrkamp.

Dahrendorf, R. (1994). *Der moderne soziale Konflikt. Essay zur Politik der Freiheit.* dtv.

Dahrendorf, R. (2002). *Über Grenzen. Lebenserinnerungen.* C.H. Beck.

Dahrendorf, R. (2007). *Auf der Suche nach einer neuen Ordnung. Vorlesungen zur Politik der Freiheit im 21. Jahrhundert* (Krupp-Vorlesungen zu Politik und Geschichte am Kulturwissenschaftlichen Institut im Wissenschaftszentrum Nordrhein-Westfalen, (4th ed., Vol. 3). C.H. Beck.

Dahrendorf, R. (2017). *The modern social conflict. The politics of liberty.* Routledge.

Deutsche Windguard (2024). Status des Windenergieausbaus an Land in Deutschland. Jahr 2023. https://www.wind-energie.de/fileadmin/redaktion/dokumente/publikationen-oeffentlich/themen/06-zahlen-und-fakten/20240116_Status_des_Windenergieausbaus_an_Land_Jahr_2023.pdf. Accessed: 2. May 2024.

Dorda, D. (2018). Windkraft und Naturschutz. In O. Kühne & F. Weber (Eds.), *Bausteine der Energiewende* (pp. 749–772). Springer VS.

Eichenauer, E., Reusswig, F., Meyer-Ohlendorf, L., & Lass, W. (2018). Bürgerinitiativen gegen Windkraftanlagen und der Aufschwung rechtspopulistischer Bewegungen. In O. Kühne & F. Weber (Eds.), *Bausteine der Energiewende* (pp. 633–651). Springer VS.

Hoeft, C., Messinger-Zimmer, S., & Zilles, J. (Eds.). (2017). *Bürgerproteste in Zeiten der Energiewende. Lokale Konflikte um Windkraft, Stromtrassen und Fracking.* transcript.

Ipsen, D. (2006). *Ort und Landschaft.* VS Verlag für Sozialwissenschaften.

Jenal, C. (2018). Ikonologie des Protests – Der Stromnetzausbau im Darstellungsmodus seiner Kritiker(innen). In O. Kühne, & F. Weber (Eds.), *Bausteine der Energiewende* (pp. 469–487). Wiesbaden: Springer VS.

Kamlage, J.-H., Warode, J., Reinermann, J., de Vries, N., & Trost, E. (2020). Von Konflikt und Dialog: Manifestationen der Energiewende in den Transformationsfeldern Netzausbau, Biogas und Windkraft. In R. Duttmann, O. Kühne, & F. Weber (Eds.), *Landschaft als Prozess* (pp. 603–633). Springer VS.

Kerker, N., Kuhlmann, L., Marg, S., Mokros, N., Küpper, B., Teune, S., et al. (Stiftung Mercator, & DEMOKON, Eds.). (2022). Die Unbeteiligten in der lokalen Energiewendekonflikten. DEMOKON—Research Paper: III. https://www.demokon.de/files/uploads/2023/06/demokon-research-paper-3-die-unbeteiligten-energiewende-konflikte-Kerke-et-al.pdf. Accessed: 30. April 2024.

Krüger, T. (2021). Energiekonflikte und Demokratiekrise. Eine radikaldemokratische Perspektive auf das Ringen um Gemeinwohlziele der Energiewende. *Zeitschrift für Politikwissenschaft, 31*(4), 539–563. https://doi.org/10.1007/s41358-021-00289-w

Kühne, O. (2017). *Zur Aktualität von Ralf Dahrendorf. Einführung in sein Werk* (Aktuelle und klassische Sozial- und KulturwissenschaftlerIinnen). Springer VS.

Kühne, O. (2018). *Landscape and Power in Geographical Space as a Social-Aesthetic Construct.* Springer International Publishing.

Kühne, O. (2019a). *Landscape theories. A brief introduction.* Springer VS.

Kühne, O. (2019b). Vom ‚ Bösen' und ‚ Guten' in der Landschaft—das Problem moralischer Kommunikation im Umgang mit Landschaft und ihren Konflikten. In K. Berr & C. Jenal (Eds.), *Landschaftskonflikte* (pp. 131–142). Springer VS.

Kühne, O. (2020). Landscape conflicts. A theoretical approach based on the three worlds theory of Karl Popper and the conflict theory of Ralf Dahrendorf, illustrated by the example of the energy system transformation in Germany. *Sustainability: Science, Practice and Policy, 12*(17) 1–20. https://doi.org/10.3390/su12176772

Kühne, O. (2024). *Redescribing horizontal geographies. A neopragmatist approach to spatial contingency, complexity, and relationships.* Springer International.

Kühne, O., & Leonardi, L. (2020). *Ralf Dahrendorf. Between social theory and political practice.* Palgrave Macmillan.

Kühne, O., & Weber, F. (2018 [online first 2017]). Conflicts and negotiation processes in the course of power grid extension in Germany. *Landscape Research, 43(4)*, 529–541. https://doi.org/10.1080/01426397.2017.1300639

Kühne, O., Weber, F., & Berr, K. (2019). The productive potential and limits of landscape conflicts in light of Ralf Dahrendorf's conflict theory. *Società Mutamento Politica, 10*(19), 77–90.
Kühne, O., Berr, K., Jenal, C., & Schuster, K. (2021). *Liberty and landscape. In search of life-chances with Ralf Dahrendorf.* Palgrave Macmillan.
Kühne, O., Parush, D., Shmueli, D., & Jenal, C. (2022). Conflicted energy transition—Conception of a theoretical framework for its investigation. *Land, 11*(1), 116. https://doi.org/10.3390/land11010116
Kühne, O., Berr, K., & Jenal, C. (2023). *The Closed Society and Its Ligatures—A Critique Using the Example of 'Landscape.'* Springer Fachmedien; Springer.
Laborgne, P., & Radtke, J. (2023). Akzeptanz und Partizipation in der Energiewende. In M. Sonnberger, A. Bleicher, & M. Groß (Eds.), *Handbuch Umweltsoziologie* (pp. 1–15). Springer Fachmedien.
Leonardi, L. (2014). *Introduzione a Dahrendorf* (Maestri del Novecento, vol. 20). Editori Laterza.
Marg, S. (2023). Zwischen überhöhten Erwartungen und fehlendem Vertrauen: Wissenschaftsgläubigkeit und-skepsis im Kontext der Energiewende. *Demokratie Gegen Menschenfeindlichkeit, 8*(1), 30–45.
Marx, K. (2014 [1872]). *Das Kapital. Kritik der politischen Ökonomie* (Ungekürzte Ausgabe nach der 2. Aufl. von 1872). Nikol.
Meifort, F. (2017). *Ralf Dahrendorf. Eine Biographie.* C.H. Beck.
Moning, C. (2018). Energiewende und Naturschutz—Eine Schicksalsfrage auch für Rotmilane. In O. Kühne & F. Weber (Eds.), *Bausteine der Energiewende* (pp. 331–344). Springer VS.
Münderlein, D. (2021). *Macht Landschaft glücklich? Ermittlung von landschaftsbezogenem Wohlbefinden und Erholung für die räumliche Planung.* Springer Fachmedien; Imprint Springer VS.
Paris, R. (2005). *Normale Macht. Soziologische Essays.* UVK.
Parsons, T. (1986 [1966]). *Das System moderner Gesellschaften* (Grundfragen der Soziologie, Bd. 15). Juventa.
Popper, K. R. (1979). Three worlds. Tanner lecture, Michigan, April 7, 1978. *Michigan Quarterly Review, 18(1)* 141–167.
Popper, K. R. (2011 [1947]). *The open society and its enemies.* Routledge.
Popper, K. R. (2019 [1987]). *Auf der Suche nach einer besseren Welt. Vorträge und Aufsätze aus dreißig Jahren.* Piper.
Popper, K. R. (1973). *Objektive Erkenntnis. Ein evolutionärer Entwurf.* Hoffmann und Campe.
Püttner, A., Liebhart, L., Wolf, P., Jaschek, C., León, C. D., Wassermann, S., et al. (Verbundvorhaben SyKonaS, Ed.) (2024). Entwicklung und Anpassung von Instrumenten zur Konfliktbearbeitung im Rahmen der Energiewende. Projektbericht Nr. 4. https://elib.uni-stuttgart.de/bitstream/11682/14104/1/SyKonaS_Bericht04.pdf. Accessed: 30. Apr. 2024.
Scheller, J. (2021). *Identität im Zwielicht. Perspektiven für eine offene Gesellschaft.* Claudius.
Schmidt, C., Hage, G., Hoppenstedt, A., Bruns, D., Kühne, O., Schuster, L., et al. (2018a). *Landschaftsbild & Energiewende. Band 1: Grundlagen.* Bundesamt für Naturschutz.
Schmidt, C., Hage, G., Hoppenstedt, A., Bruns, D., Kühne, O., Schuster, L., et al. (2018b). *Landschaftsbild & Energiewende. Band 2: Handlungsempfehlungen.* Bundesamt für Naturschutz.
Schmitt, T. (2016). Die Debatten um neue Stromtrassen als Symptomkonflikte der Energiewende. *Geographische Rundschau, 68*(11), 18–25.
Statistisches Bundesamt (2024). Stromerzeugung 2023: 56 % aus erneuerbaren Energieträgern. https://www.destatis.de/DE/Presse/Pressemitteilungen/2024/03/PD24_087_43312.html. Accessed: 2. May 2024.
Thiel, A. (2015). *Soziale Konflikte.* transcript.
Walter, F., Marg, S., Geiges, L., & Butzlaff, F. (Eds.). (2013). *Die neue Macht der Bürger. Was motiviert die Protestbewegungen? (BP-Gesellschaftsstudie).* Rowohlt.

Weber, F., & Jenal, C. (2016). Windkraft in Naturparken. Konflikte am Beispiel der Naturparke Soonwald-Nahe und Rhein-Westerwald. *Naturschutz und Landschaftsplanung, 48(12)*, 377–382.
Weber, F., Kühne, O., Jenal, C., Sanio, T., Langer, K., & Igel, M. (2016). Analyse des öffentlichen Diskurses zu gesundheitlichen Auswirkungen von Hochspannungsleitungen—Handlungsempfehlungen für die strahlenschutzbezogene Kommunikation beim Stromnetzausbau. Ressortforschungsbericht. https://doris.bfs.de/jspui/bitstream/urn:nbn:de:0221-2016050414038/3/BfS_2016_3614S80008.pdf. Accessed: 31. Aug. 2020.
Weber, F., Jenal, C., Roßmeier, A., & Kühne, O. (2017a). Conflicts around Germany's *Energiewende*: Discourse patterns of citizens' initiatives. *Quaestiones Geographicae, 36*(4), 117–130. https://doi.org/10.1515/quageo-2017-0040
Weber, F., Roßmeier, A., Jenal, C., & Kühne, O. (2017). Landschaftswandel als Konflikt. Ein Vergleich von Argumentationsmustern beim Windkraft- und beim Stromnetzausbau aus diskurstheoretischer Perspektive. In O. Kühne, H. Megerle, & F. Weber (Eds.), *Landschaftsästhetik und Landschaftswandel* (pp. 215–244). Springer VS.
Wolf, A. (2020). Landschaftskonflikte im Zuge der Energiewende: Die Windenergieanlagen von Wadgassen (Saarland). In R. Duttmann, O. Kühne, & F. Weber (Eds.), *Landschaft als Prozess* (pp. 635–656). Springer VS.

Corinna Jenal studied German language and literature, political science and philosophy at the University of Trier and completed the "Sustainability Certificate" at Saarland University's Endowed Chair of Sustainable Development. At Saarland University and Weihenstephan-Triesdorf University of Applied Sciences, she worked on various research projects, including studies on demographic change in industrial companies in Saarland, the public discourse on the health effects of high-voltage power lines, questions of social acceptance of the extraction of mineral raw materials, the development of peri-urban landscapes in Alpine metropolitan areas and the social construction and symbolic connotation of forests and old and dead wood. Since fall 2016 and summer 2019, respectively, she has been working as a research assistant and assistant professor in the Department of Geography at the Chair of Urban and Regional Development at the Eberhard Karls University of Tübingen, where she received her doctorate on the social construction of forest in 2019. Her research focuses on social constructivist and neopragmatic landscape research, energy transition, old industry as well as social construction and negotiation processes of nature and forest as their associated part.

Olaf Kühne studied geography, modern history, economics and geology at Saarland University and obtained his doctorate in geography and sociology at the Saarland University and at the University of Hagen. After working in various Saarland state authorities and at Saarland University, he was Professor of Rural Development/Regional Management at Weihenstephan-Triesdorf University of Applied Sciences and Adjunct Professor of Geography at Saarland University in Saarbrücken from 2013 to fall 2016. Since fall 2016, he has been a professor in the research area of geography at the Chair of Urban and Regional Development at the Eberhard Karls University of Tübingen. His research interests include neopragmatic landscape research, landscape and discourse theory, social acceptance of landscape change, sustainable development, old industry, transformation processes in East-Central and Eastern Europe, urban land hybrids in Southern California and the Southern states of the USA, regional development and urban and landscape ecology.

Part IV

Power Relations

Outer Space Infrastructures and Global Order: How the Control Over Satellite Constellations Reshapes State-Business Relations

Joscha Abels

Abstract

In the era of New Space, critical space infrastructure such as satellite systems are increasingly operated and owned by private corporations. This chapter explores the impact recent developments in outer space have had on state-business relations. The analysis focuses on the control of critical space infrastructure, more specifically of large satellite constellations in the field of geolocation and internet coverage. The case of global navigation satellite systems (GNSSs) demonstrates that the development of outer space infrastructures has been shaped by states' attempts to establish authority and mitigate foreign control. Yet, the rise of transnational spacecraft and tech companies significantly changed the character of outer space. Transnational corporations like SpaceX and Amazon set up mega-constellations of internet satellites. These shifts increased transnational corporations' control over critical space infrastructures and with it their structural power in the global economy. The US has reacted to this by strengthening its military-industrial space complex and financial pull to ensure the alignment of domestic companies. The EU has opted to build its own constellation IRIS2, however with uncertain outcome.

Keywords

Communication · Global order · Infrastructure · Non-state actors · Privatisation · Space · SpaceX · Transnational corporations

J. Abels (✉)
Institut für Politikwissenschaft, Universität Tübingen, Tübingen, Deutschland
e-mail: joscha.abels@uni-tuebingen.de

H.-J. Bieling et al. (eds.), *Transnational Infrastructures and the Transformation of Global Orders*, RaumFragen: Stadt – Region – Landschaft,
https://doi.org/10.1007/978-3-031-74846-2_12

1 Introduction

Outer space, once regarded an uncharted frontier beyond the confines of terrestrial geopolitics, has become a domain of strategic significance and an arena for the projection of global power. This started with the 'Space Race' of the Cold War era, a defining chapter in the geopolitical rivalry between the United States and the Soviet Union and a symbolic battleground for the ideological competition between the two blocs. The Cold War also paved the way for a broader military and industrial utilisation of space. The development of reconnaissance and communication satellites, of transport and launch infrastructures impacted the great powers' economic and military potentials, as well as their very perception of national security. It also led to the establishment of international regimes such as the Outer Space Treaty (OST), aiming at the prevention of a further militarisation of space.

While the Cold War era of outer space exploration largely reflected the rivalry between state actors, the years after the collapse of the Soviet Union were marked by a global shift towards market-liberal economics and a tightening of public budgets. In the era of 'New Space', states intensified their cooperation with commercial providers for space exploration and critical services. Private corporations, in turn, identified space as a largely untapped market for business expansion. This development has had significant consequences not just for the progress of space exploration and exploitation but also for patterns of ownership and control. Critical space infrastructure such as major satellite systems and services, launch vehicles, lunar landers, and others are nowadays frequently operated and owned by private corporations.

This chapter explores the impact these developments had on the relations between states and transnational corporations (TNCs) that are active in space, and reflects on the broader nexus between technology, infrastructure and global order. The study stresses the 'interlocking' of global orders: in this case, how the patterns of activity in outer space, the underlying norms, and the control of space-related assets are contingent and reflect back upon the dynamics of interstate and transnational relations.

The contribution focusses on the control of critical space infrastructure, more specifically of large satellite constellations in the field of geolocation and mobile broadband. Satellite systems and the services they provide have been crucial to advancements in areas such as Earth observation and environmental monitoring, navigation, transportation, logistics, global communication, as well as in warfare. As an increasing number of elements within these systems is operated by private corporations, states are forced to reconsider how to secure the cooperation of commercial actors and to what degree they can afford to grow dependent on critical infrastructure they do not directly control. These questions become even more pressing as geopolitical tensions are on the rise and the weaponisation of infrastructure dependencies is more likely to occur.

The chapter demonstrates that the development of outer space infrastructures has to a substantial degree been shaped by the dynamics of the international order and states' attempts to establish authority or to mitigate foreign control. This has been visible, for instance, in decisions by the European Union (EU) and China to build their own global navigation satellite systems (GNSSs)—Galileo and Beidou—with which they could reduce their respective dependencies on the US-controlled Global Positioning System (GPS). The rise of transnational spacecraft and tech companies however placed their drive for profit and influence alongside the national security interests of state actors. This development is reflected in the decision of TNCs to set up mega-constellations of internet satellites in Low Earth Orbit (LEO), most significantly SpaceX's Starlink, Amazon's Kuipers, and Eutelsat OneWeb, while states have shown diverging reactions to this. A key argument presented in this chapter is that these space-related developments have had substantial repercussions for the relations between states and TNCs, increasing the latter's structural power within the global economy.

The chapter proceeds as follows: in the second section, I discuss the fundamental characteristics of the contemporary order structuring outer space politics and how it interlocks with further international, transnational, and societal orders. I also outline the implications for our understanding of global politics. In the third and fourth section, I compare the state-centred competition over GNSSs with recent developments in LEO satellite mega-constellations. The sections highlight the consequences of the commercialisation of space for global order. The conclusions then summarise how space developed from a field of national security considerations into one dominated by commercial actors. It also discusses the political and academic implications of these observations. Most centrally, this concerns the increasing structural power of large tech firms and how this should refocus our analyses of global orders.

2 Infrastructures and the Ordering of Outer Space

In this volume, orders are understood as constellations of patterns of practices, institutionalised norms, and distributions of material assets among constitutive units. In principle, this definition is applicable to outer space, yet there are some specific characteristics that make it unique. First, we are talking about a realm that, much more than others, has been and still is accessible only to a select group of actors. Most individuals are—knowingly or unknowingly—dependent on outer space technology in the form of everyday necessities like navigation, broadband communication, weather reports, and so forth. Citizens contribute to the development of outer space infrastructure in the form of service payments and tax-funded programs. Yet, if we consider the very practices that structure outer space politics, most individuals are excluded from contributing to it. In fact, only some spacefaring nations and operating companies wield a practical influence in this realm. Second, outer space largely lacks regulation and the institutionalisation of norms. Some successful attempts at regulation resulted in the OST, an internationally recognised Rescue Agreement, and the International Telecommunication Union, a specialised agency of the United Nations (UN) that, among other things, manages radio frequency and orbital slot coordination. Yet, treaty-building has been stuck for decades now and, as a stateless space, no overarching political-institutional structure determines the outer space order. Finally, all man-made objects in space—satellites, probes, landers, stations etc.—fall into the category of high tech: cutting edge technology involving complex development and production processes and the input of specialised firms. Apart from these assets, distributive issues in outer space mainly concern the access to and use of spaces that do not fall within the authority or territory of states: Earth's orbits, the moon, and other celestial bodies.

If we are interested in the ordering effects of outer space infrastructures such as satellite systems, we need ask how the current order is reproduced or contested by their transformation—and how this relates to further, interlocking orders. As argued before, what is happening in outer space is contingent on the dynamics of interstate and transnational relations: they pre-determine which space assets are developed, towards which ends they are utilised, which common ground is found on mitigating risks and collective action problems, which groups reap the benefits from these developments, and so forth.

At the same time, outer space dynamics reflect back on other orders like the international—which state can leverage its position in space to its strategic advantage, which conflicts are mitigated or exacerbated—the transnational—which corporation outperforms its competition, with which state interests they align—and the societal—which social groups gain access to the public goods produced in space, which are excluded or even suffering due to infrastructures' harmful effects. As such, these orders are interlocking and there are wider ramifications of the effects of infrastructural transformations on these orders.

Thus, there is a variety of ways of how to approach the interrelationship between outer space infrastructures and global order. This chapter focusses on two central aspects: the way in which the development and operation of large satellite systems has changed the order in outer space itself—the patterns of practices of control, the distribution of assets—and how this has reflected back on interstate and state-business relations.

It approaches these questions from a theoretical perspective that strikes a balance between a more state-centric International Relations (IR) literature and the capital-focus found in many works of International Political Economy (IPE). The rise of TNCs and their increasing political power towards the end of the 20th and the beginning of the twenty-first century prompted IPE scholars to engage in the analysis and characterisation of a 'diffusion' of power on the political level (Bieler et al., 2011; Josselin & Wallace, 2001). In contrast to a predominantly state-centric IR, these works found that global politics is by no means exclusively an affair of states, but one where corporations operating across borders and their joint associations play a major role. Susan Strange (1996) even spoke of 'the retreat of the state'. As a discipline strongly dedicated to the intermediation between the political and the economic as well as the machinations of (transnational) capital, IPE was well-poised to describe these shifts in global order. Yet, at times, its conceptualisation of a 'transnational capitalist class' (Robinson & Sprague-Silgado, 2018; Sklair, 2010) suggested that the world had entered a new phase where the power of nation states was waning. Against the backdrop of the current dissolution of US hegemony and the rivalry over global influence, which is primarily organised around nation state lines, such perspectives appear premature or outright inaccurate.

Most of IR on the other hand has treated corporations traditionally as subordinate to state authority and as the prolonged arm of state strategising. This is also reflected in works on 'economic statecraft', which describe states' ability to influence and steer the activities of domestic companies to achieve political objectives. The operations and assets of private businesses are then leveraged for foreign policy measures, e.g. to sanction international competitors (Baldwin, 2020; Norris, 2018). Works on 'weaponised interdependence' received a lot of academic attention recently. They describe the ways in which states exploit infrastructural hubs they control—or, by extension, their domestic businesses—for the purpose of harming other states or making them adjust their position (Farrell & Newman, 2019; Gertz & Evers, 2020). Again, these approaches remain rooted in the assumption that businesses by and large serve as foreign policy instruments of the states.

This chapter argues that analyses of international politics and the global economy would do well to consider both the role of state actors in the organisation and enforcement of strategic interests and the influence of TNCs in these processes, without analytically favouring one group of actors over the other. Babić et al., (2017, p. 29) make the case for a perspective "juxtapositioning of state and corporate actors as two relevant and empirically specifiable actors for the study of the international political economy". In their view, state power and corporate power stand in a dynamic, non-deterministic relationship where in some cases states manage to get corporations in line with their strategic decision, but fail to do so in other cases – or even have to adjust their strategies according to the manoeuvring by TNCs.

State-business relations are thus marked by a dynamic pattern of interaction and dependencies (Abels & Bieling, 2024). States rely on businesses for the provision of essential goods, services, and infrastructure, as well as technological innovation. Growth and profitability of corporations, on the other hand, depend on the regulative and legal framework guaranteed by the state, on public infrastructure as well as public funding. State and capitalist activity are thus generally two buttressing processes that may turn antagonistic in individual cases where corporate profit-interests and states' strategic interests do not align. In the course of economic globalisation, TNCs diversified their production networks, for example to combine the know-how and industrial capacities of Western economies with the labour and sales opportunities in developing countries. This made them at the same time less dependent on their state of origin but more dependent on a functioning global economy. Under these circumstances, it would be ill-advised to assume a natural alignment of corporations with the state in which they are originally based.

States and corporations are thus key constituent units of global orders, at the same time influencing and subject to the practices, norms, and distributions in specific ways. Naturally, other actors, most centrally from civil society, do play a role. Yet, outer space is but one example where they are marginalised.

Outer space is a particularly impressive example of political realms that have been transformed by the rise of TNCs. For decades, it has been an exclusive arena of power projection by states. Activities in space and their sparse legal regulation have been a direct consequence of state rivalry. Yet, as other fields where the development and operation of costly infrastructure overstrains the limited budget of state agencies, outer space has seen the accession of corporations and a process of commercialisation of space exploration and space-related services. This period of 'New Space', in which businesses started to invest and operate in space with the intent of profit-seeking, has been further underpinned by the neoliberal shift in Western economic policy. Towards the end of the millennium, a visible policy shift reflected an ideological switch from an 'embedded realism' (Ruggie, 1982) to market-centred policies that pushed privatisations of essential services and infrastructures and restrained the role the state would play in organizing industrial and sectoral development. This shift also found its expression in the privatisation and commercialisation of space-related services and infrastructures (Maraš & Dangubić, 2022).

Nowadays, it has affected all aspects of the space industry: satellite systems and services, space stations and spacecraft, launch vehicles and logistics, space exploration and research all involve to a substantial degree contributions of large TNCs like SpaceX, Boeing, or Airbus. This does not mean that states have become irrelevant. To the contrary, the initial costs of entering the space industry are high and the timeframe towards profitability is long. Corporations are therefore heavily reliant on government subsidies and large public contracts to maintain their position in a "government-industrial space complex" (Eriksson & Newlove-Eriksson, 2023, p. 58). They also depend on infrastructure provided by state agencies. For example, SpaceX launch vehicles frequently start from NASA launch sites. Finally, as the analyses in this chapter outline, state oversight over private activities in space, although particularly pronounced in state capitalist economies such as China or Russia, still remains intact in Europe and the US.

Space is thus marked by a juxtapositioning of corporate and state actors and by dynamic political and business relationships and interdependencies. In the following two sections, the chapter outlines how contemporary shifts in control over outer space infrastructures are influencing state-business relations both in space and in other interlocking realms. The focus is on satellite systems as communication infrastructures that allow for the rapid flow of data across the globe and beyond. In line with this book's perspective, infrastructures are treated as socio-technical systems whose production and operation have social repercussions and which are thus politically contested (De Goede, 2021). I argue that the changing relation of public and private control of outer space infrastructure is both a consequence of, and a factor contributing to, a larger reorganisation of authority in global politics. This reordering enables large tech firms to act more independently of state action due to their transnational production, legal structure, and technological edge.

3 The Securitisation of Space: Navigation Satellite Constellations

Satellite systems provide a wide range of services across various sectors, including communication, navigation, broadcasting, Earth observation, weather monitoring, and so forth. Just as much as the use of such services has become part of our societal everyday, many businesses have grown dependent on them for their operations or are themselves involved in the processing and generation of satellite data. Yet, the value of satellites for state action only becomes fully apparent when one considers their military benefits. Most satellite systems are inherently dual use, meaning that the services they provide can be used for civilian and military purposes alike. Navigation satellites also enable military targeting, logistics, and troop movements; communication satellites allow for encrypted communication channels for command and coordination; Earth observation means information gathering, reconnaissance, and threat assessments. As a consequence, states consider satellite systems critical not just for their economic development and expansion but also for national security.

This makes it all the more significant that an increasing number of satellite systems are operated not by state agencies but by private companies. Just as other critical infrastructures, satellite systems were subject to state control for a long time. Around the turn of the millennium, major developments concerned the control of and access to navigation satellite systems. GNSSs provide positioning services that can localise and track an entity equipped with a receiver—with accuracies depending on the respective system. Such services are vital for everyday routines such as navigation, mapping, and logistics, and affect all mode of transportation, from automobiles to aircrafts. Satellite navigation is also extensively used in military operations for route planning, precision targeting, situational awareness, air defence, and so forth. For years, the US has been the sole provider in this field. GPS has been developed by the United States Department of Defense (DoD) and became operational in 1978. Originally intended for military use, GPS was later made available for civilians, which revolutionised navigation and positioning across the globe.

However, the dependence of third countries on this infrastructure also meant that they became vulnerable to the US restricting access to GPS. During conflicts or exercises, the US military occasionally employed measures to degrade GPS accuracy in certain regions to prevent adversaries from using GPS-guided munitions or navigation systems. Military equipment that involves GPS technology, like missiles, effectively had to be signed off by the US military. The more state agencies, armed forces, and the public of other countries grew dependent on GPS for their functioning, the higher the costs of the US potentially leveraging its control over the system. Both Russia and China began developing their own GNSSs, with initial planning commencing already in the 1970s and 1980s. However, it took decades for both systems to become fully operational. Russia's GLONASS achieved global coverage in 2011, the Chinese Beidou system followed suit in 2020.

Recognizing the strategic importance of satellite navigation and the need for an independent system, the EU initiated its Galileo project in the early 2000s. It was supposed to offer reliable and secure positioning, navigation, and timing services. Galileo should consist of a constellation of 30 satellites stationed in Medium Earth Orbit (MEO), where all GNSS are located, and a network of ground stations that control the satellites. The EU's decision to go ahead and establish its own infrastructure was motivated both by a transatlantic rift following an increasing unilateralism in US foreign policy as well as the economic prospects of promoting the EU's space-related industries (Beidleman, 2005). The initiative also fell into a period where discourses about the safeguarding of so-called 'critical infrastructure' were prevalent.

Initially, the EU intended to use a frequency for Galileo that would overlay with the M-code of GPS, its military signal. This would make it impossible for the US military to jam Galileo in a warzone without also disabling its secure communications, an alarming scenario for the US. Eventually, negotiations between the administration of US president George W. Bush and the EU led to an agreement. In exchange for Galileo receiving the approval of the US government, the EU's public signal would share its frequency with that of GPS, allowing for the distortion of both while leaving military communication intact for both sides (The White House, 2004).

The interoperability between the two systems was assured, yet the EU suffered from the general problems of the New Space era: tight public budgets and a fixation with profitability and private sector involvement (Abels & Bieling, 2023). As probabilities of success and profit margins remained hard to calculate, a lack of private investment and the failure of a public–private partnership delayed the project by several years. Galileo was only allowed to go ahead after a renationalisation of the project and a rededication of EU funds in 2008. In the meantime, GPS had further established itself as the global standard. Galileo became operational in 2017, yet at the time of writing the EU is still in the process of updating and completing the constellation.

The international push for independent and secure GNSSs has been marked by state security efforts as well as government-centred planning processes. Still, it became apparent that the public financing of comparable or larger outer space infrastructures would prove difficult in the future. TNCs were deeply involved in the production of GNSSs and, at least in the case of Galileo, there were political efforts to involve them more closely in the financing and operation. The main contractors for building navigation satellites were Lockheed Martin and Boeing in the US, and Airbus, Thales and Leonardo in the EU. Yet in the field of internet satellite mega-constellations, we are dealing with different players from the New Space era.

4 The Privatisation of Space: Internet Satellite Mega-Constellations

Internet satellite constellations are located in LEO for two primary reasons: first, as satellites are a lot closer to the Earth's surface, signal travel times are substantially lower than for example with satellites in MEO. This reduces latency and improves the responsiveness of internet services. LEO satellite constellations can provide global coverage by deploying a network of interconnected satellites that orbit Earth at different orbital inclinations and altitudes. This enables continuous coverage of all regions, including remote and underserved areas. Yet, a lot more satellites are required to achieve global coverage, which is why constellations consist of hundreds or even thousands of satellites. This leads to an increased congestion of LEO, raising concerns about collisions and space debris, and putting pressure on the spacefaring nations to develop regulations and mitigation measures.

All major internet satellite constellations are run by private corporations. Starlink is the largest and most advanced one. As of July 2024, it consists of more than 6,600 satellites and the US Federal Communications Commission (FCC) has already granted permission for the launch of up to 12,000 units (Howell & Pultarova, 2024). Starlink is operated by SpaceX, a California-based spacecraft and defence corporation, which is currently among the highest valued companies in the world that are not publicly traded (Roof et al., 2023). Business magnate Elon Musk acts as both the company's largest owner and CEO. SpaceX began deploying satellites for Starlink in 2019, which communicate with designate ground terminals to provide fast and secure internet coverage to previously underserved areas within minutes of setup. Due to the mass-production of satellites and terminals, SpaceX benefits from declining marginal costs, which facilitates the expansion of its network.

Originally presented as a service that would provide high-speed internet to individual and business customers for their everyday operations, the war in Ukraine highlighted the geopolitical relevance of such a potent internet satellite constellation (Abels, 2024). When Russia invaded Ukraine in February 2022, it was successful in jamming parts of Ukraine's military satellite networks. SpaceX took the decision to make Starlink available over Ukraine on 26 February, with the first terminals arriving just days after. Its internet services soon became indispensable to the Ukrainian military efforts. Due to the low energy requirements of terminals, broadband connection could be maintained even in the event of power outages. The Ukrainian military relied on Starlink for all operations along the front lines, where the war had destroyed ground infrastructure and other services failed. Ukrainian troops used Starlink for reconnaissance and for the execution of counterattacks, artillery fire, and drone strikes (Marquardt, 2022). It thus played an essential role in Ukraine's initial success of pushing back the Russian invasion forces. SpaceX's public perception and financial valuation in turn benefitted substantially from the showcasing of Starlink's capabilities under such intense conditions.

The US has been continuously ramping up its defence and space budget over the last years to fund its space-related programs. It relies heavily on domestic companies for virtually all stages of project implementation. SpaceX is a regular partner of the US government for all kinds of services, from launches to building satellites, and much of its business aims at securing large and profitable government contracts. The company has recognised the enormous profit potential that lies in commercial services to the military in times of geopolitical tension and has modified its portfolio accordingly. The US is highly aware of its economic pull, which has led it to view the commercialisation of space as an opportunity to cut costs and to promote US companies and sectors. John Plumb, Secretary of Defense for Space Policy, has stated "that the Department of Defense doesn't have to build its own constellation for every mission set to introduce resilience" and, with a view on LEO satellite constellation, raised the question whether "the department really need[s] to build its own when so much is available at the commercial level" (Center for Strategic and International Studies, 2022).

Yet, SpaceX's decisions soon started to divert from the declared US security interests (Abels, 2024). In summer 2022, some months after Starlink's activation over Ukraine, the defending forces reported service outages along the frontlines, which left some units cut off from command. This concerned battlefields around the oblasts of Luhansk, Donetsk, Zaporizhzhia, and Kherson, all of which Russia had occupied (Srivastava et al., 2022). In the following, SpaceX asked for additional public funds to maintain its services in Ukraine, with Elon Musk openly discussing the possibility of withdrawal (Marquardt, 2022). In February 2023, SpaceX further limited Starlink access for Ukrainian drone attacks and in Russian controlled territory.

It has become clear that, although SpaceX is a US-based company with a lot of its operations dependent on US state funding, it is not an entity the US government controls. As a transnational corporation operating in space, it follows its own logic and deals with foreign governments as well. The US initial response to these developments has been highly insightful. In principle, the US government continues to work closely with SpaceX. The Pentagon and SpaceX have been cooperating in thinning out Russian abuse of and access to the Starlink network (Capaccio, 2024). SpaceX is also building satellites and providing launch services for recent US projects. It constructs several hundreds of data relay satellites in LEO as well as a confidential spy satellite network for the US government (Roulette and Taylor, 2024). Thus, we observe the further evolvement of a US military-industrial space complex that seeks to centre the activities of domestic corporations around the national security interest and grants privileged access to those actors in return. In more recent developments, the second Trump administration has further incorporated the heads of US tech firms into the inner circle of state power - particularly SpaceX boss Elon Musk. This is likely to interlock the interests of these corporations with US state strategy even more fundamentally.

At the same time, the US was looking to diversify this corporate network in an emerging internet satellite sector. In 2024, John Plumb predicted that "more competition will emerge over this decade", including "a lot of commercial solutions that SpaceX is not involved in that the DoD would benefit from" (Capaccio, 2024). This likely alludes to further tech companies that are getting involved in the building of LEO constellations. Project Kuiper is an initiative aimed at deploying a constellation of LEO high-speed broadband internet satellites. Kuiper is expected to rival Starlink for market shares and contracts. Kuiper Systems is a subsidiary of Amazon. The company announced the project in April 2019, revealing its plans to launch over 3,200 satellites until 2029. Project Kuiper is supposed to reach almost global coverage, with the exception of Earth's most northern regions and the South Pole. It is still in the early stages, yet it has already lined up dozens of satellite launches. Amazon partners with several aerospace companies for the development and deployment of its satellites. It regularly contracts Blue Origin, a launch provider founded by Amazon CEO Jeff Bezos, yet seeks to limit its operational dependencies on direct competitors in the space business. Only in response to allegations of conflicts of interest made by shareholders, Amazon began contracting SpaceX in 2023 (Roulette, 2023).

The major European competitor in the satellite internet sector is OneWeb. The British company was founded in 2012 with the goal of providing global broadband internet access via LEO satellites. OneWeb is headquartered in London. It maintains a satellite manufacturing facility in Merritt Island, Florida, as a joint venture with Airbus Defence and Space. In 2023, OneWeb underwent a merger with Eutelsat, a French satellite operator. In the same year, it finalised its initial deployment phase of its constellation of 618 LEO internet satellites. A next generation is in planning that will raise the number of satellites in the constellation to just below 1,000 units. In contrast to Starlink, OneWeb does not target individual clients but offers global coverage to businesses and governments, including the defence sector. After the merger with Eutelsat, the major shareholders are Bharti Enterprises, the UK government, the Japanese Softbank, and Bpifrance, a French state-owned investment bank, highlighting the conflation of private and public interests in its ownership and operation.

As these examples demonstrate, it is large Western tech firms and commercial providers that dominate the internet satellite sector, whereas states are involved as clients or, investors. Yet, the transnational character of companies like Amazon and SpaceX, as well as the experiences with Starlink in Ukraine, have caused concerns with governments over the security implications of these constellations and a lack of state control. The EU, against the backdrop of its experiences with Galileo, agreed to finance its own satellite constellation called Infrastructure for Resilience, Interconnectivity and Security by Satellite (IRIS^2). It is supposed to offer broadband for critical state activities such as military operations, disaster prevention, and border surveillance.

Similar to the principles of Galileo, IRIS^2 is expected to remain interoperable with commercial systems (European Commission, 2023). Also similar to Galileo, major European corporation will be strongly involved, with the EU trying for a public–private partnership. A consortium of space industry companies submitted an offer to the European Commission in early 2024, with costs rising up to 12€ billion, twice than what has initially been estimated (Foust, 2024). Interestingly, Eutelsat will be a main contributor within this consortium, looking to benefit from IRIS^2 for its OneWeb constellation. The doubling of costs further delayed the procurement process and led to criticism from German minister of economy, Robert Habeck, who argued that the project was becoming overly expensive and risky (Fasse et al., 2024). In addition, the EU lacks reliable domestic launch companies, which made it dependent on US commercial providers for several years. IRIS^2 was originally intended to bring up to 170 satellites into LEO starting 2025, to have the system operable in 2027. At the time of writing, this date has been postponed to 2030 due to delays in procurement and the complex coordination of technological development, industrial production, and launching capacities. Under these circumstances, internet satellite constellations controlled by TNCs are likely to continue to dominate this sector of the space industry and the associated means of influence – for the near future at least.

5 Conclusions

This chapter discussed developments in outer space politics and their repercussions on other forms of global order. For that purpose, I proposed a lens that views states and corporations in a relationship of mutual dependence, yet in one where, in light of their transnational operations, corporations enjoy a larger room for strategic manoeuvre. Western states find it increasingly difficult to ensure the alignment of national companies and the control over essential infrastructures they provide. At the same time, in a period of intensifying global rivalry, states engage in more interventionist measures to reach their objectives. This has been highlighted empirically for New Space, the current era of outer space politics. State control over, and ownership of, space assets have to substantial proportions been replaced by that of private businesses, which prompted states to seek to reduce their vulnerability to the actions of corporations.

An analysis of states' competition over navigation satellite systems demonstrated the relevance of satellite infrastructures for national security considerations. Major powers such as the US, Russia, and China engaged in building their own GNSSs that would secure their access to military and civilian services and reduce their outside vulnerabilities. For the EU, however, the chapter also highlighted the political consequences of limited public budgets and an overreliance on private investment.

The second analytical section then underlined that businesses are increasingly in control of critical space infrastructure, which they are able to leverage to their advantage. In the age of internet satellite mega-constellations, corporations operating in space rely on states for advantageous regulatory frameworks and public funding. Yet, due to their technological edge and productive capacities, large tech firms are able to produce and operate constellations of hundreds of satellites on a commercial basis. Starlink, Kuipers, and OneWeb are the dominant internet infrastructures in LEO, all overwhelmingly privately owned. The US is relying on its military-industrial space complex and financial pull to ensure the alignment of domestic companies with its larger security interests. The EU, in an attempt to secure its strategic autonomy from Starlink and others, has opted for a private–public partnership model for its initiative $IRIS^2$, which maintains the prerogative of private actors in the space industry.

In outer space, private corporations own an increasing share of assets and take decisions over the accessibility of essential services, while regulation has not been catching up because of the stateless character of space. These developments have repercussions for several interlocking orders. The focus of this chapter was on a reorganisation of state-business relations. Space, to a substantial degree an unregulated realm, has allowed transnational tech firms to increase their control over critical infrastructures and with it their leverage over other commercial and state actors. With satellite constellations continuing to grow and corporations eyeing space colonisation, debris cleanup, and asteroid mining as future spheres of business activity, a reversal of this trend of privatisation seems highly unlikely.

The commercialisation of satellite infrastructure has had reordering effects on outer space: it contributed to the prevalence of profit-oriented and non-public practices, and further shifted the distribution of critical space assets towards a few central players in the private sector. Corporations can exploit their control over outer space infrastructures to influence key affairs and conflicts, changing the trajectory of global politics. In the war in Ukraine, SpaceX instrumentalised Starlink in a way that had lasting impacts on the course of the armed conflict (Abels, 2024).

Yet, the privatisation and commercialisation of outer space infrastructure is not to be viewed in isolation. Advances in technological development are particularly visible in outer space and some global trends can be observed there before they fully take hold in other realms. The depicted developments also impact on interlocking non-space orders, fundamentally reordering patterns of control and wealth on a global scale. There is a general concentration of financial and productive means in the hands of large, transnationally operating tech firms. This not only increases their structural power in the global economy but reorganises state-business relations in a way that makes issues of economic development, of foreign and security policy contingent on the interests of these corporations. Scientists would do well to take these reordering effects seriously and place the political decisions of TNCs in the focus of their analyses. An examination of the dynamics in outer space provides some indications of how global political processes, norms, and wealth distribution might develop in the future.

References

Abels, J. (2024). Private infrastructures in geopolitical conflicts: The case of Starlink and the war in Ukraine. *European Journal of International Relations, 30*(4), 842–866.

Abels, J., & Bieling, H.-J. (2023). Infrastructures of globalisation: Shifts in global order and Europe's strategic choices. *Competition & Change, 27*(3–4), 516–533.

Abels, J., & Bieling, H.-J. (2024). The geoeconomics of infrastructures: Viewing globalization and global rivalry through a lens of infrastructural competition. *Globalizations, 21*(4), 722–739.

Babić, M., Fichtner, J., & Heemskerk, E. M. (2017). States versus corporations: Rethinking the power of business in international politics. *The International Spectator, 52*(4), 20–43.

Baldwin, D. A. (2020). *Economic statecraft.* Princeton University Press.

Beidleman, S. W. (2005). GPS vs Galileo: Balancing for position in space. *Astropolitics, 3*(2), 117–161.

Bieler, A., Higgott, R., & Underhill, G. (Eds.). (2011). *Non-state actors and authority in the global system.* Routledge.

Capaccio, A. (2024, May 9). Pentagon teams up with SpaceX to block Russia from using Starlink. *Bloomberg.* https://www.bloomberg.com/news/articles/2024-05-09/russia-starlink-access-blocked-by-pentagon-spacex-ukraine.

Center for Strategic & International Studies. (2022). The state of space security: Fireside chat with the honorable John F. Plumb. https://www.csis.org/analysis/emerging-security-issues-space-policy.

De Goede, M. (2021). Finance/security infrastructures. *Review of International Political Economy, 28*(2), 351–368.

Eriksson, J., & Newlove-Eriksson, L. M. (2023). Outsourcing the American space dream: SpaceX and the race to the stars. *Astropolitics, 21*(1), 46–62.

European Commission. (2023). IRIS2 Industry Information Day, presentation. https://defence-industry-space.ec.europa.eu/system/files/2023-03/IRIS2%20Industry%20Information%20Day%20-%2030%20March%202023.pdf.

Farrell, H., & Newman, A. L. (2019). Weaponized interdependence: How global economic networks shape state coercion. *International Security, 44*(1), 42–79.

Fasse, M., Jahn, T., Olk, J., Volkery, C., & Waschinski, G. (2024, April 29). Streit um Starlink-Alternative: Kosten steigen stark. *Handelsblatt.* https://www.handelsblatt.com/politik/deutschland/raumfahrt-streit-um-starlink-alternative-kosten-steigen-stark/100035051.html.

Foust, J. (2024, April 15). EU to delay space law, constellation contract. *SpaceNews.* https://spacenews.com/eu-to-delay-space-law-constellation-contract/.

Gertz, G., & Evers, M. M. (2020). Geoeconomic competition. *The Washington Quarterly, 43*(2), 117–136.

Howell, E., & Pultarova, T. (2024). Starlink satellites: Facts, tracking and impact on astronomy. https://www.space.com/spacex-starlink-satellites.html.

Josselin, D., & Wallace, W. (Eds.). (2001). *Non-state actors in world politics.* Palgrave.

Maraš, D., & Dangubić, M. (2022). Cooperation between government agencies and private companies in space: The case of the United States. *Astropolitics, 20*(2–3), 226–237.

Marquardt, A. (2022, October 14). Exclusive: Musk's SpaceX says it can no longer pay for critical satellite services in Ukraine. *CNN.* https://edition.cnn.com/2022/10/13/politics/elon-musk-spacex-starlink-ukraine/index.html.

Norris, W. J. (2018). *Chinese economic statecraft: Commercial actors, grand strategy, and state control.* Cornell University Press.

Robinson, W. I., & Sprague-Silgado, J. (2018). The transnational capitalist class. In M. Juergensmeyer, S. Sassen, M. B. Steger, & V. Faessel (Eds.), *The Oxford handbook of global studies* (pp. 308–328). Oxford University Press.

Roof, K., Ludlow, E., & Grush, L. (2023). SpaceX value jumps closer to $180 billion in tender offer. *Bloomberg.* https://www.bloomberg.com/news/articles/2023-12-13/spacex-value-jumps-closer-to-180-billion-in-tender-offer.

Roulette, J. (2023, December 12). Amazon seeks dismissal of lawsuit over Kuiper satellite launch contracts. *Reuters.* https://www.reuters.com/legal/amazon-seeks-dismissal-lawsuit-over-kuiper-satellite-launch-contracts-2023-12-12/.

Roulette, J., & Taylor, M. (2024). Musk's SpaceX is building spy satellite network for US intelligence agency, sources say. *Reuters.* https://www.reuters.com/technology/space/musks-spacex-is-building-spy-satellite-network-us-intelligence-agency-sources-2024-03-16/.

Ruggie, J. (1982). International regimes, transactions, and change: Embedded liberalism in the postwar economic order. *International Organization, 36*(2), 379–415.

Sklair, L. (2010). *The transnational capitalist class.* Blackwell.

Srivastava, M., Olearchyk, R., Schwartz, F., & Miller, C. (2022, October 7). Ukrainian forces report Starlink outages during push against Russia. *Financial Times.* https://www.ft.com/content/9a7b922b-2435-4ac7-acdb-0ec9a6dc8397.

Strange, S. (1996). *The retreat of the state: The diffusion of power in the world economy.* Cambridge University Press.

The White House. (2004). Fact sheet: U.S.-EU summit, agreement on GPS-Galileo cooperation. https://georgewbush-whitehouse.archives.gov/news/releases/2004/06/print/text/20040626-8.html.

Joscha Abels is Postdoctoral researcher and lecturer at the Institute of Political Science, University of Tübingen. His main focus is on topics of International Political Economy and European Integration. Specific research interests lie in the fields of geoeconomics, infrastructure policy, international institutions, and the political economy of the Economic and Monetary Union. He has contributed to journals such as European Journal of International Relations, Journal of Common Market Studies, and Competition & Change. He is author of the book 'The politics of the Eurogroup. Governing crisis and conflict in the European Union' (Routledge). He is project lead of the DFG-funded project "EUInfra: Strategies of the EU in the global competition for economic expansion and geoeconomic control".

Spaces and Scales of a Street: Shifting Social Orders and Urban Transformation, as Seen From Marseille

Claire Bullen and Matteo Stefani

Abstract

When laid out in the nineteenth century, Boulevard National formed part of an urban system built as Marseille became to be an important node within France's colonial capitalism. In the early twenty-first century, it is once again linking up transport and communication systems that cross the Mediterranean Sea, and beyond. In this chapter, this urban infrastructure is used as a means of exploring the reconfigurations of spaces and scales within this former city of empire. By following the shifting significance and situation of this urban infrastructure within time–space, it becomes possible to track both the street's changing role within transnational systems and changes in Marseille's place within the re-ordering of social relations around the globe.

Keywords

Marseille · Street ethnography · Urban transport infrastructure · Urban transformation · Social reordering

C. Bullen (✉)
Institut für Soziologie, Universität Tübingen, Tübingen, Germany
e-mail: claire.bullen@uni-tuebingen.de

M. Stefani
Aix-Marseille Université, Marseille, France
e-mail: matteo.stefani@etu.univ-amu.fr

H.-J. Bieling et al. (eds.), *Transnational Infrastructures and the Transformation of Global Orders*, RaumFragen: Stadt – Region – Landschaft,
https://doi.org/10.1007/978-3-031-74846-2_13

1 Introduction

On France's Mediterranean shore, closer to Algiers than Paris, Marseille is a city whose place in the world has changed considerably over the last two hundred years.[1] Sometimes the city has been considered more "Arabic" than "European" or "French". At other times, the city is seen as marking the border between southern Europe and northern Africa. France's principal port of empire for over a century, left on the edge of the international political economy following decolonisation in the mid-twentieth century, for the last thirty years, Marseille has gained importance within French and EU initiatives to develop at once a free-trade zone around the Mediterranean Sea. As such, it offers an interesting window through which to examine urban, national, regional and global reordering, across time. In this chapter, one street, Boulevard National, will serve as the entry point to examine these changing multiscalar social relations, as they come together in Marseille.

In 2024, Boulevard National may not feel like a particularly auspicious starting point from where to begin. Boulevard National is rarely associated with the sorts of mega-projects that generally come to mind when thinking of border-crossing infrastructure: gas pipelines, submarine cables, perhaps military bases…The street does link up a two metro lines and the main railway. It is a busy bus route and channels vehicles out of the city and to the international ferry port. Yet this does not justify its choice as an entry point to explore cross-border rescaling dynamics. For many familiar with contemporary Marseille, the street is at best considered an "ordinary" street; at worst it conjures up the idea of an impoverished, stigmatised and racialised neighbourhood. When laid out in the nineteenth century, however, Boulevard National was a part of an urban transport system built as Marseille was becoming an important node within France's colonial capitalism. In the early twenty-first century, it is once again linking up transport and communication systems that cross the Mediterranean Sea, and beyond. Following the shifting significance and situation of this urban infrastructure within time–space offers one way to track both the street's changing role within transnational systems and transformations in Marseille's place within the re-ordering of social relations around the globe.

[1] This research was funded as part of the Excellence Strategy of the German Federal and State Governments. The chapter builds on the precious archival research and insights of Amel Zerourou and along the way has benefited from discussions and feedback from Daniele Karasz, Katrin Kremmel, Karolin Mattes and Franck Lamiot, and from the broader exchanges with the "Infrastructures and Global Ordering" (IGLO) project in Tübingen.

2 Conceptual Clarifications

2.1 Thinking with Infrastructure

The nuts and bolts undergirding everyday life, infrastructural forms are regularly taken for granted in everyday life. Within the social sciences conversely the case for paying attention to infrastructure as a heuristic to help to puzzle out politics, poetics and practices of entangled social relations is now well established (Amin, 2014; Appel et al., 2018; Buier, 2023; Edwards, 2002; Larkin, 2013). Numerous scholars have shown how the design, construction and governance of, for example, intercity roads or high-speed rail, urban water supplies or submarine cables can bring to the fore struggles over meanings, resources and populations in particular social spaces at particular times (Buier, 2020; Harvey & Knox, 2016; McFarlane, 2008; Ratté, 2019).

Early on within the so-called infrastructural turn, Edwards (2002) highlighted the importance of a multiscalar and power-inflected approach to infrastructural analysis. Different social groups and forces (from households, to governments and economic structures) may work within and constitute the "local", "national" and/or the "global". Yet, as Edwards (2002, p. 2) argued, the "scale" of people's relations, whether these relations are understood and experienced as local, national or beyond will always be dependent upon infrastructural projects such as telecommunications, transport networks and energy systems being in place, in good working order and accessible. These insights have been taken further in work that brings together infrastructural studies and relational thinking in the social sciences (Simone, 2014). Rather than a static *thing,* infrastructure has become to be understood in processual terms, a social-material configuration that is changing, contingent and inherently connected to multiscalar elsewheres (see also, Massey, 2005). Such a focus directs attention to the various temporal dimensions of infrastructure. As Gupta (2018) notes, the ways in which infrastructural projects are planned, rolled out and adopted (or not) and how they fit within a reordering of the world are shaped by an array of temporal frames, from historical pathway dependencies, to rhythms of the present, to visions of the future, and the potential of decay and abandonment. Thought of in these terms, the scale/s of the spatial forms of objects such as streets can be analysed as produced by contingent and power-inflected unfolding of socio-spatial relations over time. These contribute to, and are shaped by, the reconfiguration of multiscalar "social orders" (Appel et al., 2018; Graham & Marvin, 2001).

2.2 Thinking Through Social Orders

Definitions of social order vary across disciplinary fields (von Benda-Beckmann & Pirie, 2007). Coming from a sociological and anthropological tradition, we conceive social order as a relatively stable organisation of social relations, undergirded by institutionalised norms and values, practices and resources across space (see Knoblauch & Löw, 2020; Hobart & Kapferer, 2014). Typically, "the state" is considered the principal organising system of social relations. Despite critiques of "methodological nationalism" (Wimmer & Glick Schiller, 2002), a large body of social sciences scholarship continue to study social transformations from this "scale" (Bhambra, 2016). This is problematic for many reasons. The heterogeneity, partiality, dynamic and contested nature of social relations within and across state borders can be over looked. Furthermore, national governments may be the source of disruption or instability, within or beyond state borders, or may turn out to be incapable of underpinning order at the national or other scales. The latter certainly needs to be considered within an international system shaped by powerful multinational companies, where the welfare state has, in many instances, been unravelled, and groups promoting alternative normative socio-spatial fixes (including calls for regional autonomy) proliferate. Empirical investigation is thus required of the potential co-existence of multiple scaled forms of socio-spatial organisation, to make clear how different ordering processes may overlap, collide, or run in parallel.

2.3 The Ordering and the Spatiality of the Street

Streets are complex social objects. As with any urban infrastructure, how streets are planned, under which regulatory regimes, the choice, financing and sourcing of materials and the ways in which these are maintained, as well as the possibilities of "ordinary people" to intervene in the developing of the street can shed light on how local, national and—potentially—international connections come together in a specific place, and affect understandings about who is considered part of the city (Tartakowski et al., 2022; Dalakoglou & Harvey, 2012, p. 460). In this case, we are talking about a particular form of street: a "boulevard", largely similar to the model of the "Parisian boulevard".[2]

Carved out under the administrations of General Haussmann and commissioned by Napoleon III during France's Second Empire, this urban form fulfilled many functions. Wide enough and straight enough to march an army down, it linked and sped up movement between centres of political, economic and symbolic power (i.e. new railway stations, army barracks, palatial departmental stores and shopping arcades) (Harvey, 2004). The iconic Parisian boulevard was flanked by uniform yet elegant five or six-storey *Hausmannian* buildings. Wide pavements rendered the new practices of leisure and consumption (*flânnerie* and window shopping) more agreeable. Featuring in novels, newspapers and early photography, this urban transport system was soon taken as the epitome of the modernist city, an aesthetic manifestation of progress, development and "civilised"

[2] The origins of the term boulevard have been traced back to the Dutch or German word for fortification or bastion "*bollwerk*". The bollwerk referred to a wide ring road that replaced city walls that had become redundant (Lelarge 2016).

or "European" urban design (Paquot, 2015; Harvey ibid.; Werquin & Demangeon, 2000; Paquot, 2015). Travelling beyond Paris, the model arrived in big cities in the provinces—including Marseille—and was then transported, via steamship and rail to North Africa and elsewhere in the French colonies, becoming one of the urban building blocks of France's racialised colonial system (Harvey, 2004).[3]

The French boulevard embodies what Vinken (2008, cited in Knoblauch & Löw, 2020, p. 274) has called "trajectorial space", facilitating circulation of people and goods. Streets can also be made up of "places", that is imagined and experienced as spatially fixed, associated with an identity and permitting certain forms of social relations (such as neighbouring) to occur and "spaces of networks" (urban transport system, Internet, gas and water conduits etc.), a spatial figure that has been seen as the incarnation of "refigured modernity" (Castells 2001, in Knoblauch & Löw, 2020, p. 275).

Thinking with these different spatial figures, the article proceeds by first sketching out some of the social relations and aspirations that shaped how urban transport infrastructure was planned and laid out at this dawn of urban "modernity". This is followed by an examination of the street at the current time, to consider the politics, possibilities and practices of the street today, and how these have been changed and are changing in this period of "post" or "refigured" modernity (Knoblauch & Löw, 2020). Such an analytical move is particularly pertinent in a region like the Mediterranean, where urban and political b/orders are regularly rewritten, through capitalism, de/colonisation, and de/globalisation and at a time when cities are more "multi-scalar" than ever before (Brenner & Schmid, 2015).

3 A "Modern" Marseille Street

Picture Marseille in the 1830s. The early nineteenth century was a singularly unstable period in France's history. The country had undergone numerous revolts and revolutions leading to the establishment of two republics, two monarchies and two empires, first out to Italy and then extending its colonial conquest of North Africa and beyond. Notwithstanding economic shocks brought about by war and revolution, Marseille was thriving. In 1831, urban dwellers had jumped by over a third since 1811, reaching 132.000 (around a sixth of the size of the city today). In economic terms, it was a period of unrivalled growth. Sewell (1985, p. 22) described this period as Marseille's veritable "industrial revolution". The city had become the fifth most important port in the world in terms of quantity of imports and exports, predominantly from the Mediterranean (Italy, Spain, North Africa, Eastern Mediterranean) and some extra-Mediterranean trade with

[3] The urban transfer can also be traced linguistically. In North Africa, the word *bulvâr* appeared in Arabic alongside the main term for street *shâri* in the early twentieth century (Dines, 2018, p. 957; Ziadeh 2011).

northern Europe, the Americas, and South and East Asia. The commercial trade spawned industrial activity, and factories began to be thrust up across the city, transforming olive oil, wheat, lumber, sugar cane and sulphur to either ship abroad or for France's internal markets.

The rapid growth placed Marseille's urban systems under considerable strain. Within the city's fortifications, housing was increasingly overcrowded, forcing construction to spill out over the city walls, south and east of the city's port. Water supplies in this arid part of France were no longer sufficient to meet the needs of thirsty households and factories. Additionally, both port and city transport systems struggled to handle the growing size and volume of traffic. Members of Marseille's commercial and industrial elites identified the need to invest in major public works. This included the major *Canal de Provence* designed to channel water to the city. Paid for by in part by the municipality and by subscription, a grandiose arrival for the canal was conjured up, spilling out in an ornate fountain at the centre of the magnificent Longchamp Palace. This investment was an architectural proclamation of municipal pride. In today's terms, it can be seen as a form of urban boosterism, or an attempt at urban "scalar jumping" by local elites (Brenner & Schmid, 2015).

The plans to lay out Boulevard National were put forward to the city council in the end of the 1830s by a local entrepreneur of public works, M. Maurens.[4] The proposed street began in the new *quartiers* being laid out south and east of the now dismantled city walls and the Longchamp palace. It cut through agricultural land in a north-westerly direction, joining up with the Route d'Aix, which itself was part of the national road network. The plans were approved by the council in 1841, and royal approval was granted the following year.

Based on municipal decisions from the time, local historian Chantal Champet has argued that the principal aim was to free up the overcrowded roads in the old city and speed up the transportation of merchandise heading north out of the city to join France's internal markets. Within the council deliberations of 1843 meticulous details were given about the street's form.[5] It should be 20 m wide, including five-metre-wide pavements either side of the carriageway, and be lined with trees planted at ten metre intervals. The project was supervised by the city architect and Maurens was to be paid on delivery. The careful attention to the street's aesthetics and dimensions also reflects new logics of embellishment of urban space by diverse actors, working to "upgrade" the city in symbolic terms within France (Bonillo, 1992). The first buildings were constructed along the first part of the street, as Marseille's growing bourgeoisie invested in individual private hotels, Hausmannian-style town houses and a sumptuous liquor factory, inclusive of a large ballroom.

[4] 496W149, 1843-1897, Service de la Voirie, "Boulevard National: projet d'ouverture du boulevard, plans", Municipal Archives, Marseille.
[5] Ibid.

The street's name can also be read to reflect efforts by the city leaders to symbolically make connections with national-level politics. In his anthology of Marseille's street names written twenty years after the completion of the street, Fabre (2018 (1867)) bemoans the lack of imagination in coming up with Boulevard National's name. In fact, the street's original name was Boulevard d'Orleans. The choice of name can be read as a homage to one of the lines to the French monarchy. The street's name was changed at the time of the Second Republic in 1848 from this monarchist nomenclature to the more neutral Boulevard National. Both names give insights into the politics and games of positioning that were occurring in the city at the time in a city where the small dominant classes (in this largely working-class city) were largely conservative. They sought good relations to the central administration, as they were better for trade (Sewell, 1985, p. 17). The name offers a trace of the power, identity and discursive dynamics that were inherent in the city at the time.[6]

If facilitating the circulation of traffic out of Marseille via the national road network was the principal aim of decision makers in the local council—that is, the boulevard seen as trajectorial space—Boulevard National was also planned to link together two other transport systems that were yet to be built: the new port and docks and the Marseille Avignon railway line. Both these major infrastructural projects were put forward and developed by figures who embody the new "age of capital": Parisian financial investors and engineers with a keen appreciation of how transnational infrastructural investment were fundamental to the establishment of France's overseas colonial empire. This vision was most clearly expressed by the Saint-Simonian social theorist, Chevalier, who, writing in the earlier 1830s, saw Marseille as a lynchpin within a "Mediterranean system" undergirded by a transport system based on rail and steamships and roads that would extend from Britain to the Indian Ocean (Chevalier, 1832). In this vision of Marseille, the street operates according to a transnational network of spatial logic. Sewell (1985, pp. 42–43) argues that the Parisian capitalists had a broader vision of Marseille's potential than its native mercantile community, and they had the resources and the ruthlessness to undertake grandiose projects.

As the nineteenth century progressed, Boulevard National was extended to service the new port. Local investors transformed the stretch of the street between the railway and the port into a hub of industrial activity, constructing metalwork and mechanical workshops, a flour mill, sugar and oil refineries, chemical, soap and food processing factories. To meet the labour needs of this new industrial neighbourhood, a new district was planned for labourers, incorporating the boulevard into new spaces of the neighbourhood. By the end of the nineteenth century this area was predominantly inhabited by migrants from France's impoverished rural areas and from Italy. Tracing the webs of relations across multiple domains that shaped Boulevard National helps us to gain insights into how transforming socio-spatial relations in the city were intrinsically

[6] This point is made by Cailli Forrest (2018) about a very different context.

enmeshed in national and imperial systems of order (Bhambra, 2016). From the street's origins in the middle of the "modern era", we turn now to consider contemporary Boulevard National.

4 Situating Marseille Within Post-Modern Times

Marseille's role as pivot within the French colonial capitalist system had ended with the Independence movements in French colonial territories in the 1950s and 60s. Changes to trading and visa regimes had undermined the city's port-based economy (Dell'Umbria, 2006; Roncayolo, 1996). A further blow was administered when the French government chose to sever ties between the port and the municipality and to re-localise part of the port 60 kms along the coast to Fos-sur-Mer, a site better suited for handling huge cargo ships and petrol tankers.

The decision from Paris was lived badly by local economic and political leaders, depriving Marseille as it did of a considerable source of employment and tax revenue, at a time of a global downturn and patterns of deindustrialisation within many advanced capitalist states (Dell'Umbria, 2006). As the city coffers were depleted, social costs grew. The city administration was faced with growing unemployment and the obligation to respond to the needs of thousands of repatriated "Europeans" fleeing France's former colonies and (post)colonial migrant workers who arrived in Marseille in the 1950s and 60s. This exacerbated a severe housing situation (including considerable slum dwellings) that had not been resolved during the post-World War II reconstruction (Nasiali, 2016).

With little strategic oversight, and strongly influenced by racialised logics of administrators who had worked in the French colonies (Nasiali, 2016), cheap land around the city was bought up piecemeal by the municipality in order to throw up high-rise accommodation. The density of the housing units and the cheap materials used created social problems for the future in what became infamous and racialised as "*les quartiers nord*". In parallel, the city centre became increasingly rundown. Many who could afford to move out did so. Marseille's economic base was further weakened by a local conjuncture of strident industrial conflicts on the docks, pork-barrel politics, well-developed organised crime and virulent racism. Across the board, the city was presented in alarming terms in local and national press (Peraldi & Samson, 2005). These factors affected local city decision-makers' abilities to reposition Marseille nationally and internationally.

If one of the urban decision makers from 1830s Marseille were to be transported to Marseille at the end of the twentieth century, they would find many of the new institutional logics and modes of governance bewildering. Some local businesses were still involved in decision-making (Peraldi & Samson, 2005), but an increasingly complex web of local administration actors had developed with competencies being divided out across the scale of neighbourhood, the municipality, the metropolitan authority, the departmental and regional councils, and state ministries, national agencies… (Donzel,

2014). In addition, new public agencies sprung up responsible for managing different urban development across the city. Reflecting patterns visible from the neo-liberalisation of urban development across the globe, the major urban projects were increasingly developed by a handful of multinational real estate developers.

One thing that has not changed in Marseille's socio-spatial organisation is the importance of central government, both in the form of significant state subsidies and in strategic planning. The clearest manifestation of this is the Euro-Mediterranean urban development zone. This programme came about as a result of reports commanded by local and central government to transform the increasingly reductant waterfront and docklands in the 1990s (Pinson, 2002). Managed by a public authority, of which half of the board members were appointed by central state, it involved the transformation of the former docks into a "second city centre" with offices designed by "starchitects", commerces, residential and leisure, aiming to encourage outside investment and economic growth in Marseille, and those "new populations" that Alain Tarrius (1992) dubbed as "white and clean" professional classes.

The project's designation as "operation of national interest" (ONI) and its appellation as the "Euro-Mediterranean urban development project" make clear semantic connections with national and transnational scale. The French government was attempting to position France and Marseille as a strategic hub within European Union plans to forge a "Euro-Mediterranean" region. Marseille's Euromed development was underpinned by national, European and local public investment in major infrastructure projects in the 2000s, notably the extension of the high-speed train link, the TGV-Méditerranée and the development of the local airport. Locally, the project sought to give Marseille the material and symbolic resources to justify its title as capital of the metropolitan area. In short, this mega urban project reflects new orders of international governance and reflects and contributes to reordering processes at various scales. Yet, while the Euromed development did include plans to upgrade the urban fabric, the project was, in this early phase, about international repositioning *of* the city, rather than a project *for* the city (Bertoncello and Rodrigues-Malta, 2003, pp. 428–9). At the early phase of this project, it did little to affect Boulevard National's position in the world, although the street arrived at the periphery of the development zone.

4.1 Situating the Street Within This Social Reordering

Over the twentieth century, Boulevard National had lost its function as a key trajectorial space. As one urban planner bemoaned in 1950, it took longer to leave this congested, insalubrious part of the city and drive to the local airport than it took to fly from there to Algiers in Algeria or Bastia in Corsica (Nicod, 1951). To reduce travel time, national civil engineers designed a new motorway heading north that swung over Boulevard National out to the airport and towards Aix-en-Provence. Boulevard National now felt national only in name.

When one of the authors arrived in Marseille in the early 2010s, the buildings along the street were dirty and in many cases dilapidated. The street was for many associated with long, noisy traffic jams, worsened by parking methods that impeded efforts to circulate around the neighbourhood or to leave the city. Rather than being a spatial form that facilitated circulation, the boulevard had become two distinct places or urban milieus, either side of the tunnel that passed under the railway lines.

To the north of the pollution-stained, exhaust-filled tunnel, former industrial buildings had been transformed into discount stores, garages, and fast-food restaurants. Here the majority of the population were from former colonial countries. This side of the street had/has become for many included within the racialised geography of "*les quartiers nord*". On the other side, the former opulent quartier had become amalgamated into the impoverished city centre neighbourhoods, though from the 2010s, state-led investment was encouraging gentrification processes that was "upscaling" this part of the street.

The street's shift from trajectorial space to place and its displacement from its role as a key node within Marseille's connectivity at sub-regional and transnational scale, helps explain the general neglect. The state of the street also reflects the lack of resources in this highly indebted city, and years of neglect towards the poorest and racialised neighbourhoods (see Graham & Marvin, 2001). In the 2010s, however, parts of the street started to receive more attention from policy makers. We have chosen two urban development projects that show a generally growing, if uneven, interest in this part of the city and, that, more specifically, point to a reordering of socio-spatial systems.

4.2 Les Docks Libres

The plans for *Les Docks Libres* (The Free Docks) were first sketched out in the mid-2000s. The site was situated towards the northern most end of the boulevard, between one of the most economically impoverished neighbourhoods in France on the one side and on the peripheries of the Euromed development zone on the other. The project involved the demolition of nineteenth century brick warehouses to build what was described as a "multi-functional" development: several high-rise buildings incorporating flats, offices and some commercial units at street level. In the scoping documents produced by urban planners, the project was presented in terms of helping Marseille to become a new "gateway"; to where this gateway would lead was not stated; implicitly there is a semantic link to Marseille's former role within the colonial system. For the Metropolitan authorities who took over the oversight of the project on behalf of the local authorities, the state-led Euro-Med agency, and the property developer, the aim was to transform the quartier and contribute to raising Marseille's profile within the metropolitan region. Within documents setting out the vision for this project, the initiative is associated with urban development projects in Barcelona and Milan's "Santa Giulia", indexing Marseille to relatively well-positioned European cities.[7] On completion, however, these multiscalar connections fell to one side.

The finish project was described in terms of a series of courtyards, crossed by streets and footbridges (Cuordifede, 2017). In the original plans, this layout was claimed to be inspired by "Marseillaise urban tradition". The scoping documents also included architect's representations of wide pavements planted with trees, offering a visual echo with the design requirements set out for Boulevard National in the 1840s. In fact, this new-build breaks with the urban logic of the street laid out in the nineteenth century. At the launch of the project, ten years later, the Docks Libres was marketed in terms of creating a "new" neighbourhood, by transplanting a "more agreeable architecture" onto an "old and degraded neighbourhood". Interviews with the property developer behind the project indicate that aspirations to create connections with the local neighbourhood were thwarted by security concerns (Cuordifede, 2017). Within the marketing material, more reference is made to the proximity to the Euromed development zone than to the urban life along the boulevard. This comes across clearly the choice of angle of photos found on the website of the property developer, which are shot facing away from the quartier that the project was supposed to be changing, and look over to the Mediterranean Sea.

If the initial vision of the project had been based on rhetorical reference to what could be called translocal elsewheres, these were not manifested in the finished construction. Arguably, this can be put down to the lack of infrastructural investment that would have permitted such urban re-scaling. Indeed, in the words of one of the social landlords associated with the project, Les Docks Libre "had the dimensions of a small town" but not been thought about in "infrastructural terms" (Cuordifede, 2017). The logic can be understood more in terms of locally repositioning of a bounded—or barricaded—*quartier*, rather than enmeshing this space within transnational trajectories.

The second project, imagined ten years later, sees Boulevard National more clearly integrated within infrastructural projects of national and transnational re-ordering importance that begin to influence the organisation of the different spatial forms and scales of the street.

4.3 Les Quartiers Libres

In the late 2000s, local and national decision makers in Marseille started to express the need to consolidate and develop the urban public transport networks. It was argued that these should be better linked into national and transnational systems, if the maritime and urban infrastructure investments were to function appropriately (Bertoncello et al. 2009). Funded by the state, local authorities and the EU, the "Quartiers Libres" project around Marseille's central train station represents such efforts. To achieve these goals, new infrastructural investments have been focused along the boulevard.

[7] C+t architects, Immobilier Sémaphore, Ville de Marseille (2005). *Requalification urbaine du secteur Bougainville-Bellevue-Saint Mauront*. Archives de Marseille, 1311 W 197.

On the one hand, the "Quartiers Libres" sought to insert part of the city within a network logic of this national transport plan, as Marseille's central station becomes a key hub in what in France will be called the Provence-Côte d'Azur part of a "Latin-Arc", with the area where the railway lines cross the boulevard being a key intersection. An underground rail link is being built beneath the boulevard as part of these developments. The tunnel that runs along Boulevard National will be reduced in length to permit the construction of a square where different forms of transport converge, including the tramway (which will be extended along Boulevard National), buses and cycle routes (Schnyder, 2022). Together, this enables us to claim that Boulevard National be considered a part of a "Mediterranean transport system".

To bolster this assertion, it is sufficient to turn to the Regional Transport Action Plan for the Mediterranean Region 2021–2027 (RTAP, 2021). The RTAP was produced within the framework of the Union for the Mediterranean (UfM), an intergovernmental body that brings together EU member states and 16 countries from North Africa, Western Asia and Southern Europe.[8] The document seeks to increase "regional integration" by developing a free trade area, underpinned by a "well-functioning transport system". The report advocates strengthening regional and international dimensions of national transport strategies, and encouraging countries to implement sustainable urban mobility plans for their most important cities (RTAP, 2021, p. 29). The language used to help develop a Euro-Mediterranean free trade area is reminiscent of those used by Chevalier in the nineteenth century to promote a "Mediterranean system" at the time of European colonial expansion south and east of the Mediterranean.

On the other hand, and as with the Docks Libres, The Quartiers Libre project includes objectives to reinforce Marseille's socio-spatial positioning as a metropolitan capital and to transform the impoverished neighbourhoods juxtaposing the city centre. The metropolitan authority aimed to improve the profile and the functionality of Marseille's "extended city centre" by investing in university buildings, nineteenth century barracks and the surrounding neighbourhoods, to increase its economic and cultural "*attractivité*" (appeal), including linking up the impoverished 3rd arrondissement with the city's "hypercentre".

The tunnel, which continues to be a symbolic separation between the impoverished neighbourhoods and the city centre has been renovated and redecorated as part of this. As well as improvements in the street lighting, local arts associations with international profile have been called upon to decorate with "street art" the inner walls of the tunnel. "The aim is to change the way people look at the area, enhance the public spaces and beautify the streets from now on" (Grapeloup, 2024).

The choice of graffiti is a long way from the aesthetic demands of the decision-makers behind the laying out of this boulevard in the nineteenth century. In the last decades, street art has become a marker of Marseille's increasingly well-known urban culture

[8] The UfM operates with an EU policy framework directed towards countries south and east of the EU territory via the 'The European Neighbourhood Policy' (ENP), created in 2003 and the Euro-Mediterranean Partnership, instigated in 1995.

scene. At once a form of artistic expression that can be considered bottom-up appropriation of urban space by groups often left out of urban decision-making processes (Géa, 2017), it has increasingly been used within place-marketing initiatives. For this intervention, the local authorities commissioned the La Friche de la Belle de Mai, a high profile institution that makes up a key part of this "alternative" cultural industries scene, these interventions are justified in both improving the quality of life of the local inhabitants and associations. The choice of this aesthetic form can be read as contributing to the staging of this part of Marseille as a site of "authenticity" while also offering an image of Marseille that sells well nationally and internationally (Tödt, 2011). At the same time, while defended by the local authorities in terms of augmenting local adherence to an urban renewal project, this aesthetic intervention along Boulevard National contains the possibility of a reconfiguration of social relations, as the investment in cultural and urban infrastructural improvements risks leading to the displacement of certain social groups from the boulevard.

5 Concluding Thoughts

As said in the beginning, claims that Boulevard National should be considered part of a transnational transport system could seem a little overblown. Notwithstanding this, we set ourselves the task to show how, over time, Marseille's changing place in the world can be read from what could be seen as an insignificant thoroughfare, if this thoroughfare is situated in space and time. To make our case, we turned back the clocks to a period when the boulevard was being laid out. At this juncture, it is easier to see this street as a small cog within Marseille's reconfiguration as a pivotal place within the framework of France's colonial capitalism. In the mid-twentieth century, the street lost its significance within transnational infrastructural networks, as Marseille's socio-spatial position was shaken up through the combined logics of decolonisation and deindustrialisation. Yet, in the last ten years, Marseille's place within transnational transport is being reinforced. Further, current European, national and local Euro-Mediterranean policies suggest that a spruced up Boulevard National will feature within this.

The inclusion of Mediterranean thinking within local urban planning comes across strongly in the following quotation from Marseille's city mayor. In 2021, he anticipated that:

> Marseille can once again become a driving force, a beacon, a promised land. Marseille can become the leading port on the Mediterranean, the largest European hub for connections[...], a centre of energy and freedom, of economic, cultural and intellectual development towards the Mediterranean, the Maghreb, Africa and Asia.[9]

[9] Speech by Benoit Payan mayor of Marseille on the occasion of Emmanuel Macron's visit to Marseille on Thursday 2 September 2021. Our translation.

If the language echoes strongly that used by Marseille's city leaders around the time Boulevard National was planned, this is not a copy-paste from the past. In the nineteenth century, Boulevard National was laid out by a private entrepreneur, paid for by the local administration, contributing to the circulation of goods, people and ideas within the French state and France's empire. Today, the street features as a link within the local and metropolitan area run by leaders from opposing political camps, within the framework of the French state, and a "Euro-Mediterranean area" under construction.

As we have seen from the past, current re-ordering of social order around the Mediterranean is being reconfigured by multiple, often contested and divergent forces. These are differently affected by, and affect, the implementation and maintenance of transnational infrastructures. As in the past, the logics of the various institutional bodies seeking to developing regional transport links are shaped by competing ideologies and shifts in political (in)stability around the Mediterranean. This present moment is certainly one marked by a significant conjunctural shift (Clarke, 2014), as relations of power are being rewritten, bringing new social settlements into being. Nationalism and authoritarianism are increasingly present across the region, accompanied by increasingly restrictive immigration policies. This can affect plans for and the maintenance of transnational infrastructure projects. Nationalist policies do not necessarily lead to a rejection of the logics of free trade, but they can result in policies to control the circulation of people and goods in ways that racialise and exclude. Transnational infrastructure projects can also support international mobilisation for pan-Mediterranean solidarity beyond the nation-state. Conversely, both progressive and authoritarian approaches defended by diverse social groups may reinforce the importance of social ordering at the national level. In any case, at such complex times, social scientists face the challenge of better understanding changing possibilities for social relations around the world. We suggest thinking from particular places, such as a street like Boulevard National, in a city like Marseille, and being attentive to the scalar geographies of these diverse dynamics across history, can help make sense of this puzzle.

References

Amin, A. (2014). Lively infrastructure. *Theory, Culture & Society, 31*(7–8), 137–161.

Appel, H., Anand, N., & Gupta, A. (2018). Introduction: Temporality, politics, and the promise of infrastructure. In N. Anand, A. Gupta, & H. Appel (Eds.), *The Promise of Infrastructure* (pp. 1–38). Duke University Press.

Bertoncello, B., & Rodrigues-Malta, R. (2003). Marseille versus euroméditerranée. *Annales de Géographie, 632*(112), 424–436.

Bertoncello, B., Dubois, J., & Rodrigues-Malta, R. (2009). Opération Euroméditerranée, une affaire d'état. POPSU, EPAU.

Bonillo, J. L. (Ed.) (1992). *Marseille, ville & port.* Parenthèses.

Bhambra, G. K. (2016). Comparative historical sociology and the state: Problems of method. *Cultural Sociology, 10*(3), 335–351.

Buier, N. (2020). The second coming of rail: The Spanish high-speed rail-finance complex. *Antipode, 52*(6), 1603–1623.

Buier, N. (2023). The anthropology of infrastructure: The boom and the bubble? *Focaal, 95*, 46–60.

Brenner, N., & Schmid, C. (2015). Towards a new epistemology of the urban? *City, 19*(2–3), 151–182.

Chevalier, M. (1832). *The mediterranean system* (S. W. Rowan, Trans.). https://irl.umsl.edu/history-faculty/6/.

Clarke, J. (2014). Conjunctures, crises, and cultures. *Focaal, 70*, 113–122. https://doi.org/10.3167/fcl.2014.700109

Cuordifede, C. (2017, September 11). [Vivre à Bougainville] Aux docks libres, entre protection et fragmentation sociale. *Marsactu* (blog). https://marsactu.fr/vivre-a-bougainville-aux-docks-libres-entre-protection-fragmentation-sociale/.

Dalakoglou, D., & Harvey, P. (2012). Roads and anthropology: Ethnographic perspectives on space, time and (im)mobility. *Mobilities, 7*(4), 459–465.

Dell'Umbria, A. (2006). *Histoire universelle de Marseille. De l'an mil à l'an deux mille.* Agone.

Dines, N. (2018). What's in a word? Contextual diversity, urban ethnography and the linguistic limits of the street. *The Sociological Review, 66*(5), 952–967.

Donzel, A. (2014). Une écologie culturelle de la ville. *Rives Méditerranéennes, 47* (February), 19–30.

Edwards, P. N. (2002). Infrastructure and modernity. In P. Brey, A. Rip & A. Feenberg (Eds.), *Technology and modernity: The empirical turn.* MIT Press.

Fabre, A. (2018) (1867). *Les rues de Marseille (Tome 1).* Hachette Bnf.

Forrest, C. (2018). What's in a name? A feminist reflection on street name changes in durban. *Agenda, 32*(2), 53–61.

Géa, J.-M. (2017). Le panier un quartier marseillais en voie de gentrification: Reconfigurations sociales et résistances langagières. *Éditions De La Maison des Sciences De L'homme /langage Et Société, 162*, 21–45.

Graham, S., & Marvin, S. (2001). *Splintering urbanism: Networked infrastructures, technological mobilities and the urban condition.* Routledge.

Grapeloup, M. (2024, June 26). À la belle de mai, le tunnel national se transforme en temple du street-art. *Made in Marseille.* https://madeinmarseille.net/164244-belle-de-mai-tunnel-national-se-transforme-en-temple-du-street-art/.

Gupta, A. (2018). 2. The future in ruins: Thoughts on the temporality of infrastructure. In H. Appel, A. Nikhil & G. Akhil (Eds.), *The Promise of Infrastructure,* (pp. 62–79). Duke University Press.

Harvey, D. (2004). *Paris, capital of modernity.* Routledge.

Harvey, P., & Knox, H. (2016). *Roads: An anthropology of infrastructure and expertise. Expertise.* Cornell University Press.

Hobart, A., & Kapferer, B. (Eds.). (2014). *Contesting the state: The dynamics of resistance and control* (Paperback). Sean Kingston Publishing.

Knoblauch, H., & Löw, M. (2020). The re-figuration of spaces and refigured modernity—Concept and diagnosis. *Historical Social Research/Historische Sozialforschung, 45*(2), 263–292.

Larkin, B. (2013). The politics and poetics of infrastructure. *Annual Review of Anthropology, 42*(1), 327–343.

Massey, D. (2005). *For space*. Sage Publications Ltd.

McFarlane, C. (2008). Governing the contaminated city: Infrastructure and sanitation in colonial and post-colonial Bombay. *International Journal of Urban and Regional Research, 32*(2), 415–435.

Nasiali, M. (2016). *Native to the republic: Empire, social citizenship, and everyday life in Marseille since 1945.* Miller Center of Public Affairs Books.

Nicod, J. (1951). L'autoroute de la sortie nord de Marseille. *L'information Géographique, 15*(3), 113–114.

Paquot, T. (2015). Repères bibliographiques. In *Nouvelle édition* (pp. 113–124). Repères. Paris: La Découverte.

Pinson, G. (2002). *Projets et pouvoirs dans les villes europeennes. Une comparaison de Marseille, Venise, Nantes et Turin.* Rennes: CNRS/Université de Rennes I /Institut d'Etudes Politiques de Rennes.

Peraldi, M., & Samson, M. (2005). *Gouverner Marseille. Enquête sur les mondes politiques marseillais.* La Découverte.

Ratté, S. (2019). (Un)seen seas. Technological mediation, oceanic imaginaries, and future depths. *Environment and Society, 10*(1), 141–157.

Roncayolo, M. (1996). *Les grammaires d'une ville: Essai sur la genèse des structures urbaines à Marseille.* Éditions de l'École des hautes études en sciences sociales.

Schnyder, J. (2022, January 20). En 2035, la nouvelle gare Saint-Charles s'ouvrira en fin sur la ville. *Marsactu.* https://marsactu.fr/en-2035-la-nouvelle-gare-saint-charles-souvrira-enfin-sur-la-ville/.

Sewell, W. H. (1985). *Structure and mobility: The men and women of Marseille, 1820–1870.* Cambridge University Press.

Simone, A. (2014). Relational infrastructures in postcolonial urban worlds. In S. Graham, & C. McFarlane (Eds.), *Infrastructural lives.* Routledge.

Tarrius, A. (1992). *Les fourmis d'Europe. Migrants riches, migrants pauvres et nouvelles villes internationales.* Éditions L'Harmattan.

Tartakowski, D., Cornette, J., Fureix, E., Gauvard, C., & Saliou, C. (2022). *Histoire de la rue: De l'antiquité à nos jours.* Tallandier.

Tödt, D. (2011). *Vom Planeten Mars: Rap in Marseille und das Imaginäre der Stadt.* LIT Verlag Münster.

Union for the Mediterranean. (2023). Regional Transport Action Plan for the Mediterranean Region 2021–2027 (RTAP 2021–2027). https://ufmsecretariat.org/wp-content/uploads/2023/02/RTAP-2021-2027_final_EN.pdf

von Benda-Beckmann, K., & Pirie, F. (2007). *Order and disorder: Anthropological perspectives.* Berghahn books.

Werquin, A.-C., & Demangeon, A. (2000). *Boulevards, rondas, parkways...* Des concepts de voies urbaines. CERTU.

Wimmer, A., & Glick Schiller, N. (2002). Methodological nationalism and beyond: Nation–state building, migration and the social sciences. *Global Networks, 2*(4), 301–334.

Ziadeh, K. (2011). *Neighborhood and boulevard: Reading through the modern Arab city.* Springer.

Claire Bullen is a researcher at the Institute of Sociology at the University of Tübingen. An urban ethnographer with a strong interest in comparison, she has been investigating social change in cities in the UK, France and Algeria.

Matteo Stefani is a postgraduate student of anthropology at the University of Aix-Marseille. His field of study is the heritage of Marseille and its impact on the city's transformation processes.

Infrastructures of Migration Regulation: Policing Migrant "Illegality" and Deportation in India

Bani Gill

Abstract

Deportation, once a measure for exceptional circumstances, is increasingly becoming the standard response to "illegal migration". However, far from a seamless policy endeavour, deportation constitutes a complex system that involves various components—detention centres, immigration agencies, legal processes, brokers and profiteers, transportation, documentation, international agreements etc. In taking an infrastructure lens to deportation, this chapter expands upon the socio-technical apparatus of deportation processes as interlinking peoples, materials, and ideas (Larkin 2013; Xiang and Lindquist 2014). Specifically, it builds upon data from India to investigate deportation as an infrastructure of migration regulation that is constituted through the uneven intermeshing of social, material, and biometric dimensions. The chapter thus explores the violent and messy operation of deportation infrastructures (Walters 2018) and proposes future research on their transnational impacts and the transformation of global orders they potentially entail.

Keywords

Deportation · Infrastructures · Migrant "illegality" · India · Delhi · Race · Biometrics · Surveillance · Policing · Citizenship

B. Gill (✉)
Institut für Soziologie, Universität Tübingen, Tübingen, Germany
e-mail: gill@eth.mpg.de
B. Gill Max Planck Institute for Social Anthropology, Halle, Germany

H.-J. Bieling et al. (eds.), *Transnational Infrastructures and the Transformation of Global Orders*, RaumFragen: Stadt – Region – Landschaft,
https://doi.org/10.1007/978-3-031-74846-2_14

1 Introduction

The last few decades have witnessed profound polarization in imaginaries, debates, and discourses around citizenship and migration across the globe. Deportation has increasingly come to be constructed as the standard response to "illegal migration" rather than a measure used for exceptional circumstances (Bloch & Schuster, 2006). Such ideological transformations have simultaneously been accompanied by intensive material, technological, and financial investments; from a global increase in detention facilities and surveillance technologies to changes to citizenship laws and expansive international collaborations between migration regimes aimed at the identification, detention, and expulsion of illegalised populations. Such measures indicate the transnational dimensions of migration regulation and policing no longer confined to the borders of nation states or between "host" and "sending" states but as embedded within global networks and logics. Second, they demonstrate the inextricable ways in which the material edifice of deportation- from detention centres to the physical movement of populations- are inevitably enmeshed within ideological, economic, political, and social factors and vice versa. Seen in this light, deportation, as the forcible removal of "illegal" migrants,[1] emerges as much *more than* a policy-informed process aimed at the linear ejection of unwanted populations from national territory. It is more comprehensively understood as a complex set of systems, networks and processes encompassing a wide range of components- detention centres, immigration agencies, legal processes, transportation, documentation, bilateral and international agreements, technology and biometric identification systems, advocacy, and support organizations- that connect and structure the im/mobility of certain populations across local and transnational scales. In this way, deportation systems can be conceptualized as infrastructures, as "multi-layered socio-technical systems that involve the influence and utilization by different actors […] and whose components are located on various levels—global, regional, national and local." (Abels et al. Forthcoming).

This chapter is a conceptual investigation into the production and composition of deportation processes as "infrastructures", comprising social, material, and biometric dimensions, amongst others. In developing such a lens, the chapter aims to address a central, and enduring, paradox in migration regulation- i.e., why, despite the proliferation of increasingly stringent forms and modes of migrant policing, do state anxieties regarding the detection and deportation of 'illegal' migrants continue to thrive? I put forward that such a paradox stems from the unpredictable stitching together of the various dimensions of deportation processes when conceptualised as infrastructures. In taking an infrastructural approach to deportation, I build upon anthropological and sociological explorations of infrastructures as sociotechnical constellations mediating relations

[1] De Genova and Peutz define deportation as "the compulsory removal of "aliens" from the physical, juridical, and social space of the state" (2010, p. 1), such that includes a wide array of subjects at risk of deportation including foreign offenders. This chapter examines deportation specifically in relation to the expulsion of allegedly "illegal" migrants.

between goods, people, ideas, and things (Larkin, 2013), and of migration infrastructures as the "systematically interlinked technologies, institutions and actors" regulating mobility (Xiang and Lindquist, 2014, p. 6). I thus propose to examine the diverse social, material, and biometric dimensions of migration regulation and deportation policing in particular that assemble to constitute infrastructures of expulsion. In doing so, I aim to explore the ways in which the production and operation of deportation infrastructures as well as their "vulnerability to breakdown" (Larkin, 2013, p. 328) produce contradictory affordances. In further documenting how infrastructures are constituted as much of hard materiality as through legal regimes, bureaucratic enactments, racial imaginings, and biometric technologies that are inextricably intertwined with ideological questions, I contribute to literature questioning the supposed boundaries between state and society (Hansen and Stepputat, 2001; Das & Poole, 2004). In its conceptual iteration, the chapter is empirically aided by my long-term ethnographic engagements in Delhi with differently racialized migrant populations including Afghan and Somali refugees, West African migrants and Bengali migrants (Gill & Mahendru, 2017; Gill, 2018, 2020a, b, 2021, 2024a, b, c).

In the next section, the conceptualisation of deportation as infrastructures of migration regulation and, specifically, of expulsion is theoretically pursued. Taking the materiality of deportation processes as a starting point, my intervention seeks to underscore the violence of expulsion infrastructures as also constituted through social and biometric forms of policing. Thereafter, the case study of India is explored. Here, I explicate upon the uneven intermeshing between the social life of migrant "illegality" (Gill 2024a), material dimensions of policing as initiated by recent laws, and the operation of biometric modes of identification as significant determinants in the production and operation of deportation infrastructures. The last section points to avenues for future research by thinking of deportation as transnational infrastructures and the transformation of global orders it potentially entails.

2 Deportation as Infrastructures of Expulsion

The substantial human implications of the post 9/11 "deportation turn" in migration enforcement has necessitated research on the regulatory, symbolic, and political contours of state imperatives to "forcibly remove" non-citizens and undocumented migrants from their territory (Anderson et al., 2011; Fekete, 2011). The increasing securitization of migration (Bigo, 2002) has further prompted scholars, especially across Euro American contexts, to locate threats and practices of detention and deportation within the logics of the neoliberal prison-industrial-detention-centre complex (Coutin, 2015), the racialization and subordination of migrant labour and the assertion of sovereign power (De Giorgi, 2010; Golash-Boza, 2015).

At the same time, research has also indicated the complexities of deportation enforcement due to the financial constraints involved (Ellermann, 2009), the ambiguities of administrative and legal procedure (Edwards, 2009), human rights considerations and concerns of cooperation with receiving countries (Altrogge & Zanker, 2019). Anthropological work has also considered the role of informal brokerage networks (Xiang, 2013), the inconsistencies of paperwork (Horton & Heyman, 2020), and the discretionary capacity of bureaucrats and street level officials (Kalir & Schendel, 2017) that significantly temper the praxis of deportation across diverse contexts (Kalir, 2014). Such scholarship has been particularly attuned to the ways in which the allegedly weak implementation of legal regulations are, in effect, systematic forms of state arbitrariness that disproportionately affect certain populations with labour insecurity and vulnerability (De Genova, 2016; Tuckett, 2015; Chauvin, & Garcés-Mascareñas, 2012) The violence of deportation as characterized by enforcement (Kalir, 2019; Menjivar & Kanstroom, 2013) or threats of enforcement i.e. deportability (De Genova, 2002; Hasselberg, 2016) render distinct the rise of what de Genova and Peutz (2010) characterize as "the deportation regime". Scholarship in non-western contexts has however critically reassessed notions of a putatively unified and global logic of expulsion (Galvin, 2014). In decentering the priority of the state apparatus in Russia to render non-citizens legible, Reeves (2013) demonstrates how it is ambiguity instead of enforcement that is key to the enactment of state power while Gaibazzi (2017) explores how it is the modernization imperatives underlying Angola's deportation policing that has resulted in an expansion in corruption, extortion, and discretion in law enforcement. In the context of India, Ramachandran (2019) illustrates how sociocultural and racialized identities are key to the political posturing against "illegal" migrants, that have a disproportionate impact on the detention and deportation of Bengali speaking Muslim subjects, with Punathil (2022) using the framework of "precarious citizenship" to analyse such conditions.

The extensive literature on deportation has thus largely focused attention on the seemingly arbitrary yet institutionalized violence of the state, the experiences of deportable/deported subject populations (Khosravi, 2018; Peutz, 2006), and spaces of detention (Bosworth, 2014). Less explored is how legislation pertaining to detection, detention and deportation is enacted in practice, such that involves substantial policing across a range of sites, for e.g. neighbourhoods where migrants reside, police stations where their interception is processed, detention in deportation centres, actual movement involved in relocating such populations, reception of deported populations in home/arrival countries etc. Each of these seemingly disparate sites are linked together through an expansive social, material, and biometric policing apparatus which, far from being fixed or linear remains locally embedded, relationally constituted, and mediated by diverse socialities, practices and politics. How such varied dimensions- social, material, biometric- connect and fracture, and how such dis/connections shape topographies of deportation in practice has remained underexplored. Thus, this chapter argues for the pressing need to address the involvement of disparate sites, scales, geographies, actors, materials, and networks in deportation processes such that create interdependencies and tensions between 'old' (material documents, visas) and 'new' policing technologies (biometric identity cards), produce new forms of governmentality, and varying configurations of deportability and im/mobility for differently racialized subjects. Building upon insights of "migration infrastructures" (Xiang & Lindquist, 2014) and "deportation infrastructures" (Walters, 2018), the chapter conceives of such dis/connections between varied dimensions as *infrastructures of expulsion*.

Infrastructures have been the subject of much academic debate due to their inherent propensity to connect, transgress and extend across time, space, and place (Harvey et al., 2017), functioning as both "things" and the "relations between things" (Larkin, 2013, p. 239). In context of the "infrastructure turn" in migration studies, an important contribution has been Xiang and Lindquist's (2014) conceptualisation of "migration infrastructures". In focusing attention on the intensively mediated nature of migration, they identify five interrelated dimensions- commercial (brokers, smugglers, security companies), regulatory (state apparatus, documentation procedures), technological (communication, transport), humanitarian (NGOS, multi-national organisations), social (kin networks and relations)- through which migrants move and are moved (Xiang & Lindquist, 2014, p. 131). In a later article, the authors together with Lin and Yeoh further explore such "assemblages of infrastructures that produce different migrancies" (Lin et al., 2017, p. 168), thus indicating the subtle and pronounced ways in which different dimensions come together to engender different configurations of mobility. More recently, literature has analysed the hardware of infrastructure as an entry point to explore connections between migration and media (Leurs & Seuferling, 2022), religion (Heck, 2016), borders and bordering (Sur, 2021), processes of urban arrival (Meeus et al., 2019) and the role of digital technologies (Gillespie et al., 2018). Walters (2018) has specifically focused attention on material hardware and deportation by emphasising the role of aviation—airports, planes, air routes, aeronautical and navigational technologies—in moving migrants across distances of varying scales. His work considers infrastructures and the various ways in which "heterogenous elements are connected and disconnected, and the changing roles and functions they perform" (Ibid., p. 2801) as central to regulating the scale, intensity, duration of deportation mobilities.

I thus build upon an infrastructural approach to deportation by conceptualizing of infrastructures of expulsion as "socio-technical constellations" (Xiang & Lindquist, 2014, p. 143). These are constituted through intensive processes of data collection, authentication, and mediation that bring together political rationalities with practical application that create subjective modes of being-in-the-world (Larkin, 2013; Venkatesan et al., 2017). I propose that theorizing infrastructures as contingent combinations of material and culture enables one to examine the workings of expulsion infrastructures that entail diverse dimensions—recursive enactments of surveillance and detection, authentication of identity artefacts, built spaces, informal economies of bribes, mediations of market actors, the discretionary capacity of street-level bureaucrats, treaties between states—within one framework. Such an analytical investigation centres the processes and mediations through which expulsion journeys are initiated and executed, including the question of how people become vulnerable to threat of forced movement and how they are moved, which material and immaterial resources (including actors, structures, spaces, processes, practices) are mobilized for such movements, and to what effects.

Focusing on the case study of India, I now examine three interlinked dimensions of material, social and biometric policing as constituting infrastructures of expulsion. Before proceeding, it is important to remember that these dimensions by no means constitute an exhaustive account of infrastructures of expulsion that would well include other dimensions and factors (role of NGOs and international organizations, migrant networks, receiving state contexts etc.). Rather, my intention is to explore the "operational logic of intersectionality" between different dimensions (Xiang & Lindquist, 2014, p. 135) to understand how these fracture, collide, intersect, and overlap as also the intended and unintended consequences of such intermeshing. Here it is necessary to remember Larkin's assertion that infrastructures are "conceptually unruly" (2013, p. 329) and cutting of an infrastructure constitutes a "categorical act" (2013, p. 330). Answering the question of "what" constitutes an infrastructure remains an empirical question and my focus on social, material, and biometric policing is informed foremost in relation to my empirical data, observations and findings.

3 Infrastructures of Expulsion: Case Study India

About 5.2 million immigrants live in India today, mostly from neighbouring countries such as Bangladesh (3.2 million), Pakistan (1 million), Nepal (540,000) and Sri Lanka (160,000) (Connor, 2017). More recently, a fair number of African migrants have also been making their way to India for reasons ranging from education and healthcare to asylum, trade and business opportunities that hold appeal for small scale traders and entrepreneurs (Gill, 2020a, b, 2021, 2024a, b).

Despite being amongst the foremost destination for migrants (Connor, 2017), India lacks a comprehensive framework for long-term residency. Instead, supplementing what is largely colonial era migration related legislation and border enforcement, the regulation of "illegal" migration and deportation is constituted through manifold dimensions, including social policing such as informal vigilance and surveillance networks, material policing such as checking of birth certificates and passports, and biometric policing such as the issuing of national identity Aadhaar numbers. However, despite such expansive policing, there remains considerable ambiguity regarding the identification, detection, and deportation of "illegal" migrants. In part, these ambiguities stem from questions of identity, with domestic Bengali speaking migrants sharing ethnolinguistic similarity with cross-border migrants from Bangladesh. In addition, the difficulties in verifying documents, such as visas issued to African migrants, that are prone to counterfeit production, the ambivalence of the Aadhaar identifier, and the everyday relations of bribes and patronage between migrants and street-level police actors demonstrate how the state's ideological claim to expulsion is negotiated and challenged. It is against this background that in this section I explicate various dimensions of infrastructures of expulsion—

social, material, and biometric—to discover how their uneven intermeshing produces violence in the everyday life of subject populations as well as challenges for migration governance.

3.1 Social Dimensions

The social dimension of infrastructures of expulsion refer to the societal frameworks, processes, and practices that impact, influence and regulate deportation mechanisms, particularly regarding the identification, regulation, and control of "illegal migrants" based on racialised constructs such as race, religion, caste etc. It encompasses the ways in which such social dimensions shape policies, practices and perceptions related to deportation, including the use of discriminatory practices, hyper nationalist discourses as also discretionary powers as enacted by a wide-ranging set of state and non-state actors.

Scholars have long established links between the notion of migrant "illegality" and processes of racialisation, which render specific populations prone to various forms of policing (de Genova, 2002; Whitley, 2015). In India, religion and increasing islamophobia have played a significant role in this racialisation process (Baber, 2004; Mehta, 2018). The very term "illegal" in relation to migration came to gain currency in India after the 1971 Bangladesh war, marking a shift in perception towards the once-welcomed refugee population from East Pakistan, now labelled as predatory "illegals" from Bangladesh (Datta, 2013). While Bangladeshi Hindus were depicted as "victims" escaping persecution, Bangladeshi Muslims were considered "infiltrators" who threatened the demography and socio-economic stability of India (Mehta, 2018, p. 64). This narrative gained further momentum with rising Hindu nationalism of the 1990s, resulting in Bengali speaking Muslims being demonized as "illegal Bangladeshis", opportunistic job-stealers, and a 'national problem' (Mehta, 2018, p. 64). Yet, despite this rhetoric, the state apparatus has continued to grapple with detection anxieties stemming from linguistic and cultural similarities among Bengali speakers across the India-Bangladesh border. Additionally, the relative ease of acquiring counterfeit documentation has fanned anxieties about ensuing "indistinguishability" between citizens and non-citizens (Sadiq, 2008). For Bengali subjects and particularly Bengali Muslims, common practices involving language, religion, food can be enough to transition from a (Muslim) citizen to being perceived as a "Bangladeshi infiltrator" (Roy & Singh, 2009, p. 57). Even the mere suspicion of illegality based on such social markers can lead to severe consequences, including large scale evictions (Ramachandran, 2003) or incarceration in detention centres especially with the promulgation of recent laws such as the Citizenship Amendment Act (CAA) and the National Register of Citizens (NRC). Complex border histories between the postcolonial states of India, Pakistan, and Bangladesh, rising trends of majoritarianism and Hindutva nationalism combined with the normalization of a "racialized hierarchy of citizenship" (Kikon, 2021) in India are factors contributing to the objectification of Bengali Muslims. Further, the racialization of illegality is as apparent when it comes to African migrants in Delhi and the stigmatisation of blackness that stems from colonial histories of racial hierarchies (Burton, 2016) as also caste-race forms of Othering (Pandey, 2013), among other factors. In illuminating the caste-race-religion-gender informed indexes of difference that contribute to the multisensorial racialization and social policing of African migrants as "illegal" by both police and non-state actors, I have previously theorised of migrant "illegality" as enmeshed within racialized imaginaries, changing spatial economies and alternate modes of governmentality (Gill, 2024a). Blackness and Muslimness are, in this sense, deeply racialized constructs that are subject to social policing and being rendered illegal, criminal, and deportable in various ways.

3.2 Material Dimension

Material dimensions of infrastructures of expulsion refer to the tangible places, structures, and bureaucratic mechanisms as also the logistical and operational aspects—such as legal and administrative processes, travel mechanisms—embedded in the identification, detention, and deportation of individuals. Material dimensions thus range from artefacts of governmentality (visas, passports, citizenship, and residence permits, ID cards, legislation) to spatialised institutions such as detention centres, prisons, and courts.

The social and material dimensions of expulsion infrastructures do not seamlessly support each other, and there is considerable labour involved in the work, maintenance, and repair of such infrastructures by a range of state (e.g., police) and non-state (e.g. profit oriented brokers) actors. In context of the India-Bangladesh borderlands, Sur (2021) contends that the vast array of legislations, foreigner tribunals, ID cards and biometrics that the state has initiated to ostensibly ascertain citizenship have rendered the question of identity more ambivalent for it is "suspicion that shapes the politics of belonging and fail to determine the legal thresholds of either Indian citizenship or Bangladeshi migrant " illegality" (Sur, 2021, p. 169). The social dimension of suspicion is thus critical to consider in the assessment of material policing, particularly regarding India's shifting regimes of inclusion and exclusion. The recent passage of the CAA and the extension of the NRC across India are another case in point.

The CAA and NRC extension were spearheaded by the ruling Hindu nationalist Bhartiya Janata Party (BJP) in 2019 amidst widespread protests and criticism. To briefly summarize, the CAA proposes to fast-track citizenship of non-Muslim "persecuted religious minorities" who arrived in India before 2015 on "humanitarian grounds"—effectively leaving out of its ambit persecuted Muslim communities in South Asia such as the Rohingyas- and the NRC seeks to compile a database of documented citizens across India. In fundamentally altering the framework of India's citizenship laws along religious lines, the CAA must be read in juxtaposition with the NRC that places an immense burden on historically undocumented communities—i.e. urban poor, Adivasi, Dalit communities—who risk exclusion on account of inadequate or insufficient paperwork "proving" they are "Indian".

The potential impact of the NRC stands highlighted in Assam, a border state on India's eastern edge that has been the site of several anti-immigration movements since the formation of Bangladesh in 1971, and where the NRC database started to be compiled in 2015. In the first round of the NRC in Assam, 32.9 million applied and 4 million were subsequently excluded. Of these 3.6 million people reapplied, and, in August 2019, 1.9 million remained unauthenticated (Jayal, 2019). These numbers indicate the dilemmas of documentation in India arising from high levels of illiteracy, minimal access to sturdy housing and natural calamities such as floods etc. At the same time, "networks of complicity" and "networks of profit" (Sadiq, 2008) also enable for ethnolinguistically similar migrants to acquire myriad forms of, what Sadiq terms, "documentary citizenship" i.e. citizenship acquired through counterfeit or illicitly obtained paperwork. This leads to a curious situation where the inadequate documentation of some can be juxtaposed with the hyper documentation of others where, simply put, the state in India is consistently preoccupied in the task of distinguishing between *farzi* (fake) and *asli* (real) documents (Mathur, 2020).

Here social dimensions (suspicion, doubt) collide against material dimensions of infrastructures of expulsion (documentation) indicating how the uneven intermeshing between such components potentially generates paradoxical outcomes. The NRC practice of bureaucratic inscription further reveals how material dimensions are not neutral or impartial but are rather shaped through emotional and affective responses through which they are prone to breakdowns, leakages, and malfunctions. Further, the NRC is a costly task that entails intensive labour in accurately recording particulars making it as prone to mismanagement and biased pronouncements as the already existing Foreigners Tribunals (quasi-judicial bodies assessing cases of migrant illegality) in Assam (Amnesty International India, 2019). Such exercises continue despite the lack of an extradition agreement between India and Bangladesh that renders detained migrants in a perpetual condition of deportability (Punathil, 2022, p. 68), even as large amounts of land, investments, and resources are simultaneously mobilized to build new detention centres across the country (Jayal, 2019).

Detention centres constitute the exemplar of material policing, with detained subjects prone to long periods of waiting, denied the possibility to work or earn wages or even partake in recreation (Punathil, 2022, p. 64). Drawing on ethnographic fieldwork with those detained by the Foreigners Tribunals, Punathil's work further documents how Bengali speaking Muslims in Assam risk deportability despite having long constructed their social worlds as Indian citizens. Despite a 2019 Supreme Court judgement ordering the release of those detained for more than 3 years, many continue to languish in deportation centres. In Delhi, the detention centre Lampur Seva Sadan has frequently been in the news due to the harsh conditions of confinement that have prompted protests and hunger strikes by detainees (The Wire, 2017). A second centre is specifically marked for the confinement of Rohingya asylum seekers who have been branded "illegal" migrants (Rohmetra, 2022), some of whom have also been deported back to Myanmar in clear violation of non-refoulement principles. From African migrants stuck in detention centres due to lack of resources that allow them to make the journey back (Gill, 2021), to Rohingya refugees at risk of being branded "illegal" despite UNHCR mandates, from Bengali Muslim population held in detention centres to those at risk of being adjudged stateless and stripped off citizenship rights due to documentation mismatches and bureaucratic exercises like the NRC, the material dimension of infrastructure of expulsion continually demonstrate the imbrications of state and society (Das & Poole, 2004) that produces counterintuitive effects and resonances. Recent years have witnessed an increasing dependence on techno utopias and biometrics to "solve" the issue of identification, yet these present their own challenges.

3.3 Biometric Dimension

Biometric dimension of infrastructures of expulsion includes the use of biometric technologies and data in the enforcement and management of deportation processes, including fingerprints, facial recognition, voiceprints, and other physiological or behavioural characteristics. The biometric dimension of such infrastructures thus involves the integration of these technologies into border control, surveillance, and deportation procedures aiming to enhance security measures, the verification of identity and the monitoring of movements between, within, and across borders.

In 2021, the Report of the Special Rapporteur on contemporary forms of racism, racial discrimination, xenophobia and related intolerance detailed racial and xenophobic discrimination and the use of digital technologies in border and immigration enforcement (Human Rights Council, 2021). This report addressed the emergence of "digital borders" and discriminatory impact of digital technologies on migrants and refugees. Referencing colonial antecedents of racialized governance, the report explicitly highlights how supposedly neutral technology can be used to reinforce hegemonic socio-political and economic trends that stigmatize and vilify migrants. The use of the biometric based-ID document Aadhaar in India must be assessed against this background, as it threatens to institutionalize discrimination against marginalized populations while producing new paradoxes in its wake.

Neither linked to conditions of residency nor citizenship, Aadhaar is meant to define a person's identity to ostensibly streamline access to services such as banking and welfare provisions. It records particulars such as fingerprint and iris scan, photograph, date of birth, sex, address and provides a unique identification number for the holder thus generating critical personal information. While Aadhaar is theoretically accessible to any resident who can fulfil the requirements, the Government of India has, in the recent past, excluded certain non-citizen groups, such as Rohingya refugees, from access to the Aadhaar (Tiwari, 2020). The Aadhaar has over 1.2 billion enrolees (Rao & Nair, 2019) and is largely feted as a 'solution' to India's enduring crisis of fixing identity. Yet, in its everyday operation and functioning, Aadhaar is "susceptible to myriad significations and re-significations" embedded as it is in social worlds of not only citizens and state but also commercial actors and market intermediaries who broker this new arena of access to technology (Rao & Nair, 2019, p. 470). As Rao (2019) posits, Aadhaar follows on a continuum of governmental measures to record populations by adding a "new layer of procedures on top of older techniques of recognition" (p. 537). In this way, Aadhaar must constantly articulate with the anxieties of older identification forms such as paper documents that reproduce rather than resolve socially mediated production of identity. For instance, Aadhaar registration remains cumbersome for poor working-class families who may not possess material artefacts such as either a voter ID, a school leaving certificate or official marriage certificate- documents that are frequently assigned the misnomer "common" when it comes to identity registration processes. This dependence on documentary evidence weighs particularly heavy for historically marginalised populations such as Muslim or Dalit subjects regardless of citizenship status, as the previous sections have referenced. Even as technologies, such as Aadhaar, open new pathways of engaging with complexities of identity, they cannot resolve the "problem of identities being fluid and co-constituted" (Rao, 2019, p. 552) thereby complicating supposedly easy assessments between citizens/migrants, legal/illegal migrants. Elsewhere, Ghosh (2019) has described the fallacies of techno utopias with fingerprint recording machines at the India- Bangladesh border having to consistently match with other layers of identification- social, narrative, historical, documentary, bodily- for subjects to pass registers of detectability. In my own fieldwork, I have come across cases of African migrants in possession of an Aadhaar card as also those whose claims have been consistently deemed ambivalent due to conflicting information regarding eligibility (Gill 2024c). In all such cases, it is apparent that patronage and the subjectivities of mediating agents—ranging from the goodwill and knowledge of governmental operators to beneficiaries willing to provide supporting statements of good conduct and brokers manufacturing counterfeits in exchange for money- remain integral to how questions of identity and identification remain embedded within social, material, and technological registers. To think of deportation as infrastructure is thus to consistently attend to the dis/connections between these varied dimensions and the paradoxes and contradictory affordances they generate.

4 Conclusion

This chapter has analytically delved into the production and composition of deportation as infrastructures constituted through manifold dimensions—social, material, and biometric. While the chapter has introduced several empirical and conceptual observations to make sense of migration regulation and the deportation framework in India, it is as important to note that these may constitute only one half of the story since further research is required into the infrastructures through which 'return'/'departure' journey and reintegration processes commence (Drotbohm, 2016; Peutz, 2006).

As Walters (2018) reminds us, the "ingression bias" of migration studies diverts attention from the governance, cartographies and economies of deportation infrastructures that co-constitute border regimes (p. 2800). It is in this context that I have explored the analytical value of using infrastructures as a theoretical lens to engage with processes of deportation. The empirical case study of India has informed this postulation, such that it has highlighted the uneven intermeshing between the various components of deportation. The mediated processes of deportation as also the dimensions stressed here—social, material, biometric—invite a further comparative approach to understand and assess the value of an infrastructural approach. As Kleist and Bjarnesen (2019, p. 19) put it, an infrastructural approach is particularly useful "in its attention to the intersectionality of multiple infrastructural dimensions when studying the mediation of migration…". Such a focus on mediation and intersectionality regarding the maintenance, operation, and production of infrastructures thus open avenues to think of deportation infrastructures as sociotechnical and relational.

Furthering this line of inquiry, future research can well attend to the ways in which the production and operation of deportation infrastructures shape patterns of societal interaction embedded in local and transnational contexts. For instance, the production of deportation infrastructures (e.g., new detention centres) potentially (re)structure spatial and temporal dynamics in localised contexts (e.g., neighbourhoods) and create new forms of inclusion and exclusion, as also new sites, modes, and forms of resistance (protests, civil society initiatives). Yet, these also entail ordering effects on transnational political and social relations (for instance, simultaneous intensification and externalisation of border regimes, changing patterns of interactive practices between state and subject or between different subject populations). Even as this chapter has focused on infrastructures within India, deportation necessarily involves a transnational approach since it requires active relations between peoples, actors, institutions, processes, and states across multiple scales embedded as they are in the forcible circulation of people. For example, border control related EU funding to Turkey has resulted in the construction of several new removal centres (Aras and Mencutek 2019 as cited in Mencutek, 2022) that are intimately linked to political debates and *transnational* border regimes. Yet, the emergence of detention centres emplaced in *localized* contexts also invariably impacts local social relations. The actual enforcement of deportation journeys further is embedded within *regional and international* politics and bilateral treaties. On a *global* level, the use of new technologies (e.g., biometrics) to detect and deport "illegal" migrants, raises new questions about surveillance, data privacy and human rights. The ordering effects- from the local to global- so identified unfold at different scales and may complement as also contradict one another. Deportation has often been conceptualized as a geographically, temporally, spatially extended process (Drotbohm & Hasselberg, 2015; Khosravi, 2018). It is thus imperative to study the socio-technical infrastructures that facilitate, improvise, and fracture such extensions across national and transnational scales. Relatedly, in moving beyond a state-centric perspective, the expansive lens of infrastructure further "greatly expands the scope of *where* we look for resistance" and the multitude of modes, forms, and spaces where it is enacted (Walters, 2018, p. 2803). Finally, contemporary processes of deportation from the Global North to the Global South, and their contestations, have been analysed as neo-colonial forms of world-making (McNeill, 2023). This interpretation leads us to question how transnational deportation infrastructures are entwined with the production, instrumentalization and universalization of value regimes which may compete or complement each other. An infrastructural lens on deportation can thus uncover the ordering effects that transcend state boundaries, shedding insight into the ways in which infrastructures influence, produce and transform local, national, regional, transnational, and global orders.

References

Abels, J., Bieling, H.-J., Flemmer, R., & Futterer, A. (Forthcoming). Infrastructural perspectives on global ordering. A research agenda on the infrastructure-orders-nexus. Unpublished Manuscript.

Anderson, B., Gibney, M. J., & Paoletti, E. (2011). Citizenship, deportation and the boundaries of belonging. *Citizenship Studies, 15*(5), 547–565.

Altrogge, J., & Zanker, F. (2019). *The political economy of migration governance in the Gambia.* Arnold-Bergstraesser Institute (ABI).

Amnesty International India (2019). Designed to exclude. How India's courts are allowing foreigners tribunals to render people stateless in Assam.

Baber, Z. (2004). 'Race', religion and riots: The 'racialization 'of communal identity and conflict in India. *Sociology, 38*(4), 701–718.

Bigo, D. (2002). Security and immigration: Toward a critique of the governmentality of unease. *Alternatives: Global, Local, Political, 27*(1), 63–92.

Bloch, A., & Schuster, L. (2006). At the extremes of exclusion: Deportation, detention and dispersal. *Ethnic and Racial Studies, 28*, 491–512.

Bosworth, M. (2014). *Inside immigration detention.* Oxford University Press.

Burton, A. (2016). *Africa in the Indian imagination: Race and the politics of postcolonial citation.* Duke University Press.

Coutin, S. B. (2015). Deportation studies: Origins, themes and directions. *Journal of Ethnic and Migration Studies, 41*(4), 671–681.

Chauvin, S., & Garcés-Mascareñas, B. (2012). Beyond informal citizenship: The new moral economy of migrant illegality. *International Political Sociology, 6*(3), 241–259. https://doi.org/10.1111/j.1749-5687.2012.00162.x.

Connor, P. (2017, March 3). India is a top source and destination for world's migrants. Pew Research Centre. https://www.pewresearch.org/short-reads/2017/03/03/india-is-a-top-source-and-destination-for-worlds-migrants/.

Datta, A. (2013). *Refugees and borders in South Asia: The great exodus of 1971.* Routledge.

Das, V., & Poole, D. (2004). *Anthropology in the margins of the state.* School of American Research Press.

De Genova, N. (2002). Migrant 'illegality' and deportability in everyday life. *Annual Review of Anthropology, 31*, 419–447.

De Genova, N., & Peutz, N. (Eds.) (2010). *The deportation regime: Sovereignty, space and the freedom of movement.* Duke University Press.

De Genova, N. (2016). *Detention, deportation, and waiting: Towards a theory of migrant detainability* (Global Detention Project Working Paper No. 18). www.globaldetentionproject.org/detention-deportation-waiting-toward-theorymigrant-detainability-gdp-working-paper-no-18.

De Giorgi, A. (2010). Immigration control, post-fordism, and less eligibility: A materialist critique of the criminalization of immigration across Europe. *Punishment & Society, 12*(2), 147–167.

Drotbohm, H. (2016). *Frozen cosmopolitanism. Coping with radical declaration in Cape Verdean contexts of forced return migration.*" In T. H. Erikson & E. Schober (Eds.), Identity destabilised. Living in an overheated world (pp. 42–57). London. Pluto.

Drotbohm, H., & Hasselberg, I. (2015). Deportation, anxiety, justice: New ethnographic perspectives. *Journal of Ethnic and Migration Studies, 31*(4), 551–562.

Ellermann, A. (2009). *States against migrants: Deportation in Germany and the United States.* Cambridge University Press.

Edwards, A. (2009). *Rights of immigrants in voluntary and involuntary return procedures in national law.* Nottingham, United Kingdom.

Fekete, L. (2011). Accelerated removals: The human cost of EU deportation policies. *Race & Class, 52*(4), 89–97.

Gaibazzi, P. (2017). From expulsion to extortion: Deportability, predatory policing and West African migrants in Angola. *Citizenship Studies, 21*(8), 969–983.

Galvin, T. M. (2014). 'We deport them but they keep coming back': The normalcy of deportation in the daily life of 'undocumented' Zimbabwean migrant workers in Botswana. *Journal of Ethnic and Migration Studies, 41*(1), 617–634.

Gill, B. (2018). Behind the silence: Sexual violence against Afghan and Burmese refugee women in Delhi. In U. Butalia (Ed.), *Breaching the citadel: The India papers* (pp. 101–136). Zubaan Books.

Gill, B. (2020a). COVID 19, undocumented migrants, and race: A view from India. *Chakra: A Nordic Journal of South Asian Studies*, (1), 113–121.

Gill, B. (2020b). Locked down and locked in: Covid-19 and African migrants in India. COMPAS. https://www.compas.ox.ac.uk/article/african-migrants-in-india.

Gill, B. (2021). Dead papers: Migrant 'illegality', city brokers and the dilemma of exit for unauthorized African migrants in Delhi. *Journal of Ethnic and Migration Studies, 48*(9), 1961–1979.

Gill, B. (2024a). The social life of illegality: Suspicion and surveillance against African migrants in urban India. *American Anthropologist, 126*(3), 422–433.

Gill. B. (2024b). *The work of proximity: Migration as coexistence.* In R. Flemmer, B. Gill & J. Kosgei (Eds.), *Proximity as method. Concepts for coexistence in the global past and present.* Routledge.

Gill, B. (2024c). "Documentary Dilemmas in Migrant Delhi". In "Living in a Mode of Despite", edited by Rishabh Raghavan, Mascha Schulz, and Julia Vorhölter, American Ethnologist website, 3 October 2024. https://americanethnologist.org/online-content/collections/living-in-a-mode-of-despite/documentary-dilemmas-in-migrant-delhiby-bani-gill/.

Gill, B., & Mahendru, R. (2017). *The horizon is an imaginary line.* Khoj International Artists Association.

Ghosh, S. (2019). 'Everything must match': Detection, deception, and migrant illegality in the India-Bangladesh borderlands. *American Anthropologist, 121*(4), 870–883.

Gillespie, M., Osseiran, S., & Cheesman, M. (2018). Syrian refugees and the digital passage to Europe: Smartphone infrastructures and affordances. *Social Media + Society, 4*(1). https://doi.org/10.1177/2056305118764440.

Golash-Boza, T. M. (2015). *Deported. Immigrant policing, disposable labor and global capitalism.* NYU Press.

Human Rights Council (2021). *Report of the special rapporteur on contemporary forms of racism, racial discrimination, xenophobia and related intolerance.*

Heck, G. (2016). Worshipping along the routes of migration: Religion as infrastructure. *Technosphere Magazine.* https://technosphere-magazine.hkw.de/p/Worshipping-Along-the-Routes-of-Migration-Religion-as-Infrastructure-84wZwioq4HV35ZPAqceEtR.

Harvey, P., Jensen, C., & Morita, A. (2017). *Infrastructures and social complexity: A companion.* Routledge.

Hasselberg, I. (2016). *Enduring uncertainty. Deportation, punishment and everyday life.* Berghahn.

HIAS (2024). The EU pact on migration and asylum, explained. https://hias.org/news/eu-pact-migration-and-asylum-explained/.

Horton, S., & Heyman, J. (Eds.) (2020). *Paper trails: Migrants, documents, and legal insecurity.* Duke University Press

Jayal, N. G. (2019, November 1). Faith based citizenship. India Forum. https://www.theindiaforum.in/sites/default/files/pdf/2019/11/01/faith-based-citizenship.pdf (Retrieved November 27, 2020).

Kalir, B., & van Schendel, W. (2017). Introduction: Nonrecording states between legibility and looking away. *Focaal: Journal of Global and Historical Anthropology, 77,* 1–7.

Kalir, B. (2014, October 29). The deportation mess: A bureaucratic muddling of state fantasies. https://blogs.law.ox.ac.uk/research-subject-groups/centre-criminology/centreborder-criminologies/blog/2014/10/deportation-mess.

Kalir, B. (2019). Departheid: The draconian governance of illegalized migrants in western states. *Conflict and Society, 5*(1), 19–40.

Khosravi, S. (2018). *After deportation: Ethnographic perspectives.* Palgrave Macmillan.

Kikon, D. (2021, March 16). Hello chinky. Society for Cultural Anthropology. https://culanth.org/fieldsights/hello-chinky.

Kleist, N., & Bjarnesen, J. (2019). Migration infrastructures in West Africa and beyond. Merian Institute of Advanced Studies in Africa (Working Paper 3).

Leurs, K., & Seuferling, P. (2022). Migration and the *deep time* of media infrastructures. *Communication, Culture and Critique, 15*(2), 290–297.

Larkin, B. (2013). The politics and poetics of infrastructure. *Annual Review of Anthropology, 42*(1), 327–334.

Lin, W., Lindquist, J., Xiang, B., & Yeoh, B.S.A. (2017). Migration infrastructures and the production of migrant mobilities. *Mobilities, 12*(2), 167–174.

Mathur, N. (2020). 'NRC se azadi': Process, chronology, and a paper monster. *SAMAJ*, 24–25. https://doi.org/10.4000/samaj.6917.

McNeill, H. (2023). Deportation as a neo-colonial act: How deporting state influence extends beyond the border. *Political Geography, 102*(71). https://doi.org/10.1016/j.polgeo.2023.102845.

Meeus B., Arnaut, K., & van Heur, B. (2019). *Arrival infrastructures: Migration and urban social mobilities.* Palgrave Macmillan.

Mehta, R. (2018). 'Illegal' Bangladeshis in Akhand Bharat: Inscriptions of race and religion on citizenship. *Economic and Political Weekly, 53*(7).

Mencutek, Z. S. (2022). The Institutionalization of "Voluntary" Returns in Turkey. *Migration and Society.* https://doi.org/10.3167/arms.2022.050105.

Menjivar, C., & Kanstroom, D. (2013). *Constructing immigrant "illegality": Critiques, experiences, and responses.* Cambridge University Press.

Pandey, G. (2013). *A history of prejudice: Race, caste, and difference in India and the United States.* Cambridge University Press.

Peutz, N. (2006). Embarking on an Anthropology of Removal. *Current Anthropology, 47*(2), 217–241. https://doi.org/10.1086/498949.

Punathil, S. (2022). Precarious citizenship: Detection, detention and 'deportability' in India. *Citizenship Studies, 26*(1), 55–72. https://doi.org/10.1080/13621025.2021.2013444

Ramachandran, S. (2003). 'Operation pushback': Sangh parivar, state, slums, and surreptitious Bangladeshis in New Delhi. *Economic and Political Weekly*, 637–647.

Ramachandran, S. (2019). *The Contours of Crimmigration Control in India*. The Global Detention Project Working Paper 25.

Rao, U., & Nair, V. (2019). Aadhaar: Governing with Biometrics. *South Asia: Journal of South Asian Studies, 42*(3), 469–481. https://doi.org/10.1080/00856401.2019.1595343.

Rao, U. (2019). Population meets database: Aligning personal, documentary and digital identity in Aadhaar-Enabled India. *South Asia: Journal of South Asian Studies, 42*(3), 537.553. https://doi.org/10.1080/00856401.2019.1594065.

Reeves, M. (2013). Clean fake: Authenticating documents and persons in migrant Moscow. *American Ethnologist, 40*(3), 508–524. https://doi.org/10.1111/amet.12036.

Rohmetra, A. (2022). Terrorist tag, cramped space—a life of Rohingya 'refugees' at Delhi camp behind PURI- MHA row. The Print. https://theprint.in/india/terrorist-tag-cramped-space-life-of-rohingya-refugees-at-delhi-camp-behind-puri-mha-row/1089704/.

Roy, A., & Singh, U. K. (2009). The ambivalence of citizenship. *Critical Asian Studies, 41*(1), 37–60. https://doi.org/10.1080/14672710802631137

Sadiq, K. (2008). *Paper citizens: How illegal immigrants acquire citizenship in developing countries*. Oxford University Press.

Sur, M. (2021). *Jungle passports: Fences, mobility, and citizenship at the northeast India-Bangladesh border.* University of Pennsylvania Press.

Tiwari, A., & Field, J. (2020). Biometric recording of 'illegal migrant' refugee identity: The road towards discrimination, submission on Race, Borders, and Digital Technologies.

The Wire (2017). Alleging 'slave-like' treatment, foreign inmates go on strike at Lampur detention facility. The Wire. https://thewire.in/government/foreign-national-inmates-go-strike-lampur-detention-facility-alleging-slave-like-treatment (Accessed: July 2019).

Tuckett, A. (2015). Strategies of navigation: Migrants' everyday encounters with Italian immigration bureaucracy. *The Cambridge Journal of Anthropology, 33*(1), 113–128. https://doi.org/10.3167/ca.2015.330109.

Venkatesan, et al. (2017). Attention to infrastructure offers a welcome reconfiguration of anthropological approaches to the political. *Critique of Anthropology, 38*(1), 3–52.

Walters, W. (2018). Aviation as deportation infrastructure: Airports, planes, and expulsion. *Journal of Ethnic and Migration Studies, 44*(16), 2796–2817. https://doi.org/10.1080/1369183X.2017.1401517.

Whitley, L. M. (2015). More than a line: borders as embodied sites. [PhD thesis, Centre for Cultural Studies, Goldsmiths University of London].

Xiang, B. (Ed.) (2013). *Return: Nationalizing transnational mobility in Asia.* Duke University Press.

Hansen, T. B., & Stepputat F. (2001). *States of imagination: Ethnographic explorations of the postcolonial state.* Duke University Press

Xiang, B., & Lindquist, J. (2014). Migration infrastructure. *International migration Review, 48*(1_suppl), 122–148. https://doi.org/10.1111/imre.12141.

Bani Gill is a Junior Professor, Institute for Sociology, at the University of Tübingen. An ethnographer with a regional focus on South Asia and global Africa–India encounters, she has wide-ranging research and teaching interests in migration, urbanism, race, embodiment, policing, and the state. Alongside ethnographic fieldwork, she is keenly interested in methodologies of visual storytelling and collaborative semi-fictional writing. She is a Marie Sklodowska-Curie Research Fellow at the Max Planck Institute for Social Anthropology, Halle, and her current project focuses on the complexities of deportation policing in India. She is also a Research Affiliate with the Centre on Migration, Policy and Society, University of Oxford.

GPSR Compliance

The European Union's (EU) General Product Safety Regulation (GPSR) is a set of rules that requires consumer products to be safe and our obligations to ensure this.

If you have any concerns about our products, you can contact us on ProductSafety@springernature.com

In case Publisher is established outside the EU, the EU authorized representative is:

Springer Nature Customer Service Center GmbH
Europaplatz 3
69115 Heidelberg, Germany

Batch number: 08550816

Printed by Printforce, the Netherlands